Merit Pay

Linking Pay Increases to
Performance Ratings

Merit Pay

Linking Pay Increases to Performance Ratings

Robert L. Heneman
The Ohio State University

ADDISON-WESLEY PUBLISHING COMPANY
*Reading, Massachusetts • Menlo Park, California • New York
Don Mills, Ontario • Wokingham, England • Amsterdam • Bonn
Sydney • Singapore • Tokyo • Madrid • San Juan • Milan • Paris*

Library of Congress Cataloging-in-Publication Data

Heneman, Robert L.
    Merit pay: Linking pay increases to performance ratings / Robert
L. Heneman.
        p.   cm. — (Addison-Wesley series on managing human
        resources)
    ISBN 0-201-52504-6
    1. Compensation management   2. Merit Pay.   I. Title.
II. Series.
HF5549.5.C67C66   1992
658.3'225—dc20

91-27860
CIP

Reprinted with corrections, May 1992.

ISBN 0-201-52504-6
 2 3 4 5 6 7 8 9 10 BA 95949392

In memory of
my mother, Jane R. Heneman
and
my father, Herbert G. Heneman, Jr.

The Addison-Wesley Series on Managing Human Resources

Series Editor: John Parcher Wanous, The Ohio State University

Merit Pay: Linking Pay Increases to Performance Ratings
Robert L. Heneman, The Ohio State University

Assessment Centers in Human Resource Management
George C. Thornton III, Colorado State University

Fairness in Selecting Employees, Second Edition
Richard D. Arvey, University of Minnesota and Robert H. Faley,
Kent State University

**Organizational Entry: Recruitment, Selection,
Orientation, and Socialization of Newcomers,
Second Edition**
John P. Wanous, The Ohio State University

Increasing Productivity through Performance Appraisal
Gary P. Latham, University of Toronto and Kenneth N. Wexley,
Michigan State University

Managing Conflict at Organizational Interfaces
L. David Brown, Boston University

Managing Careers
Manual London, AT&T and Stephen A. Stumpf, New York University

Managing Employee Absenteeism
Susan R. Rhodes, Syracuse University and Richard M. Steers,
University of Oregon

Foreword

This is an exciting time for the Managing Human Resources Series. Originally conceived in 1977, the first six books were published between 1979 and 1982. These books were uniformly well received by academic and business professionals alike. They have been extensively cited by researchers in human resources as state-of-the-art monographs. Moreover, students—both undergraduate and graduate—have found the series books to be both readable and informative.

The series is now in its second phase. *Fairness in Selecting Employees* (1979) by Rich Arvey was revised by Arvey and Robert Faley and published in 1988. This was followed by *Managing Employee Absenteeism* by Susan Rhodes and Rick Steers. My own book on *Organizational Entry* (1980) has been revised and reissued in 1992. Two new titles also appear in 1992. The first is *Merit Pay* by Rob Heneman, and the second is *Assessment Centers in Human Resource Management* by George Thornton. The commitment from Addison-Wesley to continue and expand the series has been crucial.

As always, this series is dedicated to the articulation of new solutions to human resources problems. My charge to authors has been to produce books that will summarize and extend cutting-edge knowledge. These authors must be intellectual leaders. In addition, they must make their books readily accessible to college students and human resource professionals alike. Readability need not and must not be sacrificed at the altar of academic scholarship. Both are achievable, as evidenced by the first books in this series. The present ones continue this tradition.

John Parcher Wanous
Series Editor

Preface

Purpose

I have written this book to bring together a summary of the current knowledge on merit pay and to further advance understanding of this type of incentive pay plan. I undertook the writing of this book to fill what I believe to be a void in the compensation literature. When I began the book in 1989, there were no books devoted exclusively to the subject of merit pay. Since then, surveys have shown that merit pay is the most frequently used method of incentive compensation, and research into the merit pay process continues to grow. Surprisingly, however, other forms of incentive pay, such as gainsharing, continue to receive the most attention, as evidenced by the number of books and articles on this topic in the popular press. In response to the frequent use of merit pay in organizations and the growing body of research, a book-length treatment of merit pay is needed.

Perspectives

In presenting the current knowledge on merit pay, I have approached it from three perspectives. First, I have tried to present a balanced view. Many articles on merit pay in business magazines and journals take a strong, almost emotional stance either for or against merit pay. This book strives for more balance by presenting both sides of the merit pay argument and evaluating these arguments in the context of available research. The book examines the conditions needed for merit pay to work without taking a side for or against merit pay.

Second, I have approached the material from an interdisciplinary perspective. Generally, the treatment of merit pay in academic journals has been somewhat parochial. The conclusions you draw about merit pay may depend on the journal you are reading and the academic discipline it represents. This book, however, draws upon articles from a variety of social science disciplines, including economics, industrial relations, public administration, management, and psychology in an attempt to provide the reader with a more comprehensive understanding of merit pay.

Third, in presenting recommendations for merit pay policy and practice, I have relied primarily on theory and research rather than organizational practice. It is my belief that sound policy and practice are best drawn from theory and research rather than from current practice at other organizations. While organizational practices are used to illustrate various points in the book, it is noted when these practices appear to conflict with theory and research.

To emphasize the importance of theory and research, I have decided to begin rather than end the book with a chapter on merit pay theory. It is my belief that the reader should understand the underlying rationale for merit pay before learning the mechanics of merit pay plans. Also, I have interspersed findings from empirical studies on merit pay throughout the book, rather than relegating these findings to one chapter. My hope is that by weaving research findings throughout the book, I encourage the reader to view research as crucial, ongoing input for managing the merit pay process rather than as a side issue.

Audience

As with other books in this series, this book has been written for three audiences: students, practitioners, and researchers. For students, this book can be used as a supplemental reader in a compensation class, or it can be used along with other books in the series for an advanced topics class in human resource management. For practitioners, this book can be used as a reference guide, summarizing the empirical studies on issues arising in the design, administration, and evaluation of merit pay plans. Finally, for researchers, this book is useful as a review of the issues that have been investigated in merit pay research. My hope is that this book will encourage personnel/human resource researchers to expand the scope of performance appraisal research to include the context in which ratings take place.

Organization

The book begins with an introduction to the concept of merit pay. In the introduction, merit pay is defined and contrasted with other forms of incentive pay. The chapter ends with a model to guide the reader through the remainder of the book. The book is divided into three parts based on the model.

The first part deals with assessing the desirability and feasibility of implementing a merit pay plan. This is accomplished through a chapter on current theory and research and a chapter on diagnosing situational characteristics.

The second part of the book presents the processes used to develop and administer a merit pay plan. Included in the second part are three chapters on measuring performance, establishing pay increases based on measured performance, and administering a merit pay plan once pay increases are linked to performance.

The third and final part of the book describes anticipated outcomes associated with merit pay, methods to evaluate merit pay plans, and studies that have evaluated actual outcomes of merit pay plans compared to anticipated outcomes.

Acknowledgments

I have benefited greatly from many people who graciously gave their time and expertise in helping me write this book. I would like to acknowledge and thank them for their contributions.

Several individuals reviewed the outline and/or individual chapters: John Blackburn, Ohio State University; Lee Dyer, Cornell University; Charles Fay, Rutgers University; Norman Handshear, McDonnell Douglas Corporation; Herbert Heneman III, University of Wisconsin; Daniel Mitchell, University of California at Los Angeles; Vida Scarpello, University of Florida; and Kenneth Wexley, Michigan State University. Several other individuals also reviewed the entire manuscript: John Fossum, University of Minnesota; Edward Lawler III, University of Southern California; Steve Mangum, Ohio State University; Peter Riffel, IBM; Craig Schneier, Sibson and Company, Inc.;

and Dow Scott and Tony Townsend, Virginia Polytechnic Institute and State University.

John Wanous, Series Editor, challenged me during every phase of the book to do more than simply report the current state of affairs with merit pay. He was also a very helpful coach during the entire process. Joan Evans did an outstanding job at translating my scrawl into an organized and presentable product. The staff at Addison-Wesley provided me with assistance at every turn. Kathryn Crockett Lyon did a superb job at copyediting the manuscript and any clarity in the presentation of my ideas I owe to her.

I hope that all of the people I have acknowledged will see their influence on the final product. I remain solely responsible, however, for any errors or omissions.

Finally, I especially want to thank my wife, Renée Brausch Heneman, for her contributions to the writing of this book. She has been my sounding board and major support system from the start. Perhaps now that the book is finished, she will be able to come home after a hard day's work and put up her feet, rather than be greeted at the door by a half-crazed professor waving freshly written pages for her to immediately read.

Columbus, Ohio   Rob Heneman

Contents

1

Introduction and Overview

In this chapter, I introduce the concept of merit pay using several approaches. First, I describe my first encounter with merit pay. The questions that were raised by this experience will be used to illustrate some of the topics to be covered in this book. I also illustrate some of the topics by describing tough decisions managers face when using merit pay. Second, I provide a more formal description of what merit pay is and what merit pay is not. This will give you an idea of the boundaries of merit pay and, in turn, what you can expect to see covered in the book. Third, I present a model of the merit pay process. This model is included to show the major steps that are involved in managing merit pay and to preview the chapters of the book in the order in which they will be presented.

My First Encounter with Merit Pay

My first encounter with merit pay left me puzzled, to say the least. First, I will tell you what happened and the questions that it raised. I will then link these questions to concepts covered in this book. Perhaps some of the questions raised by my experience will be similar to your own.

After working for about five months in a job, I was pulled aside by my immediate supervisor at work one day. He told me my performance had been pretty good so far, and as a result, he was going to give me a five percent merit increase. I told him I was pleased with his assessment of my performance, but I wasn't sure what a merit increase was. He explained to me that it was an increase in my salary based on my performance. Needless to say, I was thrilled with a salary increase and walked away with a favorable first impression of merit pay.

This favorable first impression was soon replaced, however, with a number of questions. A few hours after talking with my supervisor, I ran into several other people in jobs similar to mine. It turned out they had also received five percent merit increases. They had been informed by their supervisors that this five percent increase was a market adjustment to make their salaries comparable to increasing salaries being paid by our competitors for similar jobs. After talking with these people and thinking further about the notion of merit pay, I was confused and had a number of questions. These questions, along with chapter references that point out where the questions are discussed in the book, are presented below.

1. Why was my salary increase based on my performance rather than the time I had put in on the job? It turned out that my supervisor had a theory on how to motivate employees. His theory had to do with paying people on the basis of performance rather than other factors such as seniority. Theories concerning pay-for-performance are presented in Chapter 2.

2. Why was I given a merit increase when others in the organization received a cost-of-living allowance instead? In this particular organization, increases for unionized employees were given on the basis of increases in the cost of living while increases for nonunion employees were given on the basis of performance. As shown in Chapter 3, the types of salary increases granted depend upon the organization, type of job, and situation.

3. Was I paid for my performance or was it a market adjustment? I was really stumped here. At first, I thought I had been misled by my supervisor. He told me I was paid for my performance when in reality I was paid for a change in the market that affected everyone and for which everyone was compensated. Years later, it dawned on me that maybe performance-based and market-based pay are related to one another. That is, maybe market adjustments

were granted only to those employees with adequate performance levels. To the extent that this was the case, maybe I was not misled by my supervisor after all. Issues surrounding what does and does not constitute performance under merit pay are covered in Chapter 4.

4. Why was I given a five percent increase rather than, say, a four or six percent increase? Why this specific amount and not another? Many organizations have formal guidelines that spell out the amount that employees can receive for various performance levels. Guidelines such as these are discussed in Chapter 5.

5. Why wasn't the "real" reason for my salary increase clearly spelled out to me? Organizations have various policies when it comes to the communication of pay information, and supervisors follow these policies to greater or lesser degrees. The formation of and adherence to these policies is discussed in Chapter 6.

6. What did my supervisor expect from me in return for the pay increase? At first, I thought the answer was obvious: I must maintain or improve my performance. After talking with my coworkers, however, I realized that what he expected was for me to remain with the organization. Now, I believe that merit increases are granted for both performance and retention purposes as well as for other reasons such as employee satisfaction. The returns managers expect for merit pay, including these and others, are discussed in Chapter 7.

Tough Managerial Decisions

Millions of managers in the United States are required by their organizations to make merit pay decisions. They are asked to evaluate the performance of their subordinates and decide on the size of pay increases their subordinates will receive for their performance. At first blush, this process may seem fairly straightforward and simple. It is not. Even seasoned managers will tell you that tough decisions are required of managers under a merit pay plan.

Following are some comments that represent the tough decisions managers wrestle with along with chapter references that point out where these decisions are addressed in the book:

- "Why should I give different-size raises to my subordinates? If I do give different-size raises, won't my people think they are being treated unfairly, be less likely to cooperate with one another, lose interest in their work, and be less motivated? Given these potential problems, why can't I simply give everyone the same raise under the merit pay plan?" These concerns are held by many managers and are discussed in Chapter 2. This chapter presents evidence in theory, research, and practice to support paying people different amounts to reflect differences in performance.

- "Our organization is about to take over a company that has a different product line than the companies in our current organization. My boss proposes that we extend our merit pay plan to include this new company. Does it make sense to use merit pay for employees of this soon-to-be-acquired company? Do I need to convince my boss that merit pay is not appropriate?" Although merit pay is frequently used, it is not appropriate in all situations. The issues concerning when and where merit pay should be used are addressed in Chapter 3.

- "Every few years, the personnel department distributes a new form that we are expected to use in evaluating the performance of our subordinates. Nothing seems to change, though. Everyone gripes about the forms, especially at the end of the year when we use these forms to make merit pay decisions. What can be done to improve our performance appraisal system? What can I do as a manager to better evaluate my subordinates?" A critical factor in the success of a merit pay plan is the development of a sound method to measure employee performance. Characteristics of good performance measures and ways to improve the evaluation of employee performance are described in Chapter 4.

- "I need to submit a budget for merit increases next year. How much will I need to motivate my employees? What do I need to consider in coming up with a budget figure? Is it possible to set up pay increases that will motivate my people more but cost the organization less?" Not only are tough decisions required regarding employee performance and merit pay, but tough financial decisions are required as well. Guidelines for establishing pay increases are covered in Chapter 5.

- "Money does not seem to be the issue with our merit pay plan. Our budget seems adequate. But even though the money is there, people still complain about their merit pay increases, saying that what they got is not fair. What can I do to ensure that my merit pay decisions are seen as fair?" In recent years, a number of steps have been identified that managers can take to ensure that merit pay decisions are viewed as fair and just by employees. These steps are described in Chapter 6.

- "Everyone has an opinion about merit pay. That makes sense given that we are dealing with people's pocketbooks. When all is said and done, though, is merit pay really worth the time, money, and effort?" Merit pay *does* work, but not under all circumstances. As described in Chapter 7, evaluation studies to date have reported mixed success for merit pay plans. Given the limited amount of research on the success of merit pay plans, the book concludes with a strong recommendation that organizations evaluate the effectiveness of their own plans. Procedures for doing so are presented in Chapter 7. It is premature to make blanket statements about the effectiveness of merit pay. Organizations are best advised to avoid operating on the basis of blanket proclamations concerning merit pay. Instead, they should review the evidence, implement a plan of action, and evaluate the effectiveness of the plan. This is the recommended model, described later in Chapter 1, that is followed throughout the book.

Description of Merit Pay

In this section, I briefly define merit pay, describe its history and importance, illustrate the various types of merit pay, and contrast merit pay with other forms of pay. These characteristics are described to show how merit pay fits in with other human resource practices.

Merit Pay Defined

At a general level, merit pay is one of many forms of compensation provided by an organization for services rendered by its employees. Merit pay has to do with compensation decisions rather than other personnel decisions such as staffing and training and development. Therefore, the term merit pay should not be confused with the term "merit system." A merit system is a term used in the public sector to describe hiring and promotion decisions rather than compensation decisions, based on the competence or performance of employees (Greiner, Bell, & Hatry, 1975).

At a more specific level, merit pay is a particular form of compensation known as incentive pay. Under incentive pay plans, of which merit pay is one type, pay is allocated on the basis of performance. A key characteristic of merit pay is that compensation is provided for performance rather than other factors such as the worth of the job to the employer or an employee's need for a certain form of income (e.g., retirement).

At a very specific level, merit pay can be defined as individual pay increases based on the rated performance of individual employees in a previous time period (R. Heneman, 1990). Under this specific definition, salary increases are granted on the basis of a subjective judgment of employee performance in a previous period of time. As shown in this chapter where merit pay is contrasted with other incentive plans, it is one of several different types of incentive pay plans. While a salary increase is based on previous performance, it is intended to motivate increased performance in future time periods. Hence, merit pay can be thought of as a two-stage process as shown in Figure 1.1. In stage one, pay increases are based on previous performance. In stage two, pay increases are granted to motivate future performance.

In discussing pay for performance under merit pay plans, it is important to note which stage is being discussed. For example,

Figure 1.1
Merit Pay as a Two-stage Process

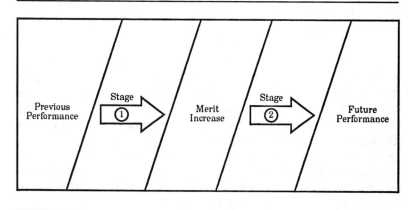

Chapter 5 looks at linking pay increases to previous performance (stage one of this process). Chapter 7, which discusses outcomes of merit pay, focuses on pay increases as motivators for future performance (stage two of the merit pay process). As shown throughout the book, attainment of stage one is a necessary but not sufficient condition for the attainment of stage two.

In summary, merit pay refers to compensation decisions rather than other personnel decisions. It is one form of organizational compensation known as incentive pay. It is a specific type of incentive pay whereby pay increases are granted on the basis of ratings of previous performance. These increases are granted with the hope of motivating future performance.

History of Merit Pay

Although the term merit pay is relatively new, the philosophy of linking pay to performance is not. According to Evans (1970), this philosophy dates back to the Protestant Reformation of the sixteenth and seventeenth centuries. During this period, pay was linked to performance in the following way: Hard work was viewed as self-sacrifice in the service of God. Hard work was assessed by the economic success one had. Hence, economic success through hard work was seen as a willingness to serve God.

Actual merit pay plans appear to have been around since the early 1900s. Schmitt and Klimoski (1991) report that the Larkin Company used merit pay for its supervisors in 1912. Cohen and Murname (1980) estimate that some 40 to 50 percent of U.S. urban school districts had merit pay plans in the 1920s. The widespread use of merit pay probably accompanied the rapid growth in the use of performance ratings after World War II (Baron, Dobbin, & Jennings, 1986; Mitchell, Lewin, & Lawler, 1990). Today, at least 80 percent of U.S. organizations have what they call merit pay plans according to recent surveys (Peck, 1984; Personnel Policies Forum, 1981; Wyatt Company, 1987). To sum up, the philosophy of pay-for-performance has been around for a long time. The translation of this philosophy into formal organizational policy has primarily taken place in the past 70 years.

Importance of Merit Pay

The importance of merit pay to organizations can be illustrated in a variety of ways, including the frequency with which merit pay plans are used, the symbolic nature of these plans, and the evaluated effectiveness of these plans. These three indicators of the importance of merit pay are considered in turn below.

Frequency of Use. One indication of the importance of merit pay is the frequent use of these plans by employers. In recent years, a number of surveys have been conducted to find out the frequency of use of merit pay plans. The figures reported in these surveys are somewhat approximate because what respondents consider to be merit pay may not be consistent from organization to organization or with the definition in this book. In general, these national surveys suggest that merit pay is probably the most frequently used method of incentive pay.

While merit pay plans are frequently used, the use of these plans is not uniform across industries. Three surveys showed that over 80 percent of private-sector employers have merit pay for at least some of their employees (Peck, 1984; Personnel Policies Forum, 1981; Wyatt Company, 1987). In contrast, surveys of public-sector employers tend to show less frequent use of merit pay plans (Greiner, Bell, & Hatry, 1975; Lawther, Bernardin, Traynham, & Jennings, 1989). Even within the private and public sectors, the use of merit pay varies. In the public sector, Lawther et al. (1989) report that 37 of the 50 state governments (64 percent) have merit pay plans, while Greiner et al. (1975) report that 48 percent of local governments have merit pay plans. In the private sector, Brown (1990) reports that the use of merit pay in manufacturing varies by industry from a low of 9 percent in the cotton textiles industry to a high of 63 percent in the household furniture industry.

Given sampling differences and methodological differences among studies, it is difficult to tell if the frequency of use is changing. In one study of primarily private-sector employers, the data suggest that the use of merit pay is increasing (Sibson and Company, 1989). In another survey of primarily private-sector employers, O'Dell (1986) reports that the use of merit pay is declining. Given a current base rate use of 80 percent or so in the private sector, it will be increasingly difficult to find many surveys indicating an increase in merit pay. For state governments, there does appear to be an actual increase in the use of merit pay, up from 27 of the 50 states in 1975 (Greiner et al., 1975) to 37 of the 50 states in 1989 (Lawther et al., 1989).

Symbolic Nature of Merit Pay. A very important and often overlooked role that merit pay plays is as a symbol of an organization's culture. Merit pay is a large-scale intervention in an organization, not just a simple change in pay policy. It is an important symbol because it signifies a prevailing organizational belief that work is to be rewarded on the basis of performance rather than on the basis of equality, need, or seniority.

Numerous examples of merit pay as a symbol of culture exist. In the federal government, merit pay is viewed as a symbol of the changing emphasis on the importance of work from time in grade or seniority to performance on the job (Perry & Petrakis, 1988). It has also been viewed by some as a symbol of the government's effort to maintain control over bureaucracy (March & Olsen, 1983). At General Motors Corporation, merit pay is seen as a shift in corporate culture from a welfare system, where all people received the same pay increase, to a competitive business, where pay increases are contingent on performance (Schlesinger, 1988). The point of these examples is that merit pay, for better or worse, commands attention from employees in work organizations. As such, it cannot be developed and administered in a haphazard fashion, but instead must be carefully managed.

Overall Effectiveness.   A final indicator of the importance of merit pay is the extent to which merit pay plans lead to desirable results. Although there are many ways to view the question "Are merit pay plans effective?" (presented in detail in Chapter 7) at least one survey indicates that the answer to this question is a tentative and qualified "yes." Peck (1984), in a survey of 521 employers, found that at least some employers under some circumstances do see merit pay plans as successful. The results of Peck's survey are shown in Table 1.1.

When and how successful outcomes are actually attained is covered throughout this book. For now, these data suggest that merit pay does indeed have some value for a number of employers. Note that these data from Peck (1984) should be treated as suggestive rather than conclusive, because it is not clear what definition of "success" employers were using when responding to the survey. As shown in Chapter 7, the results of an evaluation of merit pay effectiveness depend on which measure of success is used. Also the Peck data are somewhat dated, but a more recent survey by the Wyatt Company (1989) shows essentially the same results.

Two additional points should be made about the effectiveness of merit pay plans. First, it appears that, on average, the success of merit pay is moderate. There are, of course, deviations around this average that should also be considered. What this means is that the potential for success or failure of merit pay in any one setting may be large. The upside returns that are possible with a merit pay plan can be seen in the results of a study of managers in New York City (Allan & Rosenberg, 1986). These managers reported an increase in performance after the implementation of a merit pay plan not only in the first year but in the second and third years as well. The downside risk associated with merit pay is perhaps best illustrated by a study of federal employees and managers (Pearce, Stevenson, & Perry, 1985). In this study it was shown that over the course of 48 months after implementation of a merit pay plan, there were no improvements in productivity.

Second, even moderately successful merit pay plans may have considerable monetary value for organizations. Using a

Table 1.1
Degree of Success of Merit Pay

Industry Category	Very Successful		Degree of Success					
			Moderately Successful		Marginally Successful		Cannot Tell Degree of Success	
	Number	Percent	Number	Percent	Number	Percent	Number	Percent
Manufacturing (N=193)	50	26%*	105	54%	18	9%	20	10%
Banking (N=96)	27	28*	50	52	9	9	10	10
Insurance (N=65)	14	22*	40	62	7	11	4	6
Diversified finance (N=9)	3	33	5	56	—	—	1	11
Total	94	26%	200	55%	34	9%	35	10%

Percentages do not add up to 100 because of rounding.

Source: Peck (1984). Reprinted by permission.

procedure known as utility analysis (described in greater detail in Chapter 7), Sterling (1990) reports a three million-dollar return over three years for a simulated organization of 157 employees studied by Schwab and Olson (1990). This large monetary return was possible even under the assumption of a moderate relationship between merit pay and subsequent performance.

In summary, the importance of merit pay is reflected in the research on the effectiveness of merit pay. Overall, the success of merit pay appears to be moderate. However, it is possible to improve upon this moderate rate of success as will be shown throughout the book. Finally, even moderately successful merit pay plans give large financial returns to organizations.

Merit Versus Other Forms of Incentive Pay

Merit pay can easily be confused with other incentive pay plans. The reason for this confusion is that, like merit pay, other incentive plans are also based on the notion of pay for performance. There are, however, some differences between merit pay and other forms of incentive pay which can be used to distinguish among the various plans. The distinctions are important because what works for other incentive plans does not necessarily work for merit pay plans.

Over the years, many distinctions have been made between merit pay and other forms of incentive pay (e.g., Waldman & Roberts, 1988; Lawler, 1971; Wallace, 1990). First, merit pay is allocated on the basis of actual performance rather than potential performance. Hence, merit pay differs from skill-based pay, which is granted for the acquisition of skills that may contribute to subsequent performance.

Second, merit pay is allocated on the basis of subjective ratings of employee performance rather than on the basis of more countable indicators of performance such as sales, profit, costs, and time savings. Unlike merit pay, incentive plans like piece-rate pay, sales commissions, profit sharing, and impro-share are based on countable indicators of performance rather than ratings of performance.

Third, merit pay is granted to individual employees on the basis of individual performance. In contrast, group incentive plans and some gainsharing plans are based on the performance of the entire work group.

Fourth, merit pay is usually based on an overall assessment of long-term performance rather than an assessment of performance at one point in time. Overall performance is typically rewarded by a merit increase while one-time performance may be rewarded with a discretionary bonus. So, for example, a counter clerk at a fast-food restaurant might receive a $20 bill from management for the courtesy extended to customers during a particularly busy period. This would be a discretionary bonus. On the other hand, a counter clerk might also receive a five percent increase in weekly pay at the end of the year because he or she was courteous throughout the year, processed orders quickly and efficiently, was accurate in cash transactions, and so on. This would be an example of a merit increase. The difference, then, between merit pay and a discretionary bonus is that merit pay is based on a formal rating of performance for an extended period of time while a discretionary bonus is based on a less formal evaluation of one episode of performance.

Although these distinctions are very useful in helping to sort out the applicability of policy, practice, and research to merit pay, they are less than perfect and do become blurred from time to time. For example, Management by Objectives (MBO) is often used to measure the performance of supervisors, managers, and professional employees. Using this approach, which will be discussed in Chapter 4, performance assessment is based on quantitative measures of performance such as the number of services provided, tasks accomplished within a certain period of time, and so on. It is tempting to label a pay increase under MBO as something other than merit pay because it uses countable indicators of performance such as the time and number of services. However, in fact, these supposedly objective or countable performance measures are typically based on subjective ratings. The number of services may be measured as the number of successful services and could therefore resemble performance ratings. Given this scenario, a pay increase under MBO appears to be merit pay.

The point is that the difference between merit pay and other incentive plans is a matter of degree rather than an absolute difference. Throughout this book, I make every effort to carefully explain what I consider to be a merit pay plan, and I *do* consider MBO with pay to be a form of merit pay. The reader is also urged to carefully consider the type of plan described here or elsewhere to assess the applicability of the plan to his or her own circumstances. The distinctions provided here should be of some guidance. Also, as discussed in Chapter 3, merit and other forms of incentive pay should probably be considered as additions to one another rather than alternatives. Organizations such as Pratt and Whitney have found that an integrated reward strategy may be more effective than an "all or nothing" reward system in which one and only one incentive plan is used (Schneier, 1989b).

Although it may not be a preferred strategy, some organizations are able to use only one form of incentive pay. In general, merit pay has two important advantages over other incentive plans. First, the less tangible aspects of employee performance, such as customer service and quality, can be captured with the performance ratings used in merit pay plans. Both the aforementioned aspects of performance are being emphasized increasingly by employers in today's economy (Carnevale, 1991). Other incentive plans with more objective indicators of performance, such as piece-rate pay, tend to place more emphasis on the tangible aspects of performance such as quantity. Second, merit pay places an emphasis on the performance of the individual. Under group-based incentive plans, individuals may not be motivated to perform at their highest levels because the influence of any one person on group performance may be minimal. One employee may work hard under a group plan, but receive the same pay increase as those who do not work hard. In short, merit pay seems to be most appropriate when there is a concern for the quality of goods or services produced by individual members of an organization.

Types of Merit Pay Plans

Just as there are differences in types of incentive pay plans, so too, are there differences in the types of merit pay plans. In theory, distinctions among the various types of merit pay plans can be made along a number of lines (R. Heneman, 1984b). First, merit pay plans may differ on the standards used to assess performance. Some organizations include seniority and market adjustments as criteria while others do not. Second, the form that pay takes under various merit pay plans may differ. Under traditional merit pay plans, pay is in the form of a salary increase. Some have proposed alternative forms of pay such as benefits. Third, the method used to calculate the merit increase may vary. For example, a merit increase could be calculated as an absolute dollar amount or as a percentage increase in salary. Fourth, the permanency of the increase may vary. Under traditional merit pay plans, the salary increase is a permanent one, with the increase carrying over into the base salary in future evaluation periods. Alternatively, a lump-sum plan could be used when the salary increase is not intended to be permanent. In this case, a salary increase would be granted on a one-time basis and would not be built into base pay.

The extent to which conceptual differences exist in practice today is difficult to determine since there have not been any national surveys to take a look at these various types of merit plans. There are, however, individual case studies of many of these variations, and they will be examined at various points in the book. The important point to consider is that merit pay plans are *not* homogeneous. They vary along a number of dimensions, and what works with one plan may not work with another. Throughout the book I try to spell out when merit pay plan differences are likely to have an impact. When I discuss merit pay as a general concept, I am referring to what seems to be the typical case in merit pay: a permanent salary increase is granted on the basis of rated performance.

In summary, merit pay is an important form of incentive pay that has been around for at least 70 years. It is probably the most frequently used method of incentive pay, and there are a number of variations of merit pay plans. Overall, merit pay plans have been moderately successful.

A Normative Model of the Merit Pay Process

The normative model of the merit pay process, depicted in Figure 1.2, is intended to show the steps required for creating, using, and evaluating a merit pay plan, and to show how the contents of the remainder of the book have been organized.

At first blush, the concept of merit pay may seem straightforward and a merit pay plan relatively easy to create. However, as pointed out throughout the book, this has not been the experience of most employers. Many difficult decisions have to be made in setting up the plan. Once it has been developed, the implementation and administration steps required to gain adherence to the

Figure 1.2
Managing the Merit Pay Process

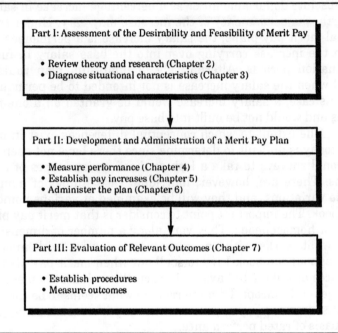

Part I: Assessment of the Desirability and Feasibility of Merit Pay

• Review theory and research (Chapter 2)
• Diagnose situational characteristics (Chapter 3)

Part II: Development and Administration of a Merit Pay Plan

• Measure performance (Chapter 4)
• Establish pay increases (Chapter 5)
• Administer the plan (Chapter 6)

Part III: Evaluation of Relevant Outcomes (Chapter 7)

• Establish procedures
• Measure outcomes

plan are difficult to enact. After the plan has been implemented, the effectiveness of the plan must be measured and decisions made as to whether to continue or discontinue the plan. Overall, the merit pay process needs to be carefully managed.

Management of the merit pay process consists of establishing three major objectives and pursuing them in the order shown in Figure 1.2. The three major objectives are an assessment of the desirability and feasibility of merit pay, development and administration of the plan, and an evaluation of relevant outcomes. These three objectives, shown in the model, correspond to the three major sections of the book. To achieve each objective, a series of steps or activities needs to be undertaken. The required activities, shown under each objective in the model, correspond to specific, consecutive chapters in the book.

The first part of the book focuses on assessing whether merit pay is feasible or even desirable in a particular organization.

To support assessment of desirability, a review of the theory and research that underlies merit pay is presented in Chapter 2. To support assessment of the feasibility of merit pay, situations where merit pay seems to be warranted are presented in Chapter 3.

The second part of the book addresses issues related to the development and implementation of a merit pay plan after it has been assessed that merit pay is desirable and feasible. Activities include the measurement of performance (Chapter 4), linking pay to performance (Chapter 5), and administering the merit pay plan that links pay to performance (Chapter 6).

In the third part of the book, the focus shifts to evaluating outcomes of merit pay after a plan has been developed and administered (Chapter 7). Activities include procedures that can be used to evaluate merit pay plans, relevant outcomes that should be assessed, and summaries of evaluation studies conducted by other organizations.

This model is normative in that it shows recommended steps for managing a merit pay plan. It is also meant to guide the reader to the appropriate sections of the book. Readers who are considering merit pay for the first time should start with Part I. Readers searching for information on how to establish and administer a plan should focus on Part II. Readers who wish to learn how to evaluate a merit pay plan should focus on Part III.

Central Themes of the Book

There are three central themes that run throughout the book. Although these themes are not used to organize the literature, they are important to consider as they represent the fundamental ideas that need to be examined to better understand and more effectively use merit pay. The major themes are as follows:

1. *Recognizing that merit pay needs to be managed.* Although the concept of merit pay is straightforward, it is not simple. Creating a merit pay policy that simply states pay is to be based on performance is likely to lead to disastrous results. Many factors other than pay and performance need to be considered and addressed in a systematic fashion, because they impinge on the pay and performance relationship. Some of these other factors include characteristics of the people making merit pay decisions, characteristics of the people

receiving merit increases, organizational conditions, and environmental conditions such as outside economic forces and the presence of labor organizations. A model is used in the book to provide a systematic way to manage these factors.

2. *Doing more with less.* In merit pay plans, a fundamental tension exists between the goals of doing more and doing it with less. Ideally, merit pay should motivate greater performance levels than would occur without merit pay, at a lower cost. A recent *Newsweek* article (Quinn, 1991) highlights the popularity of this belief. Merit pay is viewed as offering more for less because pay increases are based on performance rather than amount of time on the job. Unfortunately, there is often a conflict between the goals of achieving greater performance and reducing cost. For merit pay plans to be effective, a balance must be struck between maximizing performance and minimizing cost. To reach this balance, attention must be given to both motivational and financial considerations.

3. *Understanding that the perceived relationship between pay and performance is as important as the actual relationship.* The relationship between pay and performance in a merit pay plan can be examined from differing perspectives. One way to look at merit pay is via the *actual relationship* between performance ratings and salary increases. The actual relationship might, for example, be expressed in the form of a policy statement about the intended relationship between performance and pay. You could also audit the effectiveness of this policy by calculating the statistical relationship between ratings and increases. Another way to look at merit pay is through people's *perceptions* of the relationship between performance and pay. Some may see a positive relationship, others a negative relationship, and others no relationship at all. If merit pay plans are to be effective, the perceived and actual positive relationship between merit pay and performance must be in alignment. You cannot assume that because there is

an *actual* positive relationship between pay and performance that there is also a *perception* of a positive relationship. Many merit pay plans have failed simply because people within an organization do not see a relationship between pay and performance. An important part of managing the merit pay process is not only to facilitate the actual relationship between pay and performance but to ensure that employees see this relationship as well.

Little consideration has been given to these three issues in previous writings on merit pay. By understanding and paying close attention to these issues, however, you can better understand merit pay, which, in turn, should help make your merit pay plans more effective.

Summary of Major Points

The major points covered in this chapter are as follows:

1. *Definition.* Merit pay is a form of compensation known as incentive pay. Under a merit pay plan, pay increases are granted to individuals on the basis of their rated performance in a previous time period. Pay increases are granted with the hope of motivating future performance.

2. *Importance.* Merit pay is probably the most frequently used method of incentive compensation. It is an important symbol of an organization's culture. Its use has been shown to be related to the effectiveness of organizations.

3. *Merit Versus Other Incentives.* Unlike other incentive pay plans, merit pay is based on actual rather than potential performance, subjective ratings of performance rather than countable indicators of performance, individual rather than group performance, and overall rather than one-time performance.

4. *Types of Merit Pay Plans.* Merit pay plans can differ by the performance criteria that are evaluated, the form that merit pay takes, the method used to calculate the increase, and the permanence of the increase.

5. *Management of the Merit Pay Process.* The merit pay process needs to be managed rather than left to circumstances. Therefore, care must be taken to assess the desirability and feasibility of a merit pay plan, to develop and administer the merit pay plan, and to evaluate relevant outcomes.

6. *Central Themes of the Book.* The central themes of the book are as follows: managing merit pay; doing more with less; and understanding that the perceived relationship between pay and performance is as important as the actual relationship.

Conclusions

Merit pay is used extensively in the United States. One reason for this frequent use is that organizations hope to do more for less. "More" refers to the improved level of performance expected from the good performers due to the merit increases they receive. With across-the-board pay increases, all employees receive the same pay increase. Good performers do not receive any special recognition through larger pay increases; they receive the same increase as everyone else.

"Less" refers to the potentially lower fixed costs under a merit pay plan compared to an across-the-board pay plan. The budget needed to fund merit increases just for good performers is less than the budget needed to fund merit increases for all employees at the same level as the good performers.

Another reason for the popularity of merit pay is the method of performance measurement. By using ratings, rather than more countable indicators of employee performance such as the number of goods produced or services provided, less tangible aspects of employee performance, such as quality, can be rewarded. To compete in tough product or service markets, quality is as important or more important than quantity. Through the use of merit pay, employers can, in effect, promote the importance of these less tangible aspects of performance.

While merit pay plans are frequently used to lower costs and motivate performance, their actual success in reaching these goals is mixed. While merit pay seems to work in some situations, it does not work in others. The remainder of the book shows under what circumstances merit pay is likely to have the intended effect.

For merit pay to work, the process of linking pay to performance ratings must also be carefully managed, as shown in Figure 1.2. If the merit pay process cannot be carefully managed, for whatever reason, it is actually better to use a "peanut butter" approach to granting pay increases. Using this approach, every employee is given the same pay increase, just as peanut butter is spread evenly across toast. An explicit, across-the-board pay increase approach like this is probably less offensive to employees and less likely to lead to adverse reactions than a poorly managed merit pay plan that does not actually succeed in awarding pay for performance.

2

Pay for Performance: A Review of Theory and Research

The material presented in this chapter can be used to assess the desirability of merit pay. By the end of the chapter, the reader should be familiar with the general requirements and potential benefits and costs associated with merit pay. The first part of the chapter presents theories that provide the rationale for making pay contingent on performance. The second part of the chapter looks at the extent to which it is possible to link pay to performance. Empirical research shows the actual relationship between pay and performance in a variety of organizational settings where merit pay is used. The third part of the chapter reviews the potential risks or dysfunctional consequences that may be encountered when pay is linked to performance.

Theories Behind Merit Pay

According to a national survey of compensation administrators by Peck (1984), the number-one objective of compensation systems is to tie pay to performance. Respondents to the survey indicated that this objective was of greater importance than other important objectives of compensation, including maintaining equitable relationships among jobs, attracting job applicants, and keeping payroll costs competitive. To understand why pay for performance is given such a high priority in some organizations, it is necessary to review the theories behind merit pay. These theories show the benefits of paying on the basis of performance and also serve as the underlying rationale for merit pay plans.

Finally, and most important, these theories show *how* and *why* pay based on performance should lead to improved performance.

Theories concerning merit pay come from the fields of both psychology and economics. The reason for reviewing both psychological and economic theories here is that the similarities and differences between these sets of theories have important implications for merit pay (Kahn & Sherer, 1990). A theme common to both sets of theories is that linking pay to performance should increase performance. A major difference between these sets of theories is the view on *why* pay based on performance is likely to lead to better performance. Assumptions about the nature of man differ between the psychological and economic theories (Herrnstein, 1990; Kaufman, 1989). These differences have implications, which will be referred to throughout the book, for the development, administration, and evaluation of merit pay plans.

Before reviewing each set of theories, it should be noted that these theories were not developed solely to explain merit pay. In fact, these theories look primarily at pay *levels* rather than pay *increases*. However, under most merit pay plans, pay increases are rolled over into the pay levels received by employees. That is, a pay increase in one year becomes a part of base pay in the next year. Hence, these pay level theories do have implications for merit pay plans.

Psychological Theories

Several theories from psychology suggest that the linking of pay to performance should lead to increased performance. According to these theories, performance is increased because employee motivation is increased when pay and performance are linked. Motivation and ability are the primary determinants of performance.

Psychological theories differ in explaining why pay for performance should be motivational to employees. These different explanations, in turn, have important implications for the design of merit pay systems. In the next pages, these theories, the implications of the theories, and other related research are reviewed.

Expectancy Theory. This theory of employee motivation dates back to at least 1957 when Georgopoulos, Mahoney, and Jones (1957) looked at factors related to employee productivity. The first formal model of expectancy theory was developed by Vroom (1964) and has been refined by many authors, including Porter and Lawler (1968), since 1964.

According to expectancy theory, motivation, or the force to act, results from a conscious, decision-making process undertaken by an individual. The decision to act depends upon three sets of perceptions known as expectancy, instrumentality, and valence, which are shown in Figure 2.1. Expectancy refers to the individual's perception that a certain level of effort is required to achieve a certain level of performance. Instrumentality is the strength of the belief that a certain level of performance will be associated with various outcomes. Valence is the attractiveness of these outcomes. In making the decision to act, these perceptions are assumed to combine in a multiplicative manner. What this means is that if either expectancy, instrumentality, or valence has a value of zero, then motivational force will be zero. An example of the thought process associated with expectancy theory is shown in Figure 2.2.

Over the years, a substantial body of research has been conducted on expectancy theory. Reviews of this research have been conducted by many authors including Schwab, Olian-Gottlieb, and H. Heneman (1979) and Mitchell (1974). In

Figure 2.1
Expectancy Theory

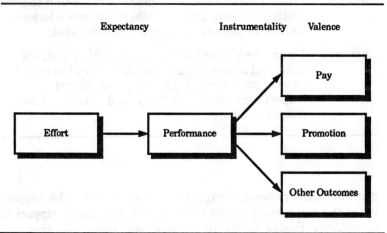

Figure 2.2
Example of the Expectancy Theory Thought Process

Expectancy

Question: If I work as hard as possible on this project, how likely is it that I will accomplish what is required?

Answer: Chances are I will not perform up to the requirements. I just don't have the time or expertise to do it. I'm just not motivated.

Answer: If I work as hard as I can, there is a good chance that I will do a good job. But, I still have to ask myself the next question.

Instrumentality

Question: So what? What's in it for me if I do a good job?

Answer: Absolutely nothing. Good performance simply is not recognized around here. I'm just not motivated.

Answer: At a minimum, my boss will say thanks for a job well done, and I may get a cash bonus. But, I still have to ask myself the next question.

Valence

Question: How attractive are these outcomes?

Answer: Praise doesn't mean that much to me, and if the truth be known, I would rather have more leisure time than more pay. I'm just not motivated.

Answer: I would be pleased with the recognition from my boss, and a cash bonus could go toward the boat I have always wanted. All things considered (expectancy, instrumentality, and valence), I am indeed motivated.

---

general, these reviews of expectancy theory tend to be supportive of the major components of the theory. Empirical support for expectancy theory tends to be stronger when the theory is focused on the individual rather than on groups of individuals (Kennedy, Fossum, & White, 1983; Wanous, Keon, & Latack, 1983). However, even when expectancy theory is used to predict motivational force across individuals rather than predicting motivational force within individuals, there is still moderate empirical support (Schwab, et al., 1979).

Expectancy theory has a number of important implications for merit pay plans (R. Heneman, 1984b; Mount, 1987). In particular, expectancy theory suggests that merit pay is likely to motivate employees when the following conditions are met:

- *Performance must be accurately measured.* If it is not, then employees cannot make the perceived link between effort and performance (expectancy) and performance and rewards (instrumentality).

- *Increased pay must be a valued outcome.* For employees to pursue high levels of performance, the end result of such performance must be attractive or have positive valence. Hence, pay increases must have greater valence than alternative outcomes such as leisure. If a pay increase is less attractive than leisure, then an employee will feel less motivated to perform when promised a pay increase rather than additional time off the job.

- *The relationship between pay and performance must be clearly defined.* The relationship between performance on the job and pay associated with performance must be clearly spelled out by the organization to ensure that performance is perceived by employees as instrumental in attaining a pay increase.

- *Opportunities to improve performance must exist.* If an employee does not have the opportunity to increase or improve performance, then it is futile for that employee to expend effort at a task. If opportunity is not present, both expectancy and resultant motivation will not be present. Employees must have the time, equipment, ability, and supervision required to perform a task—which translates into opportunity— before there can be expectations for performance.

In summary, expectancy theory suggests that merit pay is likely to motivate increased performance because performance is instrumental in the attainment of a pay increase. For merit pay to motivate increased performance, performance must be accurately measured, pay must be a valued outcome, pay must be made contingent on performance, and the employee must have the opportunity to have an impact on performance.

Reinforcement Theory. This theory comes in large part from the work on operant conditioning by B.F. Skinner (1953). Reinforcement theory has been extended from laboratory settings to the work place by a number of authors, including Luthans and Kreitner (1975). This theory suggests that any behavior, including performance, is determined by its consequences. Unlike expectancy theory where attention is given to both antecedents to and consequences of performance, reinforcement theory focuses solely on the consequences of performance (Komaki, 1986). Hence, in the language of expectancy theory, reinforcement theory provides additional explanation of instrumentality perceptions and is silent on expectancy perceptions.

According to reinforcement theory, the frequency of a behavior is likely to be increased when a valued reward is made contingent upon that behavior. The contingency between the behavior and reward is likely to be strengthened the more clearly the behavior is defined, the closer in time the reward is to the behavior, and the closer in magnitude the reward is to the behavior. If the relationship between desired behavior and its consequences is not made contingent, then the frequency of the desired behaviors may not increase.

The importance of making rewards contingent upon behavior and the careful attention that must be given to these contingencies is illustrated in the following example from a supervisor during a training program. The supervisor warned an employee, "If I catch you coming late to work one more time this year, you will not get a merit raise this year." In making this statement, the supervisor hoped to motivate the person to not be late again. Guess what happened? The person continued to be late to work, but came up with some ingenious ways to avoid getting caught by the supervisor! For the desired outcome to have occurred, merit pay should have been made contingent upon not being late again rather than on not being caught.

The usefulness of reinforcement theory in industrial settings has been covered in two major reviews of the research (O'Hara, Johnson, & Beer, 1985; Schneier, 1974). The reviews suggest that when the principles of reinforcement theory are followed, performance is indeed increased as predicted from the theory. These results tend to hold up in both public- and private-sector organizations. It should be noted, however, that most of these studies looked at short rather than long-term results and used fairly straightforward measures of performance such as quantity. The long-term effects of reinforcers on complex measures of performance such as quality are less well known. It should also be noted that many of the tests of reinforcement theory have used piece rate rather than merit pay.

As with expectancy theory, there are also implications for merit pay from reinforcement theory. These implications can be summarized as follows:

- *Performance must be clearly defined.* For desirable rather than undesirable performance to be motivated, a clear distinction must be made between desirable and undesirable performance.

- *Merit increases must be made contingent upon desired performance.* If pay is given for reasons other than desired performance (e.g., seniority), then other behaviors such as retention may be reinforced rather than performance.

- *The size of merit increases should increase with levels of performance.* If one level of merit increase is given out to all performers, then employees will be motivated to achieve only the minimum level of performance needed for an increase.

- *Merit increases should be given out close in time to the desired performance levels.* If performance is reviewed at one time and a salary increase is given out a later time, then the link between desired performance and pay will be weakened.

In summary, under reinforcement theory, merit pay should motivate increased performance because the monetary consequences of good performance are made known to the employee. For merit pay to lead to better motivation and performance, performance must be clearly defined, merit pay must be made contingent upon desired performance, merit increases should increase in size with increases in performance, and pay increases should be granted close in time to the desired performance.

Equity Theory.   The most clearly articulated model of equity theory comes from Adams (1965). It is one of several theories of "justice" reviewed by Greenberg (1987a). Compared to expectancy theory and reinforcement theory, equity theory suggests that motivation not only depends on the pay and performance relationship that the employee experiences, but it also depends on the pay and performance relationship that other employees, with whom the person compares him or herself, experience. Hence, equity theory looks at the role that social comparisons play in motivation.

According to equity theory, employees and employers enter into an exchange relationship. The employer provides outcomes such as monetary and nonmonetary rewards that include pay and verbal praise. In return, the employee provides inputs, which include performance and human capital characteristics like experience and education. When the employee perceives that the ratio of outcomes to inputs is about equal, the employee is likely to be satisfied with the exchange relationship. Under equity theory, a balance of outcomes to inputs is the goal that employees are motivated to achieve.

In considering the ratio of outcomes to inputs, employees compare themselves to other employees both inside and outside the employing organization. If the employee perceives that the ratio of his or her outcomes to inputs is less than the ratio of outcomes to inputs for others, then the employee may feel underrewarded. If the employee perceives that the ratio of his or her outcomes to inputs is more than the ratio of outcomes to inputs for others, then the employee may feel overrewarded and possibly even guilty. In cases of both under- and overreward, the employee is usually motivated to get the ratio of his or her outcomes to inputs back in line with the ratio of other people's outcomes to inputs.

The process of making the equity comparisons just described is shown in Figure 2.3. One way that organizations attempt to manage employee beliefs that pay is fair is to set up merit pay plans. By having a merit pay plan, an organization is formally acknowledging that performance is a valued input,

Figure 2.3
Making Equity Comparisons

Outcomes to self		Outcomes to others
Inputs by self	versus	Inputs by others

which will be rewarded with a corresponding increase in pay. It should be noted, however, that, according to equity theory, employees' perceptions of the fairness of merit pay may or may not be in line with the intended fairness of the plan. Sometimes employees may see the plan as not being fair and take actions to correct the situation.

One way that employees can attempt to restore equity perceptions under a merit pay plan is to alter their performance input. If employees feel underrewarded, they may increase the quantity of performance in the hope of receiving larger merit increases. If larger increases are granted, then the employees' outcomes will be increased, which will restore feelings of equity. Also, if underrewarded, employees may decrease the quality of their performance to decrease their inputs. Increasing inputs in the former case and decreasing outcomes in the latter case may restore perceptions of equity. The goal of a merit pay plan is, of course, to provide an equitable relationship between performance and merit increases so that employees do not have to resort to decreasing their performance.

If employees feel overrewarded, they may decrease the quantity of their performance. The reason for this is that an increase would lead to additional pay, which in turn would create further feelings of overreward and guilt. Alternatively, employees may increase the quality of their performance or some other aspect of performance that they believe will not lead to as large a merit increase. Equity is restored in the case of overreward by decreasing outcomes and increasing inputs. The goal of merit pay is to ensure that the relationship between pay and performance is equitably perceived so that employees do not have to resort to lowering some aspect of performance to decrease outcomes and restore equity.

The research on equity theory has been reviewed several times (Carrell & Dittrich, 1978; H. Heneman & Schwab, 1979; Mowday, 1979; Miner, 1980) and, in general, provides moderate support for the theory. In particular, support seems to be strongest in the form of predictions made about time-based pay plans under laboratory conditions. The evidence appears to be more mixed when incentive pay plans are examined in field settings. Also, while cases of overreward inequity have been reported (e.g., Garland, 1973), it would appear that the threshold for overreward is very high. That is, one must perceive that outcomes are very large indeed before feelings of guilt set in. Finally, Miner (1980) indicates that the theory sets forth few testable hypotheses, and Schwab (1980) suggests that the methods used to test the hypotheses have not been consistent with the theory. Both of these factors may account for the moderate empirical support for the theory.

Although the evidence is somewhat limited, the following are some implications for merit pay derived from equity theory:

- *Merit pay decisions cannot be made independently of one another.* Merit pay increases received by one employee are likely to have an impact on the equity perceptions and resulting behavior of other employees.

- *Inputs must be clearly defined.* Employees bring many inputs to the workplace. Employers must take care to establish the value of alternative inputs (e.g., performance versus seniority) so that an accurate assessment of the ratio of outcomes to inputs can be made.

- *Merit pay information must be communicated to employees.* If merit pay plans are not communicated to employees, then employees may make incorrect assessments of the ratio of outcomes to inputs. For example, Lawler (1965) found that managers in various industries tend to overestimate the pay of individuals subordinate to them. If these subordinates contribute less to the organization, managers may feel underrewarded and engage in dysfunctional behaviors. Feelings of equity may be restored if actual pay levels are better communicated. The communication of merit pay is addressed in Chapter 6.

- *The perceived relationship between pay and performance should be viewed as important as the actual relationship.* According to equity theory, it is the perceived relationship between pay as an outcome and performance as an input that is the determinant of motivation. It cannot be automatically assumed that the perceived relationship is the same as the actual relationship. Information regarding the actual relationship between pay and performance may become distorted as this bit of information passes from policy to practice to individual interpretation. Even well-developed merit plans may not work if not communicated properly. Hence, attention should be given to both the perceived and actual relationship between pay and performance.

In summary, equity theory suggests that merit pay is likely to increase employee motivation if it leads to equitable perceptions by employees. For merit increases to be seen as equitable rather than inequitable, merit pay decisions cannot be viewed in isolation, inputs need to be clearly defined, merit information needs to be communicated to employees, and the perceived relationship between pay and performance needs to be given as much attention as the actual relationship between pay and performance.

Goal-Setting Theory. The theory of goal setting as it relates to incentive pay was first established by Locke (1968). According to goal-setting theory, goals are motivating to employees when they are specific, challenging, and accepted by employees. Goals need to be made specific, as "do your best" or general goals do not give a target toward which the employee can direct effort. Goals need to be challenging. Goals that are too easy to attain may suggest to the employee that the goals are not important. Goals that are too difficult to reach may suggest to the employee that effort to attain them is futile. Goals need to be accepted by the employee before he or she can internalize and act upon these goals. Incentives such as merit pay should contribute to the motivational effects of goal setting in several ways (Locke, Bryan, & Kendall, 1968; Wright, 1989). First, merit pay provided for goal attainment may create greater commitment to the goal. Second, merit pay may result in the setting of more difficult goals to earn larger rewards. Third, merit pay may result in the setting of more goals to justify larger merit increases.

Over the past 20 years, considerable research and support for goal-setting theory has been generated (Mento, Steel, & Karren, 1987; Tubbs, 1986). Goal specificity, difficulty, and acceptance have all been shown to relate to performance in a variety of situations. In contrast, the relationship between incentives and goals is not very well understood. There is little empirical research on this relationship, and the research that has been conducted on this topic has some methodological limitations (Wright, 1989). In one well-designed study, however, Wright (1989) found that incentive pay does indeed increase the level of goals as well as commitment to those goals. Even the results of this study are somewhat tentative, as the study was conducted with undergraduate students, and the magnitude of the results was only moderate.

Given this line of theory and research, some logical extensions can be made to merit pay. Goal-setting theory tentatively suggests the following:

- *Merit increases should be contingent on specific rather than "do your best" goals.* Employees may have very little idea as to what constitutes "do your best" in the eyes of the supervisor or person allocating merit increases. Hence, specific criteria need to be established.

- *Merit increases should be based on goal difficulty as well as goal accomplishment.* If goal difficulty is not factored into rewards, employees may be motivated to set lower goals because they are easier to accomplish and still rewarded.

- *Goals and merit increases should be discussed at the same time.* The limited research suggests that the setting of goals and allocation of rewards serve as additions to rather than substitutes for one another. That is, motivation is greater when goals and rewards are coupled together rather than being treated separately by managers. Hence, they should be discussed at the same time rather than separately.

In summary, goal-setting theory suggests that merit pay increases motivation because merit increases result in the setting of more goals, the setting of more difficult goals, and greater commitment to goals. Adhering to this theory, merit increases should be based on the attainment of specific goals that have been weighted by difficulty. Goals, weights for each goal, and merit increases should all be discussed at the same time to have the desired motivational effect.

Economic Theories

Another set of theories that addresses the pay and performance relationship comes from the field of economics. Theories from economics have not received the widespread attention that psychological theories have in the merit pay literature. Nevertheless, they do have the applicability to merit pay and are referenced and discussed at several points in the book.

The economic theories reviewed here are similar to the psychological theories just reviewed in that both sets of theories suggest that individuals direct their efforts toward the maximization of outcomes, such as pay, which will provide the greatest level of satisfaction (Kaufman, 1989). The theories differ from one another, however, in several ways. First, economic theories tend to be directed to the operation of the firm or market rather than the motivation of individuals within the firm or market. Second, the pay and performance relationship tends to be examined from the employer's rather than the employee's perspective. Third, when economic theories do address the issue of individual rather than organizational performance, as is the case, for example, with efficiency wage theory, they place a greater emphasis on the opportunity costs to the employee that are associated with employment decisions, such as deciding at what level to perform at work. Psychological theories tend to emphasize the attractiveness of outcomes to individuals more than the costs. As a result, economic theories yield a somewhat different set of implications for merit pay than do psychological theories, which in turn leads the reader to a more comprehensive understanding of merit pay.

Marginal Productivity Theory. According to Tobin (1985), this theory can be traced back in the United States to the work of Clark (1889). Under this theory, employers pay employees at the value of their marginal products. What this means is that employers provide higher rates of pay to those employees whose inputs result in higher rates of profit to the organization. In a competitive market, where an employer must minimize costs to remain in business, employers will grant pay increases only up to the point where pay is equal to the input or performance contribution of the employee. Clearly, employers need to carefully define the performance input and pay according to this input to contain labor costs and be competitive in the market.

By paying on the basis of marginal productivity or performance, firms receive three types of benefits, according to Bishop (1987). First, this system serves as an incentive to employees to expend greater effort. Second, it tends to attract workers who are willing and able to work hard. Third, it helps diminish the chances of the best performers leaving the organization and the worst performers remaining with the organization. All three of these benefits are in line with maximizing the profits of the organization.

The research on marginal productivity theory suggests that it is extremely doubtful that employers pay exactly at the level where wages equal marginal productivity, even under ideal circumstances. Frank (1984) found that even in highly competitive industries such as auto and real estate sales, where marginal productivity theory is most applicable, employees are not exactly paid to their marginal products. Bishop (1987) suggests that there are a number of reasons why pay cannot be linked precisely to marginal productivity, including the difficulties involved in measuring performance and the overhead costs involved in doing so.

While the research does not show a one-to-one correspondence between pay and marginal productivity, as would be expected under marginal productivity theory, the theory still has several important implications for merit pay, as follows:

- *Performance must be carefully measured.* To contain costs, performance must be carefully measured to determine the contribution of the employee to the organization so that employees can be paid in line with their contributions.

- *An upper boundary for merit increases must be established.* The demand for the labor of an employer is derived from the demand in the market for the employer's goods and services. Merit increases, which are in part dependent upon the demand for labor, need to be set at a level consistent with the demand for goods and services.

In summary, marginal productivity theory suggests that pay is issued on the basis of performance to minimize labor costs and remain competitive in the labor market. To do this, attention must be paid to the measurement of performance and to the demand for goods and services. While research indicates that pay and performance are not always directly related, it is a goal that employers work toward. A recent survey by Sibson and Company (1989) indicated that the use of additional incentive pay was being considered by 48 percent of the surveyed organizations to help control fixed compensation costs, and by 22 percent to improve pay competitiveness.

Implicit Contract Theory. Many have heard the phrase "A fair day's pay for a fair day's work." This saying captures the notion of an implicit contract between an employer and employee. In exchange for services provided by the employee, the employer promises to pay the employee. In exchange for pay from the employer, the employee promises to provide services to the employer. In essence, then, an implicit contract is formed between the employer and employee.

According to Rosen (1985), the phrase "implicit contracts" was first coined by Gordon (1974). The theory was developed in response to two of the major assumptions sometimes attributed to marginal productivity theory (Nalbantian, 1987). First, some presentations of marginal productivity theory assume that performance is a homogeneous input in work organizations. Second, it is also sometimes assumed that performance, or marginal productivity, can be perfectly measured. Bishop (1987) reviews these two assumptions and other criticisms of marginal productivity theory.

Implicit contract theory does away with these two assumptions. It suggests that for many jobs, performance varies from person to person. To the extent that employers pay the same wage to all employees, employers may be incurring additional costs by overpaying those who produce the least with an average wage. Implicit contract theory also suggests that it is difficult to measure performance in many jobs. As shown in Chapter 4, measures of employee performance may not only capture actual employee performance but may also capture the effects of other variables that have an impact on the employee's actual performance. For example, sales may be greater for one individual than another not because of a difference in effort, but simply because one individual was assigned a better sales territory. As a consequence of less than perfect measurement, employers may end up overpaying employees for performance results unrelated to their individual efforts. Therefore, to minimize these potential costs, it is to the employer's advantage to set up contracts with individuals in which the relationship between pay and performance is clearly specified rather than assumed.

A common practice for outside sales positions, where the employee is on the road selling goods and services rather than selling in a retail establishment, is to establish sales commissions with "bogeys" (Patten, 1976). Under this incentive arrangement, a contract is clearly established, with pay increases allocated on the basis of sales. But, as you can well imagine, some products sell better than others, and sales are more plentiful in some regions than others. Therefore, sales results are adjusted to reflect the differences in products or regions before pay increases are granted. These adjustments, or bogeys, are made to ensure that pay increases or commissions are issued for performance that is under the direct control of the outside sales representative.

Two reviews of the empirical literature suggest that there is some support for the notion of implicit contracts. Bishop (1987) reviews and provides evidence suggesting that marginal productivity of employees does indeed vary and is not homogeneous as assumed under classical marginal productivity theory. Rosen (1985) reviews evidence that suggests that marginal revenue product and, in turn, wages are indeed affected by exogenous factors, or elements outside of employees' control. For example, wage rates in manufacturing have been shown to be related to local labor market conditions, but not to aggregate output measures.

Taken together, the theory and research behind the concept of implicit contracts suggests the following for merit pay plans:

- *Performance must be measured, not assumed.* If an employer assumes that all employees are equally productive, the employer may end up with payroll costs that are larger than necessary. Poor performers who are being paid an average wage on the basis of equal performance will be overpaid. Therefore, the employer must measure performance to contain costs.

• *Performance ratings should be adjusted for factors outside an employee's control.* Without an adjustment, some employees may end up receiving greater merit increases than they deserve for their individual contributions while other employees may receive less than they deserve for their individual contributions.

In summary, implicit contract theory suggests that merit pay is a form of an implicit contract. This contract is formed by employers to minimize labor costs. Employers must measure the performance of each individual rather than assuming that each person performs at the same level. An employee can then be paid on the basis of his or her actual contribution. Also, to minimize labor costs, the employer must take care to adjust performance ratings for factors outside the employee's control before tying pay to these ratings.

Efficiency Wage Theory. The final theory to be considered can be traced back to the work of Salop (1979). In essence, efficiency wage theory suggests that effort is determined by the level of wages. In general, a premium wage is paid to ensure that employees perform up to their maximum levels (Stiglitz, 1987). The reason to provide a premium wage is because employees have an incentive to perform at less than their maximum level (Nalbantian, 1987). By working less hard than someone else and receiving the same rewards, an individual employee maximizes his or her net returns. That is, employees may attempt to get more for less.

When a wage premium is offered, which could be in the form of a merit increase, employee performance should be improved over what would be expected if a premium were not offered, for a variety of reasons (Katz, 1986; Levine, 1989; Thaler, 1989). First, an employee is less likely to shirk job responsibilities. If an employee shirks his or her duties, or in other words, does not perform his or her assigned duties, the employee is likely to lose his or her job. It will then be difficult for the employee to find a similar job at the same premium rate. Hence, the loss of a job for which an efficiency wage is paid is very costly to the employee. Second, voluntary turnover is likely to be minimized because alternative jobs at premium wages are not readily available in the labor market. Hence, an employee receiving an efficiency wage is unlikely to leave. Third, employees may feel obligated to perform at higher levels in return for the more-than-fair treatment being offered by the employer.

In paying an efficiency wage, an employer bears an additional cost not faced by others in the labor market; namely, the premium wage that is being paid. In a sense, however, it may be worth it because the employer expects to see a return on investment. In particular, the employer expects to see lower turnover, more qualified applicants, and less shirking. An employer may incur some large wage costs up front in the hope of regaining these costs through better performance in the future. By paying efficiency wages, the employer is able to minimize turnover and thereby reduce the costs associated with turnover. When an individual leaves the organization, it costs the employer money to replace the person because the recruitment and hiring process must be repeated. Also, while the person was employed by the organization, there were costs to the organization to train and pay the person. These costs will not be offset by the services of the person to the company if the person leaves. Interestingly, Henry Ford paid nearly double the going wage rate back in 1914 and argued, in line with efficiency wage arguments, that raising wages was actually a cost-saving measure (Raff & Summers, 1987).

Another reason that costs may be lower for an efficiency wage employer is that the cost of monitoring and controlling employee performance may be minimized. The employer has, in a sense, an insurance policy by paying efficiency wages. Employees are less likely to shirk their duties because they may not be able to find similar work at such a premium efficiency wage elsewhere in the market place. As a result of this high-wage insurance premium protecting against poor performance, employers may not need to assiduously monitor and control employee performance. Employees will monitor their own performance to retain their jobs.

Katz (1986) provides a very insightful review and evaluation of the research on efficiency wage theory. There is some support for efficiency wage theory in studies that examine wage differentials among industries. Employers in some industries, such as mining and petroleum (Krueger & Summers, 1988), pay a high wage even after controlling for the effects of union, job, and worker characteristics (Thaler, 1989). Precisely why this interindustry wage effect is present is a subject of continuing debate. Even if this differential is attributable to efficiency wage theory arguments, we do not know which arguments are best supported. To date, there are no well-controlled studies testing the shirking, turnover, or obligation hypotheses from efficiency wage theory at the level of the individual employee.

Although the evidence for efficiency wage theory's positive effect on employee behavior is sparse, the theory does seem to have the following implications for merit pay:

- *Merit pay levels should be aligned with the competitive market.* In determining the sizes of merit increases, employers should consider increases being offered by their competitors. By doing so, it may be possible to minimize the shirking of job duties and voluntary turnover.

- *Merit increases are particularly important in low-wage organizations.* By offering attractive merit increases as additions to the base wage, it may be possible to provide a premium to high performers in low-wage organizations, thereby minimizing turnover. In high-wage organizations, merit increases may be of lesser importance to employees as a premium is already being offered in the form of base pay.

- *Merit pay should lead to better self-monitoring of performance.* The employer may not need to devote as much time to monitoring employee performance because employees are more likely to monitor their own performance. Employees may self-monitor to ensure that they retain efficiency wages.

In summary, efficiency wage theory suggests that pay be set high to obligate employees to fully perform, not shirk their duties, and remain with the organization. When employers pay a premium wage, it is costly for their employees to lose their jobs. One way to establish a premium is on the basis of merit. For merit to be a premium, merit increases would need to be set relative to the competition. The initial investment in a wage premium may be offset later by better performance and lower monitoring costs.

A Summary of Theories

As reviewed in the previous discussion, there are a variety of theories that have a bearing on merit pay. These theories are integrated in Figure 2.4.

As shown in Figure 2.4, the theories can be summarized using the components of expectancy theory. The arrows leading from various psychological and economic theories to expectancy theory simply show which components of expectancy theory are related to each theory. Both efficiency wage theory and goal-setting theory address the issue of expectancy, or the perceived relationship between effort and performance. Efficiency wage theory suggests that if merit pay is provided, employees may feel

Figure 2.4
Summary of Psychological and Economic Theories Related to Merit Pay

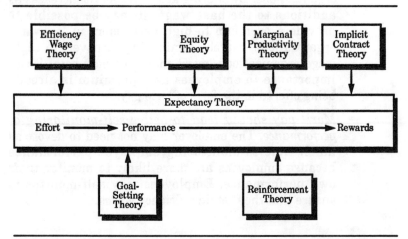

obligated to exert effort and not shirk their duties. Goal-setting theory suggests that merit pay may lead to increased effort because it may induce the setting of and commitment to more difficult performance goals.

Equity theory, marginal productivity theory, and implicit contracts all seem to address the notion of instrumentality, or perceptions of the relationship between performance and rewards. Equity theory suggests that there must be a balance between performance and pay for merit pay to strengthen instrumentality perceptions. Marginal productivity theory indicates that there is, from the organization's perspective, an upper boundary to the amount of merit pay that can be allocated to strengthen the pay and performance link. Implicit contract theory indicates that, for instrumentality perception to be made, performance must be carefully measured, and the contribution of the individual to the firm needs to be separated out from factors outside the employee's control.

Finally, reinforcement theory is related to both instrumentality perceptions and to the concept of valence, or the perception of the attractiveness of outcomes such as merit pay. Reinforcement theory suggests that merit needs to be made contingent on performance for there to be instrumentality perceptions. Also, merit increases must be viewed by employees as more attractive than alternative outcomes, such as leisure, to motivate improved performance.

The Pay-for-Performance Relationship

The previous section showed that there are some sound reasons, from both economic and psychological perspectives, for an organization to have a policy of paying on the basis of performance. The objective of this section is to review research that looks at the extent to which organizations actually *do* link pay to performance. Having a policy of pay for performance does not necessarily guarantee that pay will actually be tied to performance in practice.

In reviewing the research on the pay-for-performance relationship, two points should be kept in mind. The first point is that pay for performance can be viewed in relationship to *previous* performance and in relation to *subsequent* performance. For merit pay to lead to subsequent improved performance, it must first be related to previous performance as discussed in the earlier overview of theories. This chapter reviews studies that examine pay for previous performance. Chapter 7 deals with pay for subsequent performance.

The second point to bear in mind is that the pay-for-performance relationship can be examined both in terms of actual relationship and in terms of people's perceptions of the relationship. Both the actual and perceived relationship between pay and performance are important to consider if a merit pay plan is to be effective. Sometimes employees' perceptions of the relationship are different than the actual relationship, which can cause problems for managers of merit pay plans. For example, as presented in the discussion of equity theory, employee motivation is a function of perceptions of the ratio of pay to performance rather than the actual ratio of pay to performance. Because of the importance of this distinction, the studies reviewed here are broken down into actual and perceived relationships.

Actual Relationship Between Pay and Performance

It is indeed possible for organizations to establish an actual link between pay and performance. This is illustrated in Table 2.1.

In the first column, the authors and date of the study are listed. This citation can be used to find the full reference for the study in the reference list at the back of the book. The second column describes the types of jobs or occupations held by the participants in the study. The third column assigns a general label to the type of organization in which the participants worked. Study type, listed in the fourth column, notes whether the study was conducted in a setting where merit pay was actually being used (field) or in a setting where the researchers simulated a situation involving merit pay (laboratory). The fifth column shows the sign linked to the results of the study. A positive sign indicates that there was a positive relationship observed between previous performance and the size of merit increases. That is, as ratings of employee performance increased, merit pay increased as well. A negative sign indicates that as ratings of employee performance increased, merit pay decreased. Significance of the results, shown in the sixth column, indicates the degree of certainty that we can have in the

Table 2.1

Summary of Studies Showing Relationship Between Merit Increase and Previous Performance

Authors		Participants	Organization	Study Type	Sign	Results Significance (p<)
Alexander & Barrett (1982)	4,582	Managers, Scientists, Students	Int'l. Research Group	Lab.	+	.001
Bass (1968)	113	Students	University	Lab.	+	?
Birnbaum (1983)	10	Faculty Members	University	Lab.	+	?
	125	Students	University	Lab.	+	?
Bishop (1987)	456	Professionals	Various Private Sect.	Field	+	.01
Dreher (1981)	1,414	Employees	Manufacturing Co.	Field	+	.05
Fossum & Fitch (1985)	20	Students	University	Lab.	+	.001
	40	Managers & Professionals	Various Private Sect.	Lab.	+	.001
	42	Managers & Professionals	Various Private Sect.	Lab.	+	.001
Foster & Lynn (1978)	56	Managers	Various Private Sect.	Lab.	+	?
Gerhart & Milkovich (1987)	5,550	Admin. & Professionals	Diversified Firm	Field	+	.01
	840	Admin. & Professionals	Diversified Firm	Field	+	.01
Goodman (1975)	65	Students	University	Lab.	+	.05
Greene (1973)	62	Managers	Manufacturing Co.	Field	+	.01
H. Heneman (1973)	68	Managers	Retail Firm	Field	+	.01
R. Heneman & Cohen (1988)	175	Employees	Manufacturing Co.	Field	+	.01
Hills et al. (1988)	1,255	Employees	Transit Authority	Field	+	.001
Huber et al. (1987)	229	Managers	City Government	Lab.	+	.001
Ivancevich (1983)	104	Engineers	High Tech. Firm	Field	+	.01
	66	Scientists	High Tech. Firm	Field	−	n.s.

(continued)

Table 2.1 *(continued)*
Summary of Studies Showing Relationship Between Merit Increase and Previous Performance

Authors		Participants	Organization	Study Type	Results Sign	Results Significance (p<)
Johnson & Kasten (1983)	32	Faculty Members	University	Field	+	.05
Kaun (1984)	144	Faculty Members	University	Field	+	.01
Koch & Chizmar (1973)	229	Faculty Members	University	Field	–	.01
Kopelman (1976)	142	Engineers	Tech. Based Co.	Field	+	.01
	138	Engineers	Tech. Based Co.	Field	+	.01
	119	Engineers	Tech. Based Co.	Field	+	.01
Leventhal et al. (1972)	120	Students	University	Lab.	+	.01
	44	Students	University	Lab.	+	?
Landau & Leventhal (1976)	120	Students	University	Lab.	+	.01
Magnusen (1987)	40	Faculty Members	University	Field	+	?
Markam (1988)	71	Managers	Manufacturing Co.	Field	+	n.s.
Medoff & Abraham (1980)	2,763	Employees	Manufacturing Co.	Field	+	varied
	2,491	Employees	Manufacturing Co.	Field	+	varied
Medoff & Abraham (1981)	7,078	Managers & Professionals	Manufacturing Co.	Field	+	varied
Scott et al. (1987)	800	Employees	Transit Authority	Field	+	varied
Sherer et al. (1987)	11	Managers	Hospital	Lab.	+	.01
Teel (1986)	?	Professionals	Various Private Sect.	Field	+	?
Turban & Jones (1988)	25	Managers	Rehabilitation Center	Field	+	.05
Vecchio & Terborg (1987)	67	Students	University	Lab.	+	?
Wyatt Company (1987)	1,415	Professionals	Various Private Sect.	Field	+	?

Source: Adapted from R. Heneman (1990). Reprinted with permission.

results. The smaller the number in this column, the less likely the reported result is due to chance associated with the selection of the study sample.

In some 40 of 42 studies that looked at the relationship between pay and performance in organizations with merit pay, there was a positive relationship between current merit increases and previous performance. In a small number of the studies, the results were not statistically significant, but this could be due to small sample size. The actual positive relationship between pay and performance appears to be robust. It has been observed in laboratory and field settings, private- and public-sector organizations, service and manufacturing jobs, and at many job levels, as demonstrated by this collection of studies.

The data clearly indicate that it is possible for organizations to successfully implement the concept of pay for performance. However, it is just as important to note that theory and practice do not always perfectly coincide with one another. The magnitude of the relationship between pay and performance in these studies is *not* large. As shown in a previous review (Heneman, 1990) and in many places throughout the book, there are many factors, in addition to previous performance, that influence merit pay. In practice, these other factors result in less than "picture perfect" merit pay plans.

Perceived Relationship Between Pay and Performance

In contrast to the numerous studies on the actual relationship between pay and performance, very little research has been conducted on the perceived relationship between pay and performance. In general, the data suggest that a moderately positive perceived relationship does exist under merit pay plans. Vest, Hills, and Scott (1989) reported an average of 2.6 on a scale with the following parameters: 1 = weak perceived pay-for-performance relationship to 6 = strong perceived pay-for-performance relationship. Todd, Thompson, and Dalton (1974) reported that there was a significantly greater number of strong than weak perceptions of pay for performance for a sample of accountants. Wisdom and Patzig (1987) found that about 60 percent of private-sector employees perceived a strong relationship while only about 40 percent of public-sector employees saw a strong link. Similar results were reported by Rainey (1979).

Three additional studies shed further light on these moderately positive findings. First, Peck (1984) reported the results of a large-scale survey by Opinion Research Corporation. The overall relationship between effort and rewards was weak for a huge, combined sample of merit- and nonmerit-based organizations. This study, along with the ones just mentioned, suggests that pay-for-performance perceptions are somewhat stronger in merit-based companies alone than in a combined sample of merit-based and nonmerit-based companies. Logically, this suggests that pay-for-performance perceptions are somewhat stronger in merit-based than nonmerit-based companies.

Second, Heneman, Greenberger, and Strasser (1988) found that in a hospital without a formal merit pay plan the average pay for performance relationship was about 2.4 on a scale where 1 = weak pay-for-performance relationship and 6 = strong pay-for-performance relationship. Comparing the perceptions found in the organizations just reviewed, it appears that pay-for-performance perceptions are somewhat stronger in merit- versus nonmerit-based organizations. However, this difference is by no means large.

Third, Jenkins and Lawler (1981) conducted a study where the organization appears to have shifted from a nonmerit- to a merit-based system. Pay-for-performance perceptions decreased during this change by a small and insignificant amount. The results of this study cast some doubt on the notion that pay-for-performance perceptions are strengthened under a merit pay plan. However, these results are not conclusive. Some factor other than the introduction of a merit pay plan may have been responsible for the lack of a significant change. The study design did not allow for the testing of other factors.

In summary, the perceived relationship between pay and performance under merit pay plans appears to be moderate. These perceptions do appear to be somewhat stronger in merit pay-based than in nonmerit pay-based organizations. But, a shift from a nonmerit- to a merit-based system does not seem to automatically strengthen these perceptions. Given the small number of studies, the potential methodological difficulties with these studies, and the general comparisons made here, these conclusions are tentative.

Potential Pitfalls with Merit Pay

The information presented so far indicates that there is both theoretical and practical substantiation for trying to link pay to performance with a merit pay plan. Overall, merit pay appears to be a desirable method of pay because of the potential for improved performance. It has also been shown, however, that there are some specific requirements that must be met for merit pay to have the desired end result of improved performance. These requirements are reviewed throughout the book.

The tradeoff between performance and resources is an important factor in determining the overall desirability of merit pay. Merit pay may not be as desirable because of the resources that need to be devoted to creating and implementing the plan. (The resources that need to be committed to a merit pay plan are described in Chapters 4, 5, and 6.)

Also, in assessing the desirability of merit pay, management must examine the line of arguments that have been made against merit pay over the years. In this section, some of the potential risks or pitfalls with merit pay are addressed, including the potential for a decrease in intrinsic motivation, cooperation, self-esteem, and equity. These pitfalls are illustrated in Figure 2.5 and will be discussed in turn.

Decreased Intrinsic Motivation

Deci (1972) advanced the argument that when people are paid on the basis of performance, the pay reduces the amount of pleasure or intrinsic motivation they receive from performing the task. That is, by rewarding people for what they already enjoy doing, motivation will decrease. In support of his argument, he conducted a laboratory study in which pay was made contingent upon the completion of an enjoyable task (solving a puzzle). He found that the amount of time the participants spent on the puzzle during their free time was actually less for those granted pay on the basis of performance than for those not granted pay on the basis of performance. Thus, the laboratory study supported his argument.

While interesting, Deci's work has been subject to criticism. Dyer and Parker (1975) found that the concept of intrinsic motivation is very difficult to define, let alone measure. Given this definitional problem, it is difficult to know when merit pay

Figure 2.5
Problems Believed to be Associated with Merit Pay

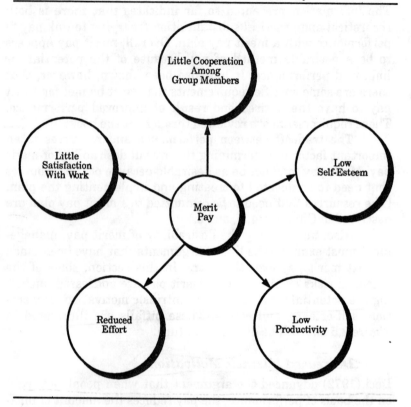

does or does not affect intrinsic motivation. Even when there appears to be a reasonable measure of intrinsic motivation, empirical studies conducted by other authors do not lend much support to Deci's argument. For example, in a recent, well-designed study by Scott, Farh, and Podsakoff (1988), it was shown that pay for performance did not reduce intrinsic motivation. Instead, the trend was for pay for performance to increase intrinsic motivation. This study suggests that, at a minimum, merit pay will not reduce intrinsic motivation and, in fact, may actually increase intrinsic motivation. The results of these two studies and others indicate that a decrease in intrinsic motivation does not appear to be a likely outcome of merit pay.

Decreased Cooperation

Another criticism that has been made against merit pay is that merit pay decreases cooperation among work group members. That is, individual rewards, such as merit pay, foster conflict rather than cooperation as work group members compete against one another for pay. Conflict arises because the size of most merit pay budgets is fixed. This argument is especially damaging when individuals are dependent on one another for the completion of work. This line of reasoning dates back to at least Whyte (1955) and has recently been summarized by Pearce (1987).

Over 120 studies have examined the impact of cooperation and competition on performance. These studies have been reviewed by two sets of authors (Cotton & Cook, 1982 and Johnson, Maruyama, Johnson, Nelson, & Skon, 1981). Although they reviewed the same studies, these two sets of authors reached different conclusions about the desirability of competitive rewards because of differences in the two review procedures used. Also important to note is the fact that these studies do not directly address merit pay. Nevertheless, the findings from these reviews do have implications for merit pay. The implications differ depending on whether you are looking at the Cotton and Cook or the Johnson et al. reviews.

A liberal interpretation of the more than 120 studies is offered by Johnson et al. (1981) who conclude that cooperation is superior to competition in increasing productivity. Is this conclusion at odds with the concept of merit pay? If a merit pay plan emphasizes individual goal attainment over group goal attainment, then the answer may be "yes," because productivity may decline. However, this need not be the case. As pointed out by Patten (1976) many years ago, performance standards can and should be developed to reflect the amount of collaboration individual employees have with their fellow work group members. That is, cooperation can be a rating standard for individual performance. An example of this can be seen in university settings where collegiality is sometimes used by department heads as one measure of performance. Collegiality might, for example, be rated higher for a faculty member who covered the classes of a colleague who was out sick.

Another example of using cooperation as a dimension for assessing individual performance comes from Johnsonville Foods,

Inc., the Wisconsin-based maker of bratwurst. As can be seen in Figure 2.6, cooperation or teamwork is defined by performance standards such as contribution to groups, communication, willingness to work together, and attendance and timeliness. Both employees and their supervisors (coaches) are required to evaluate employee performance using these standards.

A more conservative interpretation of the 120-plus studies is offered by Cotton and Cook (1982). Their review suggests that competition is "healthy" and may be more conducive to productivity increases than cooperation when task interdependence is low, the task is simple, or groups are small (fewer than six people). This conservative assessment suggests that it is not always desirable to use cooperation as a performance standard under merit pay plans. Indeed, under some conditions, competition is to be encouraged.

Although the cooperation/conflict argument has not been addressed directly in the literature on merit pay plans, the indirect evidence suggests that it would be incorrect to conclude that merit pay inevitably causes competition and that, in turn, this competition causes decreased performance. Instead, it seems that management can design merit pay plans that promote either cooperation or competition by setting performance standards accordingly. And, either cooperation or competition can increase performance, depending on the nature of the task. Cooperation is more likely to lead to increased performance when tasks are interdependent, complex, and worked on in large groups. Competition is more likely to improve performance when tasks are independent, simple, and worked on individually or in small groups.

Decreased Self-Esteem

Meyer (1975) has long criticized merit pay on the grounds that merit pay threatens an employee's self-esteem. He bases this assertion on his research at General Electric Company in the late 1960s. There he found that when employees were asked to evaluate their own performance relative to others, the average self-rating was at the 77th percentile. This rating indicates that, on average, each General Electric employee felt that he or she was better than 77 percent of all other General Electric employees. By comparison, when managers evaluated these same employees, the average rating was at the 60th percentile.

Figure 2.6
Performance Standards to Evaluate Cooperation

JOHNSONVILLE FOODS, INC.
COMPANY PERFORMANCE-SHARE EVALUATION FORM

Please check one: _____ Self _____ Coach

II. TEAMWORK

A. Contribution to Groups
How would I rate my contribution to my department's performance? Am I aware of department goals? Do I contribute to a team? Do I communicate with team members?

Score _____

B. Communication
To what extent do I keep others informed to prevent problems from occurring? Do I work to promote communication between plants and departments? Do I relay information to the next shift? Do I speak up at meetings and let my opinions and feelings be known?

Score _____

C. Willingness to Work Together
To what extent am I willing to share the responsibility of getting the work done? Do I voluntarily assist others to obtain results? Do I demonstrate a desire to accomplish department goals? Do I complete paperwork accurately and thoroughly and work toward a smooth flow of information throughout the company? Am I willing to share in any overtime?

Score _____

D. Attendance and Timeliness
Do I contribute to the team by being present and on time for work (including after breaks and lunch)? Do I realize the inconvenience and hardship caused by my absence or tardiness?

Score _____

Source: Stayer (1990). Reprinted by permission of *Harvard Business Review.* Copyright © 1990 by the President and Fellows of Harvard College; all rights reserved.

According to Meyer (1975), similar results were obtained in several other studies of employees in various jobs and companies. These distributions of self-ratings are shown in Table 2.2.

The way these results tie in with merit pay is that most employees with inflated self-ratings are disappointed with their merit increases, because they feel the increase is too small a reward for their superior performance. However, in most organizations, merit increases are limited by budget constraints. The disappointment felt by employees translates into threatened self-esteem in Meyer's view. To cope with this threat to self-esteem, employees may work harder to improve their performance; withdraw effort at work in the form of tardiness, absenteeism, and reduction in output; or adjust their unrealistically high opinions of their own performance. According to Meyer (1975), most employees opt for the middle option of withdrawing effort at work.

Conceptual arguments and empirical studies tend to cast doubt on Meyer's (1975) assertions. At a conceptual level, both

Table 2.2
Self-Rating Distributions for Several Employee Groups

	Employee Groups			
Self-Ratings	Blue-Collar Group Plant A	Blue-Collar Group Plant B	Engineers in Research Laboratory	Accountants in Several Companies
Top 10%	46%	40%	29%	37%
Top 25%	26	28	57	40
Top 50%	26	28	14	20
Bottom 50%	1	2	0	3
Bottom 25%	0	0	0	0
Bottom 10%	0	0	0	0
No response	1	2	0	0
	100%	100%	100%	100%

Source: Herbert H. Meyer, "The Pay-for-Performance Dilemma." Reprinted, by permission of publisher, from *Organizational Dynamics,* Winter 1975, © 1975 American Management Association, New York. All rights reserved.

Patten (1977) and Lawler (1976) have argued that organizations can help employees adjust their unrealistic expectations by the manner in which salary increases are allocated and communicated to employees. Lawler (1976) also argues that the threat to self-esteem is more problematic for lower rather than higher performing employees. To the extent this is true, it may be that low- rather than high-performing employees leave the organization. This outcome may be desirable, rather than undesirable, for some employers.

Although the exact model of Meyer's (1975) arguments has never been fully tested, the related research is not supportive of Meyer's argument that low self-esteem leads to low performance. As shown by Brockner (1988) in his review of the self-esteem literature, this relationship has not received empirical support. Perhaps this is to be expected when a general trait, like self-esteem, is studied for its effect on specific behaviors at work, like performance (Herman, 1973). Merit pay may, in fact, be related to low self-esteem in isolated cases, but even when it is, it may not lead to negative consequences for the organization such as lower productivity.

Decreased Equity

It has also been argued that merit pay leads to decreased employee perceptions of equity. Two causes, the Matthew Effect and overreward inequity, have been advanced to explain this potential decline in equity.

Matthew Effect. Gabris and Mitchell (1988) borrow a quote from the Apostle Matthew in the Bible (Matthew 13:12): "For to him who has shall be given, and he shall have abundance: but from him who does not have, even that which he has shall be taken away." They use this quote as an analogy to the alienating impact of merit pay plans on lower performing employees. According to the Matthew Effect, merit increases are frequent and plentiful for good performers. But, poor to average performers suffer because money is taken from them to pay large merit increases to the good performers. The lower performers perceive inequity because their pay is reduced to reward the better performers. Proponents of the Matthew Effect assert that merit pay is not at all motivational to lower performing employees.

Pursuing this reasoning, merit pay simply motivates those who are already motivated.

While this is indeed an interesting line of reasoning, it has not received much empirical support (Gabris & Mitchell, 1988; Porter, Greenberger, & R. Heneman, 1990). While it does appear that merit increases may be somewhat more motivational to higher than lower performing employees, there is no evidence that it is not motivating to average performers. Since the bulk of employees are average performers, this criticism of merit pay has limited applicability to employees other than low performers. Moreover, for low performers, dissatisfaction with merit pay may be advantageous to the employer if it encourages poor performers to leave the organization and be replaced with better performers.

Overreward Inequity. The other argument that asserts a decreased perception of equity due to merit pay plans is the concept of overreward (Adams, 1965). To the extent that high performers receive disproportionately high merit increases compared to low performers, high performers feel guilt and, consequently, withdraw effort. This argument suggests that merit pay may decrease the motivation of high performers. In contrast to the Matthew Effect prediction that lower performers will withdraw effort, overreward inequity argues that it is the higher performers who will withdraw effort.

Empirical research casts doubt on the overreward inequity prediction. In reviewing equity theory research, Miner (1980) suggested that in a few studies overreward did produce a withdrawal of effort by high performers. However, he notes that, generally, people have a high threshold for this type of guilt reaction to overpayment. Leventhal (1976) suggested that most studies show that overreward results in *more* rather than *less* effort because the so-called overpaid employee may feel indebted to the person who allocated the overpayment. Finally, Schwab (1980) reviewed studies that indicate employees expend greater effort for overpayment, perhaps out of fear of losing their jobs or to bolster self-esteem. These arguments are, of course, consistent with efficiency wage theory. In summary, while we still are not exactly sure why the overreward prediction of reduced effort does not hold, such reduced effort does not seem to occur with much frequency. Gross instances of overreward *may* produce a reduction in effort. But only organizations that are extravagant in their merit increases need worry about such an effect.

Because of these arguments against merit pay, some have argued that merit pay should not be used (e.g., Meyer, 1975). But, given the empirical evidence related to each of the arguments, this appears to be too strong a conclusion (Lawler, 1976). Instead, it appears that these arguments should be considered as potential rather than actual pitfalls associated with merit pay. They should, of course, be considered in assessing the desirability of merit pay, but should not *a priori* lead to an outright rejection of the merit pay concept.

Summary of Major Points

Below are the key points covered in this chapter.

1. *Reasons for Merit Pay.* Psychological and economic theories provide the rationale for merit pay. According to these theories, the linking of pay to performance should lead to improved performance because motivation is increased. In turn, this increase in performance helps organizations maximize profits.

2. *Implications of Theory.* Both psychological and economic theories have implications for the design and administration of merit pay plans. These implications center around the measurement of performance, the establishment of pay increases, and the linking of pay to performance. It takes time, money, and effort to build these features into a merit pay plan.

3. *Pay-for-Performance Relationship.* Many studies have examined the actual and perceived relationship between pay and previous performance. The results do suggest that it is possible to put the theory of merit pay into action. This is seen in a variety of organizational settings where there is a moderate relationship between actual performance and pay when a merit pay plan is in place. Studies that have looked at the perceived relationship between performance and pay also show moderate results in terms of the magnitude of the relationship.

4. *Potential Pitfalls with Merit Pay.* Along with the potential advantages of merit pay, such as improved performance, there are some potential drawbacks. These drawbacks or pitfalls include decreases in intrinsic motivation, cooperation, self-esteem, satisfaction, and equity. The research that considers these issues does not provide strong support for any one of these arguments. Nevertheless, they should be considered relative to the potential benefits of merit pay when assessing the desirability of a merit pay plan.

Conclusions

The rationale behind merit pay is not the product of idle speculation. Instead, the concept of linking pay to performance is well grounded in theories from economics and psychology. Moreover, the tests of these theories, which have been conducted through empirical research, have, for the most part, been supportive. In short, the rationale behind merit pay has been clearly established.

The idea of linking pay to performance under a merit pay plan is grounded in practice as well as in theory and research. As shown in Table 2.1, organizations have indeed been able to put pay for performance into practice. In almost all of the studied organizations, a positive relationship was observed between pay increases and performance ratings. This relationship was observed in a variety of organizational settings, with many different study participants, and in both laboratory and field settings. It does indeed appear possible to take the theory of pay for performance and put it into practice.

Because there is a solid rationale behind merit pay, and because it is possible to put it into practice, merit pay may be a desirable pay policy for many organizations. However, as shown throughout the book, having a merit pay plan does not guarantee that merit pay will lead to the desired result of improved performance. The entire merit pay process must be carefully managed for merit pay to have the desired results. The initial consideration of merit pay feasibility is just one step in managing the process. As shown in this chapter, for example, linking actual pay to actual performance ratings, does not necessarily guarantee that employees will see the relationship between pay and performance. If employees do not perceive this relationship, then it is doubtful merit pay will lead to the desired result of improved performance.

It should also be recognized that along with the theory that supports the notion of pay for performance, there is also some theory that casts doubt on its potential for positive outcomes. Given the limited amount of research that has been conducted on these alternative theories, however, it is inappropriate to argue that merit pay should never be used. Also, the limited research that has been conducted simply does not lend much support to the arguments made against merit pay. Finally, even when there is some empirical support for a theory that argues against pay for performance, it may be possible to take these potential pitfalls into account in the design and administration of a merit pay plan. For example, if it is believed that merit pay will decrease cooperation, then one aspect of performance that can be both measured and rewarded is cooperation, which should increase rather than decrease cooperation.

The arguments presented here should put an end to those who argue that merit pay should never be used. There *are* some desirable features to merit pay. Unfortunately, there are some organizations that have stopped using or never considered using merit pay because of the counterarguments, which have limited empirical support. Some of these organizations could and should be using merit pay. Also, as discussed in Chapter 3, there are organizations currently using merit pay that should not be given the circumstances that they face. Merit pay is not appropriate in all situations.

The theories presented here provide an excellent starting point for developing a formal organizational policy regarding merit pay. They can be used to create a document spelling out the intent of merit pay (e.g., "The intent of this merit pay plan is to reward past performance to motivate future performance . . ."), the standards that will inform the organization when the intended objectives of the plan have been met (e.g., "It is expected that the quarterly department productivity reports will show improvement throughout the year . . ."), and the procedures to be followed to ensure that the standards are met (e.g., setting specific and challenging performance goals, adjusting performance ratings for factors outside the employee's control, and so on). In addition, these theories represent a framework for continuing research into merit pay. As it stands now, the economic theories, in particular, are ripe for further exploration through research, as most of the research to date has focused on the psychological theories.

3

Diagnosing Situational Characteristics

In the previous chapter, general information was presented to help organizations assess the desirability of merit pay. This chapter will address the feasibility of using merit pay in specific organizational settings. The objective of the chapter is to describe some of the situations where it may be advantageous to use a merit pay plan.

To accomplish this objective, settings where merit pay plans are likely to be found are identified, using the limited empirical research as well as the logical arguments advanced by various authors. The reasons *why* merit pay plans are used in some situations and not in others are discussed to diagnose when merit pay is appropriate. However, a word of caution is in order at this point. Many of the arguments are speculative. Much of what has been written has to do with what should be done. There is very little research on what is actually done. There is almost no research on how effective merit pay plans are under various organizational conditions. Hence, the arguments presented here need to be considered carefully by the reader.

Guidelines are offered concerning the conditions that are needed for merit pay to be a viable compensation plan. Both monetary and nonmonetary additions to merit pay are reviewed to guide the reader to other sources if merit pay is not considered feasible or in line with the objectives of a particular organization.

A Merit Pay Framework

Given the heavy emphasis on pay for performance under merit pay plans, it is tempting to focus attention on pay and performance in discussing merit pay plans. To do so, however, would be a disservice, ignoring characteristics of a situation that could hinder or impede the linking of pay to performance. A discussion of the context is important for all reward allocation decisions, including merit pay (Freedman & Montanari, 1980; R. Heneman, 1990; Leventhal, 1976).

The importance of considering factors in addition to pay and performance became quite clear to me a few years ago in a study of merit pay I undertook with Debra Cohen (Heneman & Cohen, 1988). We conducted the study in a midwest manufacturing firm. We were told by the firm that all personnel decisions, including pay increases, were made strictly on the basis of performance without regard to any other factors. The written policy of the organization regarding pay raises also made this point very clear. As you might expect, we did find a significant positive relationship between the performance of employees and their pay increases.

We also found, however, that characteristics of the supervisors who granted the pay increases were related to the pay increases received by their employees. Characteristics of the supervisor such as age, seniority, and salary predicted employee pay increases almost half as well as did actual performance levels of employees. What this example illustrates is the need to focus on the context in which merit increases are given. Ignoring contextual characteristics may lead to incorrect assumptions about the reasons for merit increases. In turn, if we are unaware of the actual reasons, then we may have a very difficult time managing the merit pay process.

As shown in Figure 3.1, pay-for-performance decisions under merit pay plans are embedded in a rich context. This context includes characteristics of the allocator, recipient, organization, and environment. In this chapter, specific attention will be given to each of these characteristics to help the reader establish the feasibility of merit pay.

Characteristics of the organization that could have a bearing on merit pay include obvious features, such as the size of the budget, type of organization, and type of work performed. They

Figure 3.1
Merit Pay Framework

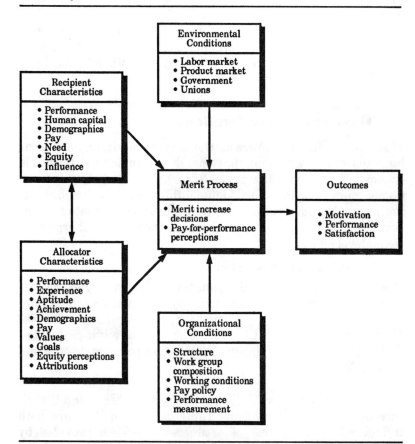

Source: R. Heneman (1990). Reprinted with permission.

also include less obvious features, such as the culture of the organization and government subsidies received. Both obvious and less obvious organizational features influence the degree to which merit pay plans can be used.

The environment consists of factors outside the immediate boundaries of the organization which should be considered in making decisions regarding merit pay. Environmental factors may include the present and anticipated state of the economy, laws and regulations, and the presence or absence of labor organizations. Like organizational characteristics, these environmental conditions can either facilitate or hinder the use of merit pay.

Finally, the feasibility of merit pay may also be determined by the preferences of organizational members. Allocators' and recipients' preferences for merit pay over other forms of pay are also reviewed here.

Economic Considerations

When rewarding employees on the basis of merit, organizations have to contend with sometimes harsh and sometimes favorable economic conditions. The present and anticipated status of economic conditions has a formidable influence on the feasibility of merit pay. Economic conditions that must be taken into account occur at both the economy level and at the individual organizational level as well.

Economy-Level Influences

The economy represents the sum total of monetary exchanges for goods and services. These monetary transactions can be categorized by industry, geographic area, and occupation. Several features of the economy have direct bearing on merit pay. These features include the stability of prices, tax rates, and wage and price guidelines.

Price Stability. Money that is available to fund merit increases and the purchasing value of merit dollars are both influenced by the prices of products or services provided by employers. Periods of either rising or declining product and service prices can make the feasibility of merit pay difficult. During inflationary times, when product prices are increasing, the purchasing value or real value of merit increases declines. For example, if the prices of goods and services are rising by 12 percent and an employee receives a 5 percent merit increase, the value of the raise is less than it would be had prices been rising by only 4 percent. The raise has less value because the amount of goods and services that can be purchased is less when price inflation is 12 percent rather than 4 percent. As a result, employers might expect that the motivational mileage they can get from merit plans will be altered during periods of inflation. A good example comes from a survey conducted by Miller (1979) during a period of double digit inflation in the United States. Respondents to his survey of *Personnel* readers indicated that not only is motivational impact reduced when merit increases are less than the level of inflation, but motivational clout is also lost even when merit increases are 1 to 2 percent *above* the inflation rate!

Another view of inflation with regard to merit pay is that the size of the merit increase is illusory. Employees may think they are getting more when they actually are getting less. That is, employees may only look at the absolute size of their merit increases. During inflationary periods, these raises may be larger in an absolute sense, but less in terms of actual purchasing power. Increases may be larger because, as noted in the earlier discussion of marginal productivity theory in Chapter 2, wages are derived from the demand for goods and services. To the extent that the absolute amount rather than real amount of merit pay is the focus of employee efforts, it could be argued that employees will be more motivated during periods of rising prices. This illusion, however, is probably only short-term for some employees. You would expect that most employees would eventually see the real value of their merit increases as reflected in their smaller-than-anticipated baskets of goods and services.

Periods of price stability or deflation also have an influence on the feasibility of merit plans. Cook (1987) pointed out that during tight economic times such as the middle 1980s in the United States, employers did not have much flexibility to adjust product or service prices upward. As a result, funds for merit increases were limited, as were the sizes of increases in many organizations. In this situation, merit pay may also lose its motivational value. While the purchasing power of merit increases is better in tight economic times, the absolute amount that is available for purchases is limited.

This discussion of the stability of prices suggests that it is difficult, if not impossible, to implement a new merit pay plan during periods of very high or low price inflation. Also, the discussion suggests that merit pay plans already in place may lose their motivational impact during periods of high or low inflation. Finally, organizations should plan ahead for anticipated economic conditions. Organizations need to look at the forecasted rates of inflation if a merit pay plan is to be implemented at a future time.

Wage and Price Guidelines. One response to periods of high inflation is for the government to step in and impose mandatory controls or voluntary wage and price guidelines. For example, this was done by the Nixon administration during the early 1970s in response to inflation in the United States. Wage and price guidelines are also sometimes imposed in response to national priorities. For example, controls were imposed in the early 1940s to help the United States war effort during World War II.

When guidelines or controls are imposed, the ability of the employer to grant salary increases on the basis of merit or other factors is again limited. As shown in a survey by Miller (1979), compensation administrators feel that wage and price guidelines detract from the motivational impact of merit pay, especially when the ceiling for guidelines is below the rate of inflation. Bruce Ellig, Vice President of Compensation and Benefits at Pfizer, Inc., during 1979, summarized this point as follows in the Miller (1979) article:

> "The federal guidelines become a limiting factor because in many instances the *average* increase must be *less than the rate of inflation*. It becomes a Hobson's choice: Increase the number of 'no increases' (thereby lowering the purchasing power and increasing the dissatisfaction of many employees) in order to adequately reward the top performers (and thereby minimize the risk of their leaving), or establish a very narrow range of increases (thereby protecting the purchasing power of most employees but increasing the risk of losing the top performers)."

(Reprinted, by permission of the publisher, from *Personnel*, July/August 1979, © 1979 American Management Association, New York. All rights reserved.)

Tax Rates. Along with the influence of price stability and wage and price guidelines at the economy level, tax rates also need to be considered. Cook (1979) showed one potential consequence of changes in tax rates. Lower marginal tax rates on ordinary income may result in greater purchasing power for merit pay increases. The real value of the increase will be greater to the employee because less of the increase is being held by the government. One might expect, therefore, that the motivational impact of merit increases was somewhat greater during the 1980s than the 1970s because, in part, of the lowered marginal tax rates enacted by the Reagan administration in the 1980s.

Another potential consequence of the tax structure has to do with the funding of merit pay plans. If tax breaks are given to employers for one component of the total compensation package (e.g., benefits), then employers may shift their portfolio of compensation funds away from other components of the total compensation package (e.g., direct pay) where the employer does not receive a tax break. For example, an employer may limit the size of the merit budget to put additional money into private pension plans thereby receiving the tax savings available for qualified pension plans.

Another example of the influence of tax rates is the shifting of merit increases from cash to paper. Such was the case at Primerica, a company that set up an Employee Stock Ownership Plan (ESOP) in 1989 for its 1500 middle managers (Bernstein, 1991). Managers at Primerica were rewarded for good performance with a paper increase in the form of company stock rather than a traditional merit pay increase in the form of cash. The reason for this shift from cash to paper was to take advantage of the tax savings associated with ESOPs. Under ESOPs, organizations are given tax breaks in return for granting employees ownership in the company via shares of company stock.

Firm-Level Influences

The economic picture at the individual organizational level also exerts an influence on the desirability of merit pay. Two aspects of the economic picture include government subsidies sometimes received by employers and the adequacy of the merit pay budget.

Government Subsidies. From time to time the government offers subsidies to employers for helping in matters of national priority. One example from the 1970s is on-the-job training subsidies offered to employers who hired and trained the hard-core unemployed. The hard-core unemployed are workers with limited skills and long durations of unemployment. This subsidy was authorized under the Comprehensive Employment and Training Act (CETA). A study by Bishop (1987) showed that employers who received this subsidy tended to grant larger merit increases than those employers who did not receive this subsidy. This result suggests that when employers are subsidized by the government, it may be more feasible to have a merit pay plan. The Bishop (1987) study suggests that money that could have gone to special training needs of the hard-core employed may have been used by employers for incentive pay instead.

Adequacy of Budget. Another economic variable at the firm level is the size or adequacy of the budget for merit increases. Even if the economy is cooperative in terms of price inflation, individual organizations need to be of sound financial status to be able to fund merit increases. A study by Miceli and Near (1987) found that satisfaction with pay was greater, for middle managers and executives in a government agency with merit pay, when perceptions of the adequacy of the budget for merit increases were strong. This result, based on *perceptions* of the budget rather than *actual* budget figures, underscores the importance of factoring in budget considerations when assessing the feasibility of merit pay. Unfortunately, current research offers no direction with regard to this consideration. As ridiculous as it may seem, researchers have not yet looked into the impact of actual budgets on merit increase decisions.

Summary

In summary, it has been shown that the feasibility of a merit pay plan depends, in part, upon economic considerations at both the economy and firm level. Economic conditions that are conducive to the use of merit pay plans include stable prices, absence of wage and price guidelines, low marginal tax rates, subsidies from the government, and an adequate merit pay budget.

Institutional Arrangements

Along with economic conditions, another set of conditions that has a bearing on the feasibility of merit pay plans are institutional arrangements, or the policies formed by organizations in response to their business environment. These considerations have to do with the interaction of the organization and environment as shown in Figure 3.1. In particular, these considerations can be grouped into the following categories, which are each covered in turn: product or service markets, organizational life cycle, structure of the organization, business strategy, allocation norms or culture, labor unions, job characteristics, politics, and human resource practices.

Product or Service Markets

Differences between and within product and service markets appear to have an influence on the use and effectiveness of merit pay. Comparisons have been made between manufacturing and service sectors, high- versus low-technology organizations, and the public- versus private-sector. These comparisons will be considered in turn.

Manufacturing Versus Service. Service-sector organizations, in comparison to manufacturing-sector organizations, tend to have less tangible products, more customer involvement in service output, and consumption of services at the time of production (Jackson, Schuler, & Rivero, 1989). A recent study by Jackson, et al. (1989) indicated that merit pay is used more frequently in the service sector than in the manufacturing sector of the economy. The reason for this finding, according to the authors, is that performance ratings are more readily available in the service sector as a check on the quality of the service provided. More countable indicators of performance, such as number of products (associated with other incentive pay plans like piece-rate systems), are more readily available in the manufacturing sector.

High- Versus Low-Technology. A distinction that is often made, but difficult to define, is between high- and low-technology organizations in manufacturing. According to Milkovich (1987), high-technology firms are those in which innovation and invention are emphasized in the business strategy, a high level of resources is devoted to research and development, competition is world-wide and in short-cycle product markets, and a high percentage of the work force is comprised of engineers and scientists. Merit pay plans are less likely to be used in high- than low-technology firms for two reasons. First, high-technology firms tend to be less risk-averse and more innovative. Hence, they are less likely to use traditional merit pay plans and more likely to use recent innovations in compensation, such as long-term stock option plans. Second, there is some evidence that group incentive plans are more effective than such individual incentive plans as merit pay for engineers and scientists in research and development organizations (Gomez-Mejia & Balkin, 1989).

Although we might expect merit to be used more frequently in high-technology firms, one study by Jackson et al. (1989) suggests that this is not always the case. They reported that there was not a statistically significant difference in the use of merit by high-technology and low-technology firms. Hence, this distinction, which is troublesome to define, does not seem to have much bearing in the actual practice of merit pay.

Public- Versus Private-Sector.   A major difference between these two sectors of our economy is ownership. Although there are some exceptions, in general, ownership of organizations in the public sector is held by the public, and ownership of organizations in the private sector is held by private parties. This difference in ownership has resulted in differences in personnel practices such as merit pay. In turn, these different personnel practices have had different levels of effectiveness for merit pay. A more detailed explanation of these differences follows.

Perry (1986); Rainey (1979); Silverman (1983); and Scott, Hills, Markham, and Vest (1986) describe some of the situational characteristics found more often in the public sector than in the private sector, which limit the effectiveness of merit pay plans. These constraints include, among other things, limited merit pay budgets, limited discretion in merit pay decisions, accountability to conflicting constituencies, and a long history of pay based on longevity rather than performance. These limiting situational characteristics and others are shown for government organizations in Figure 3.2.

These constraints, which have led to limited success of merit pay plans in the public versus the private sector, are reflected in the result shown in Table 3.1. For example, as shown in Table 3.1, which compares public and private merit systems, pay-for-performance perceptions appear to be weaker in the public sector. Also, the perceived effectiveness of merit pay may be lower as well. Table 3.1 shows the number of organizations (N) and percentage of organizations (%) who agree with

Table 3.1
Effectiveness of Public and Private Merit Systems

Question: "If your company does have a merit system, what is your opinion of the program's effectiveness in motivating the employees to improve performance?"

Sector	Very Effective		Somewhat Effective		Not Effective	
	N	%	N	%	N	%
Public	26	7.2	214	59.0	123	33.9
Private	1130	22.3	3178	62.7	759	15.0

Statistical Summary: Chi Square = 111.77 Df = 2
Significance = .001

Performance - Reward Expectancy

Question: "If I perform well in my job, I am likely to get a promotion or a pay raise."

Sector	Strongly Agree		Agree		Neutral		Disagree		Strongly Disagree	
	N	%	N	%	N	%	N	%	N	%
Public	26	6.6	97	24.7	78	19.9	142	36.2	49	12.5
Private	1198	18.8	2652	41.6	1296	20.3	887	13.9	341	5.3

Statistical Summary: Chi Square = 209.67 Df = 4
Significance = .01

Source: Wisdom & Patzig (1987). Reprinted with permission of the International Personnel Management Association.

each statement. The statistical summary refers to the degree to which the results for this sample of organizations can be generalized to a larger population of organizations. The smaller the significance level, the greater the confidence that we can have that the results will be similar for a larger population.

While it appears that it is more difficult to link pay to performance in the public sector, the potential returns for doing so may be even greater than in the private sector, as shown in Figure 3.3.

Figure 3.2
Reasons for Merit Pay Failures in Government Organizations

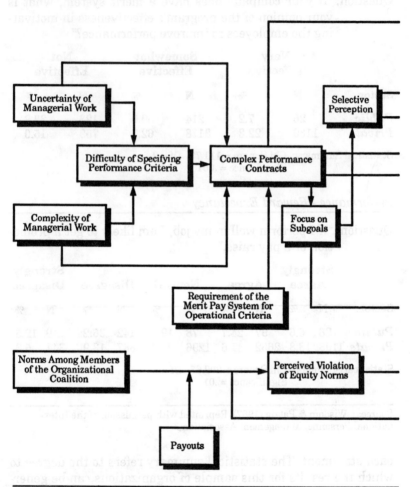

Source: Perry (1986). Reprinted with permission.

Giles and Barrett (1971) found that pay satisfaction and fairness perceptions increased for each additional dollar allocated to merit increases in the public sector. In contrast, pay satisfaction and fairness perceptions actually declined when allocation of merit pay dollars reached a certain point in the private sector.

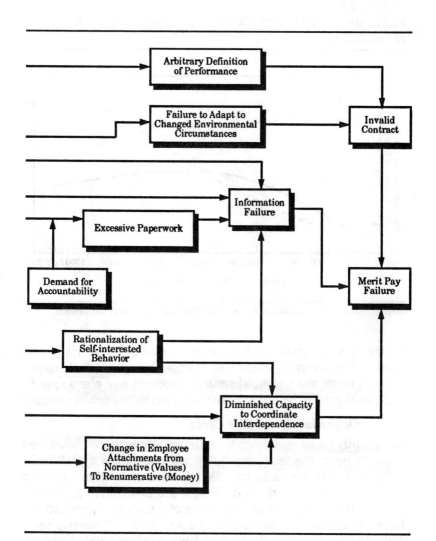

All told, it would appear that conditions tend to be less favorable for implementing merit pay in the public than private sector. While the results of merit plans in the public sector have not been overwhelmingly positive to date, neither have they been a total disaster (R. Heneman, 1990). Other studies,

Figure 3.3
*Pay Fairness-Pay Satisfaction Perceptions as a Function
of Pay Increase*

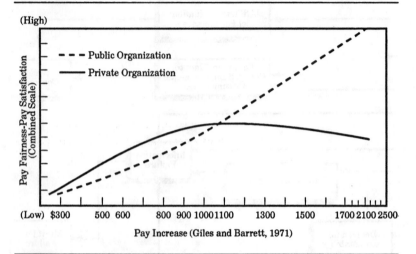

Source: Schuster, Colletti, & Knowles (1973). Reprinted with permission.

reviewed in Chapter 7, show positive results for merit pay in
some public sector organizations. Although perhaps problematic
to implement, the potential returns on merit pay plans may be
somewhat greater in the public sector than in the private sector.

Organizational Life Cycle

Some authors have argued that the effective use of merit pay
depends upon the stage in the organization's life cycle (Seals,
1984; Balkin & Gomez-Mejia, 1987). Human *systems* go through a
cycle of life just as humans do. People are born, develop, mature,
and eventually die. Collections of people, such as organizations,
have life cycles that parallel the human stages of development.
The growth of organizations over time involves several phases,
including start-up, growth, maturity, and decline. Start-up is
characterized by the small organization with low current profits
and a high potential for future profits. The growth phase is characterized by an increase in size from a small- to medium-sized
firm with high profitability and high potential. The maturity
phase occurs when the organization becomes medium to large in
size with high profitability and low potential. The decline stage is

characterized by a large- to medium-sized firm with low profits and low potential.

Under this organizational life cycle theory, merit pay would seem to be more appropriate in some phases than others as a reward system. For example, merit pay would not be appropriate during the decline phase. Then, the organization may be cutting back its resources and, as a result, employee trust may be low and the budget for merit increases limited. Pagaio (1985) describes the disastrous results of merit pay during a reduction in force at the U.S. Department of Health and Human Services.

Merit pay would also seem to be less appropriate during the start-up phase, because more emphasis may be required for long-term incentives to achieve the high potential for profits.

Merit pay would seem to be most appropriate during the growth and maturity phases when current profitability is high, and merit pay can be used to reinforce and maintain the behaviors contributing to profitability. In support of these ideas, Balkin and Gomez-Mejia (1990) found that the use and effectiveness of merit pay was greater in the growth than in the maturity stages of manufacturing firms.

Balkin and Gomez-Mejia (1984) also present data from a study of high-technology firms that suggest merit pay be given less emphasis in the growth than maturity stage. During the growth stage, innovation is likely to be emphasized, with both merit pay and cash bonuses used to reinforce this emphasis. However, cash bonuses might be the incentive of choice for the successful completion of specific projects. In summary, merit pay would seem to be most applicable in the maturity phase, followed by the growth phase. It would be much less applicable in the start-up and decline phases.

Organizational Structure

The way that work is arranged and coordinated in organizations may also influence the degree to which merit pay is used. Jackson et al. (1989) reported that some, but not all, indicators of organizational structure were related to the use of merit pay.

Jackson et al. (1989) also found in their study that organizations with "flexible, specialization technologies" used merit pay more frequently than did organizations with "mass production technologies." In the former organizations, work is organized into jobs with wide scope and task diversity. In these types of jobs, not only are employees responsible for performing the work, they also have a voice in how the work is to be done and may be authorized to alter work arrangements as needed. In the latter organizations, work is arranged into simple and repetitive tasks like those found on an assembly line. Perhaps the difference in the use of merit pay is due to the availability of performance measures. You might expect to find countable indicators of performance, that lend themselves to piece rate pay, in mass production organizations. On the other hand, in flexible specialization firms, you might expect to find the more subjective ratings of performance usually associated with merit pay. For example, there was no difference in the use of merit pay between organizations arranged along product lines and those arranged along service lines. Also, there was no evidence of any differences in the use of merit pay in small versus large organizations.

In another study, Brown (1990) expected that merit pay would be used more frequently in smaller organizations because the costs of monitoring employee performance are greater in larger than in smaller organizations. While Brown (1990) expected this effect, his study showed the opposite of what he predicted. Large firms used merit pay more often than small firms. However, this result should not be surprising. Large organizations are more likely to have the resources to meet the requirements of a merit pay plan, as discussed in Chapter 2. Also, while the total costs of monitoring employee performance may be greater in larger firms, the fixed costs per employee are less.

It should also be noted that simply because industries with "flexible specialization technologies" are more likely to have merit pay plans, these merit plans are not guaranteed to be effective. In a study of the Environmental Protection Agency (EPA), which can be characterized as flexible in structure, managers were *not* receptive to a merit pay plan because it was seen as imposing a rigid set of performance standards that threatened the managers' autonomy (Gaertner, Gaertner, & Akinnusi, 1984). This study demonstrated the importance of considering culture as well as structure in assessing the feasibility of merit pay.

Business Strategy

The compensation policy of the organization should be tailored to the strategic mission of the firm for the organization to survive, grow, and prosper in its product or service markets. Many methodologies are available for helping organizations to decide upon the appropriate role of incentives in furthering the business strategy. These methodologies have been summarized by Hurwich (1986) and include financial, planning, statistical, and organizational effectiveness models.

One organizational effectiveness model is described by Carroll (1987) as it relates to merit pay and incentive plans. The model he describes is the one by Miles and Snow (1978), which suggests that the structure of the organization needs to be congruent with the business strategy for the organization to meet its goals. Carroll's discussion of this model suggests that merit pay is more likely to be appropriate for organizations that pursue a "defender" rather than a "prospector" business strategy. A defender organization is one that is protecting rather than expanding its current product or service markets. Typically, a defender organization is highly structured, with stable tasks. Under these structured and stable conditions, performance measures are somewhat easier to develop and use than under the unstructured and unstable conditions found in organizations pursuing a prospector strategy.

Unstructured and unstable conditions are present in the prospector firm as it seeks to locate and develop new product and service markets. Under these conditions, performance is difficult to define and measure. Since measures of performance are better developed in defender than prospector firms, we are more likely to find merit pay being used successfully in defender rather than prospector firms.

Although not a direct test of Carroll's (1987) arguments, some indirect empirical support was generated in a study by Balkin and Gomez-Mejia (1990). In this study of compensation officials from manufacturing companies, they found that merit pay was more frequently and effectively used by single product manufacturers rather than diversified manufacturers who carried multiple product lines. One might argue that the strategies of single product carriers are similar to defender firms while the characteristics of diversified organizations are more like prospector organizations. Regardless of interpretation, however, these data do suggest that the desirability of merit pay is related to the strategy of the organization.

Organizational Culture

Another organizational characteristic related to the feasibility of merit pay is the culture of the organization. Culture refers to the shared set of beliefs and values held by members of the organization (Ott, 1989). One would expect that merit pay would work better in organizations in which there is a shared belief, that pay increases should be granted on the basis of performance. Also, one would expect that merit pay would work better in organizations where recipients of merit pay share the same belief as the allocators of merit pay in pay for performance. As discussed below, not all employees are necessarily in favor of granting pay increases on the basis of merit.

Pay can be allocated in a variety of ways (Leventhal, 1976; Kopelman, 1976). Some of these methods of pay allocation are as follows (Gardner, 1961): birthright, egalitarianism, and competition. *Birthright* refers to pay allocated on the basis of nepotism or some other form of favoritism. *Egalitarianism* refers to pay based on parity, where everyone receives the same pay increase. An example would be a general increase offered to all employees once a year. *Competition* refers to pay allocation on the basis of merit or best performance. Also, the notion of *Marxian justice* could be added to this list whereby pay is allocated in accordance with people's needs (Lerner, 1977; Greenberg, 1987a). For example, pay increases may be larger for those with a larger number of dependents. Finally, pay could also be allocated according to the principle of *equity* or relative contributions (Birnbaum, 1983; Vecchio & Terborg, 1987). Pay allocated on the basis of equity might include an *adjustment system,* in which persons equally underpaid receive equal raises, or a *relative system,* in which persons with equal merit receive equal percentage raises. As can be seen from this list, the competition model, in which pay is based on performance, is only one of many ways to allocate pay increases.

Empirical studies on these various methods of allocating pay suggest that beliefs in these systems depend upon many factors. Alexander and Barrett (1982) provided evidence to suggest that belief in these systems of pay allocation depends on one's nationality. They found that Japanese managers are more likely to follow a merit strategy than are managers in the United States, Austria, Germany, Italy, and the United Kingdom.

Managers in these other countries are more likely to evaluate factors other than performance in determining salary increases. Kidder, Bellettirie, and Cohn (1977) provided some evidence from the laboratory that suggests that men tend to follow a reward strategy of equity while women follow a reward strategy of egalitarianism. Meindl (1989) found that the allocation strategy followed by managers depended upon the situation (e.g., task interdependence) and person (e.g., leadership style).

The studies reviewed here suggest that not all organizational cultures are supportive of merit pay. For merit pay to be an accepted organizational strategy, the philosophy of pay for performance must be congruent with the present culture of the organization. Although it may be possible to use merit pay as the vehicle to change the culture from, say, one of egalitarianism to one of merit, it could be problematic if not accompanied with other programs of organizational development (Patten, 1977). An example is offered by Kroeck, Avolio, Small, and Einstein (1987) who found that it is possible to shift resource allocation preferences for managers in a laboratory environment when panel discussions are conducted. A more conservative route would be to only use merit pay when the culture is in line with the merit philosophy. At least one study (H. Heneman & Young, 1988) showed that disruption of the social system through merit pay may lead to negative consequences for the organization.

Labor Unions

It is sometimes mistakenly assumed that merit pay is not used in unionized settings. In fact, merit pay is used in some unionized settings. For example, at General Motors the United Auto Workers have agreed to a merit pay plan of sorts as the time span is shortened for the automatic pay increases to be received by outstanding performers (Milkovich & Newman, 1987). Under this arrangement, pay increases are granted more frequently to outstanding than to average performers. Another example comes from Boeing Helicopters where the United Auto Workers agreed to two percent semiannual selective adjustments. These adjustments are made on the basis of performance (Cimini, 1990). A very recent example comes from Harley-Davidson. Local 175 of the Machinists Union agreed to a merit pay plan for production and maintenance employees at the York, Pennsylvania, assembly plant (Cimini, 1991). While merit pay *is* used for some unionized employees, as shown in these examples, it is used less frequently for unionized than nonunionized employees. Surveys conducted by The Conference Board, U.S. Department of Labor, and the Bureau of National Affairs indicate that only between 10 to 16 percent of unionized employees are eligible for merit pay increases (Weeks, 1979; Mitchell, 1989; Balkin, 1989).

In part, the infrequent use of merit pay for unionized employees may be attributable to resistance to merit pay plans by some labor unions. Unions and other employee organizations may be against merit pay for several reasons. First, it has been suggested that unions may fear that management will use merit pay to take money away from lower level union jobs to reward high-level management officials. For example, this concern was expressed by federal workers in the wake of the firing of striking air traffic controllers by President Reagan (Wildstrom, 1986). More recently, Chrysler workers expressed their dissatisfaction with merit pay for much the same reason. Higher level salaried employees were given merit increases at roughly the same time that lower level unionized employees were asked to take a reduction in salary (Naughton, 1990). To prevent pay from being taken from lower level jobs, unions have sought to standardize wage increase criteria within organizations (Balkin, 1989; Freeman, 1982).

A second and related concern that members of labor unions may have about merit pay is the subjective rating involved in the process, especially when employees' ratings do not include actual indicators of an employee's contribution to the organization. This concern was voiced by Ray Pasmore, Business Manager of Local 1466 of the International Brotherhood of Electrical Workers (Alloy, 1988): "If you happen to be an individual that's very good at your job, but you don't happen to have the right kind of personality to where you get along with your supervisor, your raise may show what your supervisor feels about your personality rather than your work." (Reprinted with permission.)

Third, labor unions are political institutions. As pointed out by Freeman (1982), solidarity and organizational strength are likely to be bolstered when workers are paid the same wage increase rather than different wage increases. Merit pay is viewed by some unions as the imposition of an artificial barrier between workers. Also, as pointed out by Freeman (1982), and later by

Balkin (1989), unions tend to emphasize indirect pay in the form of benefits over direct pay in the form of salary increases. Because labor union members' preferences are for benefits over salary increases, labor union officials may bargain more forcefully for benefits than merit pay. The incentive for labor union officials to push for benefits is the need to represent their members' preferences to be reelected by these members.

Fourth, the administration of merit pay plans may be troublesome to union members (Barkin, 1948). Given the complexity of administering merit pay plans, as discussed in Chapter 6, it is costly for unions to enforce the agreed-upon terms and conditions of a merit pay plan. For example, the costs of monitoring the extent to which actual employee performance is being measured, rather than nonmerit considerations such as personality, may be very high.

In summary, while merit pay is indeed used from time to time in unionized firms, it is unlikely to be used in unionized firms frequently. There is union resistance because of the subjectivity of the merit process and the goals of the labor movement. Therefore, merit pay appears to be less feasible in union than nonunion organizations.

Job Characteristics

As discussed in the next chapter, a major stumbling block to implementing merit pay successfully is the measurement of performance. Some jobs lend themselves better to the performance measurement than others. As a result, it is more feasible to link pay increases to performance in some jobs than others. Given the current state of the empirical literature, it is not possible to say precisely which jobs lend themselves better to merit pay. It is possible, however, to sketch out the general characteristics of work that should be factored in when determining the feasibility of merit pay.

Two characteristics of jobs seem to lend themselves to merit pay (Konrad & Pfeffer, 1990; Lawler, 1989; Mohrman, Resnick-West, & Lawler, 1989). First, an employee must be responsible for performing a whole piece of work. What this means is that there must be a distinct start and finish to the product or service being generated by the employee. If this is not the case, it may be difficult to assess what it is that the employee is contributing to the organization. Second, the employee

must have the opportunity to have a noticeable impact on performance. In some jobs, employees are given so little autonomy,
discretion, or authority in performing their tasks that again it is
difficult to establish their contributions to the organization.

Both of these conditions seem to be required for merit pay
to be feasible. In some jobs, while discrete units of work are
being performed, the employee has little discretion in performing the job. For example, on an assembly line, there may be an
identifiable part placed repeatedly on the product. However, the
speed at which the number of parts are placed is outside the control of the individual employee and determined by the speed of
the assembly line. Hence, if the number of parts placed on the
product in a given time period is the performance standard,
there will not be enough variability in performance to make a
case for merit increases for higher performers.

Perhaps because both discrete units of work and discretion in performance are required, national surveys show (e.g.,
Peck, 1984) that exempt jobs are associated with merit pay
much more frequently than nonexempt jobs. According to the
Fair Labor Standards Act, which is a federal law, exempt jobs
must, by definition, have an inherent component of discretion
over the work to be performed. Nonexempt jobs do not have this
job characteristic. In exempt jobs, you are likely to find both the
performance of whole units of work as well as more employee
autonomy in the way work is performed. Hence, merit pay is
well suited for exempt positions because both the job characteristics required for an effective merit pay plan are present. It
should be noted, however, that even when both conditions are
present, performance measurement may still be problematic, as
shown in the next chapter. In nonexempt jobs, employees do not
have authority to control the way in which work is performed.
As a result, merit pay is less suited for nonexempt positions
because employees do not have an impact on performance.

Politics

In some organizations, or in some positions in organizations,
the climate may be so driven by office "politics" that it is not
feasible to use merit pay. Politics refers to deliberate attempts
by the allocator to enhance or protect his or her self-interests
to the extent of creating inaccurate performance appraisals
(Longnecker, Sims, & Gioia, 1987). In these types of situations,

it may be impossible to use merit pay because performance is based on political factors rather than performance. For example, ratings and, in turn, merit increases may be more a function of who you know than what you do. Politics may also interfere with merit pay even when performance *is* being accurately measured. For example, a large merit increase to a good performer may be attributed by others to favoritism rather than actual good performance.

While politics in organizations, both actual and perceived, can create problems in organizations and decrease the feasibility of merit pay, it should not be concluded that politics always lead to dysfunctional consequences for organizations. As pointed out by Longnecker, Sims, and Gioia (1987) and Ungson and Steers (1983), politics in organizations are sometimes very functional for the organization and may need to be encouraged. For example, in a study of managers' perceptions of politics in performance appraisal, Longnecker et al. (1987) found that some managers viewed it as legitimate to give out lower ratings than a particular employee deserved to "shock" that employee back to higher levels of performance.

While this example suggests that politics may be useful from time to time for developmental reasons, it is doubtful that a merit pay plan would be successful in a politically charged environment.

As pointed out by Lawler (1971) and empirically verified by Vest, Hills, and Scott (1989), trust is an important component of reward systems. If pay is based on politics but alleged to be based on performance, employees may have less trust in organizational decision makers. In such a situation, these employees conceivably could seek employment elsewhere or seek representation by a third party such as a labor organization.

Human Resource Management Practices

Reward systems such as merit pay are only one component of the many human resource management activities undertaken in organizations. Other human resource management activities, such as staffing and training and development, also influence the feasibility of merit pay. In general, the more successful an organization is with other human resource activities, the less merit pay is needed. With success in other areas of human resource management, the base rate of success is high. That is, the ratio of an organization's successful employees to its total employees, or the base rate as it is called, is high. When the base rate is already high because of other human resource activities, it is difficult to significantly improve the base rate through merit pay. In other words, in truly excellent organizations, it is difficult to make human resources even more productive. The organization has already hired the best available talent, carefully manages work practices, provides training when needed, and provides a sound pay package. Under these circumstances, it is difficult for merit pay or any other new human resource procedure to improve upon the existing situation.

In the opposite situation, if the base rate is very low, merit pay may not make much of a difference. Under a low base rate, other human resource activities may be so poorly performed, that merit pay cannot increase the base rate enough to make up for the poor practices in other areas of human resources.

Hence, merit pay seems most applicable under circumstances of a moderate base rate. When there is a moderate base rate, human resource operations can be improved. At the same time, human resource operations are not so poor that the results of a merit pay plan will be swamped by the ineffectiveness of other human resource procedures. When there is a moderate base rate, other human resource activities play a strong supporting role for merit pay. For example, as shown throughout the book, training in the merit pay process is an essential component to the proper administration of merit pay. In turn, merit pay also supports other human resource management activities. For example, merit pay can be used to reinforce the principles learned in training back on the job.

Summary

In summary, it has been shown that institutional arrangements need to be considered along with economic factors in determining the feasibility of merit pay. Conditions that seem to facilitate or hinder the use of merit pay are shown in Table 3.2.

Preferences for Merit Increases

In addition to considering economic conditions and institutional arrangements, attention should also be given to organization members' preferences for merit increases. Salary increases can,

Table 3.2
Institutional Arrangements Contributing to the Feasibility of Merit Pay

Merit Pay More Feasible Under These Conditions	Merit Pay Less Feasible Under These Conditions
Service sector	Manufacturing sector
Private sector	Public sector
Middle stages of organizational life cycle	Early or late stages of organizational life cycle
Flexible specialization technologies	Mass production technologies
Competitive culture	Egalitarian culture
Nonunionized	Unionized
Low politics	High politics
Moderate base rate	High or low base rate
Well-defined job characteristics	Poorly defined job characteristics
High discretion in work performed	Low discretion in work performed

of course, be based on many factors other than performance, including seniority, cost of living, and promotions. Other examples include "comparability adjustments," sometimes granted in an attempt to equalize pay in the public sector relative to the private sector, or "general increases" granted to every current employee of an organization. A merit pay plan would be more feasible when organizational members prefer merit increases over these other options.

As might be expected, merit pay is not always preferred by all organizational members. Over the years, many surveys have been conducted in which organizational members are asked to rank order their preferences for merit pay and other types of pay increases. One such survey is shown in Table 3.3. The figures in this table can be interpreted as follows.

In each of the three studies, participants were asked to indicate the importance of each criterion for merit pay decisions

Table 3.3
Importance of Pay Increase Decision Criteria: Means, Standard Deviations, and Rank Order

Criterion	Study 1			Study 2			Study 3		
	Mean	SD	Rank	Mean	SD	Rank	Mean	SD	Rank
Level of job performance	4.70	.66	1	4.93	.27	1	5.00	.00	1
Size of salary increase budget	4.30	.77	2	3.58	1.30	3	4.44	.80	2
Cost of living increases	4.10	.73	3	3.88	.99	2	2.93	1.01	4
Tightness of the labor market for this type of job	4.00	.65	4	3.53	1.13	5	3.35	1.16	3
Degree of disruption that would occur if the job holder quit	3.90	.85	5	3.55	1.28	4	2.78	1.38	5
Length of service	3.30	.86	6	2.93	.92	6	2.33	1.00	6

Source: Fossum & Fitch (1985). Reprinted with permission.

Note: Study 1: 22 students in undergraduate personnel course and graduate compensation class; study 2: 40 full-time professional and managerial employees in MBA personnel class; study 3: 42 employees of 21 midwestern private-sector organizations in personnel and line management positions.

on a scale from 1 = least important to 5 = most important. The mean shown in the table refers to the average numerical score assigned by the participants to each criterion. The higher the mean, the more important the criterion to the participants. The standard deviation (SD) shows the dispersion in values assigned by participants around the mean. In essence, the smaller the SD, the more agreement by study participants on the importance level of this criterion. The rank refers to the rank ordering of means from the highest to the lowest. Along with the mean, it is another summary statistic of the importance of each criterion to the participants in the study. The results of this survey and others will be reviewed in this section to help assess which organizational members are likely to prefer merit pay. Preferences for merit pay seem to vary by the following categories, which will be discussed in turn: job type and level, merit pay plan characteristics, income and performance, gender, and motivation.

Job Level and Type

Surveys of both managers' and employees' preferences for merit pay have been conducted (Bureau of National Affairs, 1988; Dyer & Theriault, 1976; Fossum & Fitch, 1985; Koys, Keaveny, & Allen, 1989; Mahoney, 1964; Nigro, 1981; Pearce & Perry, 1983; Scott, Hills, Markham, & Vest, 1987). The results of these surveys suggest that managers' preferences for merit pay are stronger than employee preferences. In these surveys, managers are more consistent in ranking merit pay as their number one preference than are employees. Hence, preferences for merit pay seems to be related to job level.

It should be noted, however, that just because managers, on average, *prefer* merit pay does not necessarily mean that their *actual* decisions are based solely on merit. Sherer, Schwab, and H. Heneman (1987) reported a correlation of .65 between preferences and actual weights used for performance and other factors in merit pay decisions. A correlation of .65 means that only about 42 percent of those who favored merit pay actually made pay decisions on the basis of merit. It should also be noted that just because managers prefer merit pay does not mean that they are in favor of the current system under which they are required to operate. For example, Hyde (1988) reports the results of a study by Clark and Wachtel (1988): In this study of 4000 federal managers, 90 percent favored the concept of merit pay; however, 74 percent felt that the current system was unfair.

Types of jobs are also related to preferences for merit pay. It appears that merit pay preferences are stronger for white-collar than blue-collar employees (Beer & Gery, 1972; Koys et al., 1989). White-collar jobs include technical, professional, and clerical positions, while blue-collar jobs include more traditional manufacturing jobs. In the Koys et al. (1989) study, cost of living was the preference of first choice for blue-collar employees while merit pay was the preference of first choice for white-collar workers.

Taken together, the results of these two sets of studies suggest that those individuals who are in higher level, white-collar types of jobs tend to have stronger preferences for merit pay. It should be noted, however, that there are exceptions to the rule. For example, H. Heneman and Young (1988) found that school administrators had unfavorable perceptions about merit pay. The implication of this general finding is that it may be easier to "sell" some parts of an organization on the feasibility and desirability of merit pay than other parts of the organization.

Merit Pay Plan Characteristics

In two very interesting empirical studies, it was shown that characteristics of the merit pay plan also have a bearing on an employee's preferences for merit pay. Koys et al. (1989) found that preferences for merit pay were stronger when it was perceived that merit pay did not decrease teamwork. Beer and Gery (1972) reported that preferences for merit pay vary by type of merit pay plan offered. In their sample of white-collar workers, a merit increase based solely on performance was preferred over one that includes both performance and a general increase for all employees. But, both of these merit plans were preferred over a high-risk merit plan where only above-average performers are rewarded. This type of plan is high-risk because no merit increase is granted to anyone rated less than above average. These studies suggest that in surveying organizational members about their preferences for merit increases versus alternative arrangements, considerable care should be taken to specify the *type* of merit plan in the survey.

You would also expect that preferences for merit pay would be related to perceptions of performance appraisal.

Performance appraisal is an essential component of the merit pay process, as discussed later in Chapter 4. The research on this issue, however, is mixed. Koys et al. (1989) found that the perceived validity of the appraisal system used to make merit decisions did *not* have an impact on preferences for merit pay in a university setting. Pearce and Perry (1983) found that there was a significant positive relationship between perceptions of a fair and objective appraisal system and preferences for merit pay in federal agencies.

These findings concerning performance appraisal suggest that the present performance appraisal system may not always be an obstacle in the eyes of organizational members when considering the adoption of a merit pay plan. It would be wrong, however, to conclude that the perceived validity of the appraisal system is not important. As will be shown in Chapter 4, the perceived validity of the appraisal system *does* have an impact on people's reactions to merit pay *after* such a plan has been implemented.

Income and Performance

Individuals with higher levels of performance (Beer & Gery, 1972) and income (Mahoney, 1964) have been shown to prefer merit pay over alternative increase policies. Perhaps this is because high performers are more likely to receive a raise than low performers under a merit pay plan. Also, high-income employees may favor merit pay because they have income to rely on should their merit increases be less than adequate. People with larger incomes, from work and/or other outside sources, may be more willing to "risk" pay-based-on-performance ratings because whether they get an increase or not, they still have other sources of income to meet their basic needs. By comparison, someone with a lower income, perhaps without any source of outside income, may be less willing to run the risk of not getting a merit increase, because they cannot afford the loss. In short, employees with low incomes may prefer the security of a small increase each year over the gamble of a large increase—or no increase—in any given year. Increases are seldom guaranteed under a merit pay plan.

Gender

Koys et al. (1989) also reported a gender effect in preferences for merit pay. Men preferred merit pay more than women did.

Perhaps this is because, as the authors note, women allocators prefer to distribute pay across the board to all employees rather than on the basis of merit (Majors, 1988). Brenner and Bertsch (1983) found that gender preferences may be moderated by personality. Assertive men preferred pay increases based on merit, while assertive women preferred pay increases based on seniority.

Motivation

In two studies, employee motivation was examined as a correlate of merit pay preferences. Meyer and Walker (1961) reported that individuals high in achievement motivation preferred merit pay more than those low in achievement motivation. Those who are oriented toward task mastery and accomplishment may prefer merit pay because it provides employees with feedback on how well they are doing.

Beer and Gery (1972) also concluded that merit pay was preferred by individuals high in the need for achievement. They based their conclusion on the finding that employees with high needs for advancement, responsibility, and interesting and challenging work preferred merit pay over those employees low in these needs. Also, they found that people high in the need for security, vacation, and money preferred a general increase for all employees more than employees low in these needs. Beer and Gery (1972) reasoned that these latter employees were more concerned with security and therefore preferred a general increase because it was less risky than merit pay. A general increase usually involves less risk because it is granted to all employees regardless of performance. On the other hand, increases under a merit pay plan involve more risk because increases are usually granted only to those employees who perform at or above a certain level.

Summary

The research available on preferences for merit pay is somewhat sparse, disjointed, and dated. However, it does strongly indicate that not all organizational members prefer merit pay. The limited research suggests that merit pay is more likely to be preferred by those in higher level, white-collar positions; by those who are male, good performers, and achievement oriented; and by those who like to work in a climate where performance differences are emphasized and teamwork is not diminished. Organizations need to consider the preferences of their members prior to the implementation of a merit pay plan. Also, merit pay may have an influence on the recruitment of new members to organizations. Individuals with a preference for merit pay may be more likely to be attracted to organizations with a merit pay plan.

Alternatives or Additions to Merit Pay

After considering the environmental constraints, organizational considerations, and employee preferences, the reader may conclude that merit pay is not feasible in his or her organization. However, even if merit pay is not an appropriate choice, the reader may still be faced with the difficult prospect of motivating his or her work force. Alternatively, perhaps the reader will want to combine merit pay with other reward systems.

This section offers readers some alternative motivational programs that can be considered. For those readers who have concluded merit pay *is* a viable option for their organization, this section suggests some additions to merit pay. For those who decide against merit pay, this section provides alternatives.

In many organizations, more than one reward system is needed (O'Dell, 1986; Wallace, 1990), and these systems need to be integrated with one another (Schneier, 1990). Multiple reward systems and the integration of these systems will be addressed here. Readers desiring even more information on other reward strategies will be referred to other sources.

Promotions

Meyer (1987) has forcefully argued over the years that it is very difficult to effectively administer a merit pay plan. He advocates that employees be motivated on the basis of promotions rather than a salary increase based on merit. The reason for using promotions rather than monetary rewards, according to Meyer (1975), is that more objective criteria accompany promotion decisions than pay increase decisions. Also, Meyer (1975) asserts that the cut-throat competition associated with merit pay can be avoided if promotions are made on the basis of peer nominations. (See Chapter 2 for a look at the notion of competition.)

Meyer (1975 and 1987) takes a very broad view of promotions as a reward. In his view, promotions do not include just the traditional model of technical employees moving up and through the managerial ranks. Instead, Meyer considers the creation of technical career tracks as promotions. Under this approach, employees can continue to move up in the organization without necessarily becoming a manager. Meyer also includes lateral moves in his definition of promotions. Under this type of arrangement, employees are "promoted" when they acquire new skills or different job responsibilities even when this occurs at the same level as their previous job.

Lawler (1976) disagrees that promotions should be substituted for monetary rewards. He suggests that the problems of competition and the subjective criteria associated with some merit pay plans are also likely to be associated with promotion decisions as well. Moreover, he argues that promotions place more emphasis on potential than actual performance. Therefore, if only promotions are used, actual performance may not be taken into account by the organization, and motivation will decline.

Looking at both sets of arguments, it would seem that both monetary and promotion systems are needed in organizations. Merit pay or other monetary pay systems can be used to reward and motivate actual performance. Promotions and/or pay based on the acquisition of new skills (e.g., Lawler, 1981) can be used to reinforce the potential for performance.

As a practical matter, organizations today may need to place more emphasis on merit pay than on traditional upward promotion systems. Many organizations are in the process of downsizing by eliminating middle-management positions. At the same time, there is a large population of "baby-boom" employees, born in the late 1940s through early 1960s, that is competing for higher level positions. When there is a large number of people for a small number of jobs, as is presently the case, the motivational impact of an upward promotion system is diminished because advancement is less likely. One way to deal such a situation is to place more emphasis on merit pay than on promotions as a means to motivate employees.

Other Monetary Incentive Plans

As indicated in several parts of this chapter, conditions may favor using another type of incentive pay strategy. For example, countable indicators of performance may exist in some jobs and, as a result, a piece-rate pay plan may be more appropriate to reinforce continued production. In other organizations, jobs may be highly interdependent with performance determined more by the overall functioning of the group than by any one individual. Under these circumstances, a group incentive plan may be appropriate. Extensive reviews of the empirical research on piece-rate and group incentive plans can be found in Guzzo and Bondy (1983); Jenkins (1986); Locke, Feren, McCaleb, Shaw, and Denny (1980); and Katzell, Bienstock, and Faerstein (1977). Current advances in alternative monetary reward strategies are discussed in O'Dell (1986). Some of the old and new incentive pay plans reviewed by O'Dell (1986) are described in Figure 3.4.

In many organizations, several incentive pay plans are needed rather than just one. Different plans accomplish different objectives. For example, skill-based pay is used to facilitate the acquisition of new skills, group incentive plans are used to motivate performance of the group, and merit pay is used to motivate individual performance. Although multiple incentive plans are desirable, these plans need to be integrated and coordinated.

Examples of integrated incentive-pay systems can be seen at Pratt and Whitney and at Pacific Gas and Electric Company. Schneier (1989a,b) details an integrated reward system, put in place at Pratt and Whitney, known as the Performance Management, Recognition, and Reward System (PMRR). This system uses merit increases, bonuses, special cash awards, and prerequisites, along with nonmonetary rewards. It is integrated by being tied into and reinforcing the business strategy of the organization.

Pacific Gas and Electric Company (1989) has an integrated incentive plan for its managers. This plan, which is also tied to the strategic mission of the organization, provides incentive pay for corporate, work group, and individual performance. One of the oldest, and perhaps best-known, examples of an integrated incentive plan can be found at Lincoln Electric Company in Cleveland, Ohio (Lincoln, 1951). At Lincoln, incentive pay plans are viewed as a means to manage, and have been in use for over 80 years. Financial rewards are provided for individual and group performance, profits, and employee suggestions (Perry, 1990).

In summary, other incentives can and should be considered in addition to, or instead of, merit pay. These plans need to

Figure 3.4
Some Definitions of Nontraditional Reward Practices

Earned Time Off

Due to exceptional performance, employees are eligible to earn time off from work with pay.

Gain Sharing Plan

Unit-wide bonus system designed to reward all eligible members for improved performance. Gains are shared with all employees in the unit according to a single predetermined formula or target (several measures may be included in the formula).

Examples of common gain sharing plans are Scanlon, Rucker, Improshare, and unit level (other than corporate level) cash profit-sharing, but limited to these. If profit sharing is corporate-wide and/or deferred, consider this practice "Profit Sharing Plans" (below).

Small Group Incentives

Similar to gain sharing plans, except that bonuses are based on small-group performance rather than single-formula, unit-wide performance. Formulas and bonuses can vary from group to group within a unit, depending on nature of the work and performance.

Individual Incentives

All or part of an individual's pay is tied to individual performance. This would include all standard hour incentive plans, engineered incentives, production incentives, piece rate, etc. *Does not include merit raises or executive compensation packages.*

(continued)

Figure 3.4 *(continued)*

Lump Sum Payment/Bonus	Eligible employees are given one-time, lump sum payments or bonuses instead of all or part of a base wage or salary increase. Bonus does not become part of base pay. This is independent of any incentive or gain sharing pay.
Pay For Knowledge	Hourly or salaried pay, or pay progression, is determined by the number of jobs an employee can do, not the job (s)he actually performed on a given day. Often seen in "team concept" operations instead of traditional job classifications, or part of an effort to reduce the number of job classifications in a unit.
Profit Sharing Plans	Annual bonus or share based on company/corporate profit performance. An employee's share could be paid in cash, or deferred into a retirement fund.

Source: O'Dell (1987). Reprinted with permission.

be selected based on their intended objectives and the facilitating conditions discussed in detail by other authors. If multiple plans are used, considerable care must be taken to integrate and coordinate these plans. Integration and coordination can be achieved by using these plans as a routine part of the managerial process and by tying each plan to the mission of the organization.

Nonmonetary Rewards

A variety of nonmonetary rewards are available to organizations in addition to the monetary rewards just reviewed. Examples of nonmonetary rewards are shown in Figure 3.5. Some of these rewards may be more feasible for organizations

Figure 3.5
Examples of Nonmonetary Rewards

Formal commendation

Formal recognition

Informal recognition (e.g., a "pat on the back")

Unofficial time off (e.g., allowing late arrival or early departure)

Vacation scheduling (giving favorable vacation times)

Favorable job assignments (e.g., easy, comfortable, involves challenge)

Informal performance feedback

Mentoring, coaching, and development

Participation in unit decision making

Off-job socializing and friendship

Considerate, personally supportive behavior (e.g., giving personal advice or help)

"In-group" membership (giving inside information, special consideration, etc.)

Career advice, counseling, and help

Source: Hinkin, Podsakoff, & Schriescheim (1987). Reprinted with permission.

as they are virtually cost free. Also, nonmonetary rewards may actually be more attractive to some employees than monetary rewards. For example, in this age of busy work and family schedules, some employees may prefer time off over an increase in pay. As shown in the discussion of expectancy theory (Chapter 2), outcomes with more positive valence to an employee are likely to be more motivational.

In using nonmonetary rewards, two points should be considered. First, if these rewards are to be used to maintain and improve performance, they must be made contingent on performance (Hinkin, Podsakoff, & Schriesheim, 1987). Only by making these rewards contingent on performance will they take on the motivational properties needed to improve performance. Second, it is sometimes possible to couple these nonmonetary rewards with monetary rewards. For example, an organization might not only reward a good performer with additional time off from work but also provide pay during this time off. One reason to use monetary and nonmonetary rewards as complementary incentives is that there is some evidence that monetary rewards are associated with higher levels of productivity than are nonmonetary rewards (Locke, Feren, McCaleb, Shaw, & Denny, 1980).

Organizations may use nonmonetary rewards as substitutes for monetary rewards from time to time. A good example is the situation described later in Chapter 5 in which it may not be possible to provide good performers with merit increases because there are maximum amounts employees can earn—ceilings—that allow the employer to control labor costs and earn a profit. Over a number of years of good performance, an employee may reach the maximum that can be paid to a person holding that job. As any manager who has faced this situation will tell you, it is very difficult to maintain the employee's good level of performance when it is no longer possible to grant a merit increase.

What sometimes does work in this situation is to grant nonmonetary rewards instead of merit pay to continue to motivate good performance. For example, the manager may give the employee a greater voice in decisions that have a bearing on how work is performed in the unit. Along with greater participation in decision making, the manager might also involve the employee in training less senior employees. Even when monetary rewards are not possible, as in this example, there are still additional ways to motivate good performance as shown in Figure 3.5.

Summary of Major Points

1. *Feasibility of merit pay.* Merit pay is not appropriate in all situations. Even if merit pay appears to be desirable, an assessment needs to be made of conditions that may facilitate or hinder the use of merit pay.

2. *Conditions that need to be diagnosed.* At a general level, attention must be given to characteristics of the environment and organization in which merit pay decisions are made. Attention also needs to be directed toward the allocators and recipients involved in and affected by merit pay decisions.

3. *Economic conditions that favor using merit pay.* One aspect of the environment and organization that has a direct impact on the use of merit pay is present and anticipated economic conditions. Economic conditions favorable to the use of merit pay include the following:
   - Price stability
   - No wage and price guidelines or controls
   - Low marginal tax rates
   - Government subsidies
   - Adequate budget

4. *Institutional arrangements that favor merit pay.* The interaction of the organization and environment result in various institutional arrangements that influence the use of merit pay. Institutional arrangements that seem to favor merit pay are as follows:
   - Service-sector organizations
   - Private-sector organizations
   - Middle stages of organizational life cycle
   - Flexible specialization technologies
   - Competitive culture
   - Nonunionized
   - Low politics
   - Well-defined job characteristics
   - High level of discretion in performing work

5. *Preferences for merit pay.* Not all employees favor pay increases allocated on the basis of performance. Some employees prefer alternative allocation procedures such as pay increases based on seniority. Groups that tend to favor merit pay are as follows:
   - Males
   - White-collar employees
   - High performers
   - Achievement-oriented employees
   - Those who already work under a merit plan where performance differences are emphasized and teamwork is not diminished

6. *Alternatives or additions to merit pay.* If the reader concludes that merit pay is not feasible, or that merit pay needs to be supplemented, a variety of other reward systems are available. These reward systems include promotions, other incentive plans, and non-monetary rewards.

Conclusions

In Chapter 2 it was argued that merit pay does indeed have some desirable features, and that those who reject merit pay under all circumstances have gone too far. Based on the material presented in Chapter 3 on the feasibility of merit pay, it can be concluded that those who endorse merit pay in all circumstances have also gone too far. Some managers seem very committed to the belief that merit pay is *the* method to be used to decide pay increases. Simply put, there are times when merit pay should not be used. There are some organizations currently using or contemplating using merit pay that should not use merit pay.

Merit pay should clearly *not* be used under the following three sets of circumstances:

- The budget is too small or economic conditions are too tight to allow the granting of large increases to good performers.

- Employees value leisure, recognition, or some reward other than pay increases, or they prefer the allocation of rewards on the basis of equity, seniority, or some basis other than merit.

- Institutional arrangements are such that ratings of employee performance do not capture performance valued by the organization.

When faced with these circumstances, an organization needs to find alternatives to merit pay. One obvious approach is to use an across-the-board increase for all employees. As discussed in Chapter 1, this approach could be less offensive to employees than a merit pay plan under any of the circumstances listed above. It may be more effective to tell employees, "Pay increases will be the same for each employee because of the current economic crunch, your preferences for equality, and the limited capabilities we have to measure performance," than to simply tell employees, "You should be motivated by a merit increase," which employees know is less than inflation, is the same for each employee, and is based on a poorly defined standard of performance.

It should also be noted that alternatives other than across-the-board increases can be used as well. These alternatives include other incentive plans, promotions, and nonmonetary rewards. There is no reason to be stuck with a merit pay plan when it will not work.

Three issues need to be considered when deciding if merit pay is feasible. These three issues are shown in Figure 3.6.

First, organizations need to assess whether current conditions favor the use of a merit pay plan. The summary of major points in this chapter can be used as a checklist. If conditions do favor merit pay, then it can be used and, as described in Chapter 3, there are many potential benefits to the organization in using it.

Figure 3.6
Deciding Whether Merit Pay Should Be Used

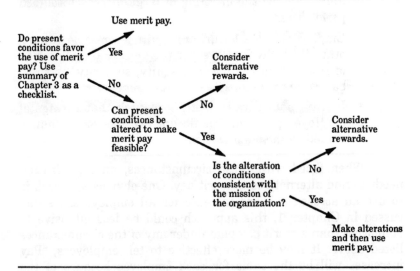

Second, if conditions faced by the organization do not favor merit pay, then the question is whether the current conditions can be altered or managed to create a more feasible environment for merit pay. Some of the conditions described in this chapter are more easily altered than are others. For example, an organization has greater influence over the way jobs are designed than they have over price inflation in the United States. If conditions are not favorable to merit pay and cannot be altered, merit pay should not be used.

Third, if conditions can be altered to make merit pay more favorable, the desirability of these alterations and their impact on other aspects of business needs to be considered *before* going ahead with them. The alterations should be consistent with the mission and strategic plan of the organization. If the conditions are alterable and the alterations do make "business sense," then the alterations can be made, and merit pay becomes a feasible pay plan.

4

Measuring Performance

It is essential that adequate performance measures be developed if pay increases are to be linked to performance under a merit pay plan. In this chapter, it is argued that the measurement of performance is a set of judgments rather than an end state, product, or form. This set of judgments is called validation and refers to the extent to which performance standards measure what they purport to measure. It will be shown that: (1) There are several different types of performance standards ranging from traits to behaviors to results to relative comparisons; (2) There are multiple indicators of the extent to which we can infer that these standards of performance possess validity; and (3) There are several steps that can be taken in developing and using performance standards to maximize our chances of meeting these indicators, which allow us to infer validity.

The Importance of Adequate Performance Measures

As pointed out by many observers of incentive pay plans, a critical component of the success of these plans, including merit pay, is the adequacy of performance measures (Lawler, 1971; Hamner, 1975; Winstanely, 1978; Pearce & Perry, 1983; Ball & R. Heneman, 1990). There seems to be much stronger support for this view than for other contentions regarding aspects of merit pay. This support can be found in theory, research, and practice.

Both psychological and economic theories, reviewed in Chapter 2, support the importance of adequate measures of performance. From a psychological perspective, an adequate measure of performance is needed so that employers can see that improved performance is instrumental in the attainment of a salary increase. An employee can only make the association between a desirable outcome, such as pay, and performance if performance is adequately measured. From an economic perspective, adequate measures of performance are needed for both the employer and employee to minimize costs. If performance is not adequately measured, an employer may end up overpaying employees whose performance was rated higher than it should have been and underpaying employees whose performance was rated lower than it should have been. In either case, unnecessary costs may be incurred by the employer and employee because of inadequate performance measures.

A pair of empirical studies also point to the importance of adequate performance measures. While the adequacy of performance measures appears to have only a moderate impact on actual merit pay decisions (Schwab & Olson, 1990; Huber, Neale, & Northcraft, 1987), adequacy of measures does have a larger impact on employee perceptions of the extent to which pay is tied to performance. As noted throughout the book, these perceptions are just as important as the actual link between pay and performance when it comes to employee motivation. Miceli and Near (1988) found that pay-for-performance perceptions and satisfaction with pay were stronger when allocators adhered to formal performance appraisal standards than when they did not adhere to such standards. Vest, Hills, and Scott (1989) found that low-performing employees in a transit agency were more likely to perceive a relationship between pay and performance when they believed that performance was accurately measured than when they believed that performance was not accurately measured. Although far from conclusive, the Miceli and Near (1987) and Vest et al. (1989) studies do provide support for the importance of adequate performance measures as they relate to pay-for-performance perceptions.

Finally, employer practices and experiences also demonstrate the importance of adequate performance measures. National surveys of employer practices (Cleveland, Murphy, & Williams, 1989; Bureau of National Affairs, 1983) show that the number one reason for using performance appraisals is for making compensation decisions, merit pay decisions in particular (Peck, 1984).

While deemed important in these surveys, performance measurement has also been reported as being problematic as well in another national survey. Downs and Moscinski (1979) reported that one of the most frequently mentioned weaknesses of large companies' current performance appraisal systems is the subjectivity of ratings. A large-scale case study of the federal government's experience with merit pay also points to the importance of adequate performance measures. Pearce and Perry (1983) attributed the lack of success with merit pay in the public sector to a number of causes, including a performance appraisal system that was not adequately pretested. This resulted in inaccurate measures of performance being used to make merit decisions. Both national surveys and individual case studies point to the importance of adequate measures of performance.

Types of Performance Measures

Pay increase decisions are made on the basis of performance ratings under a merit pay plan. Performance ratings are appraisals or evaluations of employees' individual contributions to an organization. To assess the contribution of the employee to the organization, the employee is compared to a standard. Both absolute standards and relative comparisons are used. They are considered in turn in this chapter.

Absolute Standards

Employee performance can be rated by comparing characteristics of the employee to definitional statements about the contribution or value of certain characteristics to the organization. Standards that are used in making these absolute comparisons include traits, behaviors, and results.

Surveys are conducted periodically to assess the extent to which each of these sets of standards is actually used by organizations (Bernardin & Klatt, 1985; Bureau of National Affairs, 1983; Bretz & Milkovich, 1989; Downs & Moscinski, 1979; Peck, 1984; Sibson & Company, 1989). The results of these surveys indicate that results are the most frequently used performance standards, followed by traits and then behaviors. In recent times, however, there seems to be a move toward a greater use of behaviors than traits (Sibson & Company, 1989) and a greater use of behaviors and results as a combined standard (Bernardin & Klatt, 1985). Each of these three sets of standards—traits, behaviors, and results—will be described in turn, along with a discussion of their advantages and disadvantages for the purposes of merit pay.

Traits.   Employee traits refer to personality characteristics of the employee. An example of a trait-rating scale on which employees are compared is shown in Table 4.1.

As can be seen in this table, traits have an obvious appeal. Although the traits listed in the table were for the job of production supervisor, they would seem to be applicable to virtually all jobs. One advantage of using traits as a standard is that they appear to be applicable to a wide range of jobs. A second advantage to traits is that they can be generated fairly quickly. It takes very little prompting to get organizational members to develop lists of desired personality characteristics. Perhaps this is because we think about performance using trait-like categories (Feldman, 1981).

Although traits are frequently used as a standard, they are very troublesome in measuring performance for merit pay.

Table 4.1
Sample Items from a Trait-Rating Scale
for Production Supervisors

	Strongly Disagree	Disagree	Neutral	Agree	Strongly Agree
Is active and energetic	1	2	3	4	5
Seldom sticks to business	1	2	3	4	5
Is self-controlled	1	2	3	4	5
Has common sense	1	2	3	4	5
Is proud of work	1	2	3	4	5

Source: R. Heneman (1984a).

One disadvantage of traits is that they are vague and subject to varying interpretations by different raters (Borman & Dunnette, 1975). To illustrate this, ask a group of people, one at a time, to give their definition of traits like "aggressive," "dominant," or "self-starter." Then see how many different definitions of the same trait people come up with. Because of the likelihood of differing interpretations, merit pay decisions that rely too heavily on the evaluation of traits may be very inconsistent.

An implication of goal-setting theory (see Chapter 2 for a review) is that performance must be clearly specified for merit pay to help maintain or improve current performance. A disadvantage of traits is that they cannot be specified clearly enough. It is very difficult, if not impossible, to improve employee performance when it is related to a personality characteristic that is difficult to define and probably unalterable.

Behaviors. Employee behavior refers to the manner in which employees carry out their activities or duties. An example of a frequency-of-behavior scale, similar to behavioral observation scales (Latham & Wexley, 1981), is shown in Table 4.2. With a frequency-of-behavior scale, employees' behavior is compared to desired behaviors. The more frequently employees exhibit these desired behaviors, the better their performance.

Measuring behavior offers two advantages over measuring traits. First, behavior appears to be less vague, more clearly defined. You would expect to get more consistent merit pay decisions when using behavior as a standard. Also, you would expect improved motivation by using a more specific definition of expected performance. For example, you often hear about the need to be "professional" at work. While we all probably agree this is a desirable trait, what does it mean? What is required? Clearly, the trait "professional" needs to be spelled out in behavioral terms for employees to understand what is expected of them. An example for the position of salesperson is as follows: Be courteous to customers; Submit sales reports in a timely and accurate manner; Keep shelves stocked with goods; and so forth. These behavioral standards give employees concrete performance objectives to work toward.

The second advantage that measuring behavior offers is that behavior is under the control of individual employees. Employees can more directly influence their behaviors than

Table 4.2
Sample Items from a Frequency-of-Behavior Scale for Receptionists

Desired Behaviors	Almost Never	Seldom	Some-times	Fre-quently	Almost Always
	0	1	2	3	4
1. Answers the phone by the second ring.	0	1	2	3	4
2. Takes correct names and numbers on messages.	0	1	2	3	4
3. Does not keep a person on hold any longer than two minutes without getting back and explaining why.	0	1	2	3	4
4. Answers the phone in a pleasant manner and is always willing to help people.	0	1	2	3	4
5. Offers guests coffee.	0	1	2	3	4
6. Offers to take the guest's coat.	0	1	2	3	4
7. Sorts mail no longer than 30 minutes after it arrives.	0	1	2	3	4
8. Distributes mail to the correct personnel.	0	1	2	3	4

Source: Reprinted with permission from the National Church Residences, Columbus, Ohio.

their traits or their results (described in the next section). Traits are a combination of innate characteristics and early learning. Results may be influenced by factors outside the employee, such as coworkers and budget constraints. Hence, it is more possible for the employee to alter behavior than traits or results to work toward the desired merit increase.

The use of behaviors as measurement criteria, however, comes with a cost. Creating behavioral measures of performance is a more cumbersome, difficult, and time-consuming process than creating trait measures. However, these costs are probably offset by avoiding the potential legal liability associated with performance measures that rely solely upon traits (see Chapter 6).

Results. Results-oriented measures of employee performance evaluate employee contributions in terms of actual products or services provided by an employee. A common approach here is to use Management by Objectives (MBO). An example of items from an MBO plan for lawyers in a large law firm is shown in Table 4.3.

As shown in this example, the major advantage of results-oriented measures is that they are highly specific and well defined. As a result, when these standards are set at challenging levels and accepted by employees, they have desirable motivational

Table 4.3
Sample Items from an MBO Plan for Attorneys

Statistic	Desired Results	Actual Results	Improvement Plans
(1) Fee credits billed	$220,000.00		
(2) Cash receipts	$220,000.00		
(3) Realization (2÷1)	100%		
(4) Billable hours	1700 hrs.		
(5) Nonbillable hours	400 hrs.		
(6) Total hours	2100 hrs.		

Source: Adapted with permission from the law firm of Porter, Wright, Morris, & Arthur, Columbus, Ohio.

properties, as discussed under goal-setting theory in Chapter 2. In addition to their motivational potential, another advantage of results-oriented measures is that results can be directly coupled with merit increases of a specific size.

There are also, however, some distinct disadvantages to results-oriented measures of performance like MBO. Results may be outside the control of individual employees. For example, billable hours for associates in a large law firm may be determined as much by the assignments they receive from partners as by their own efforts. Results may also fail to capture important aspects of employee performance. Using the same example, while billable hours might be an indicator of the *quantity* of service provided, those hours may indicate very little about the *quality* of service.

Relative Comparisons

Another standard is comparing employees to other employees. This is known as the process of relative rather than absolute comparisons, which we just reviewed. The simplest method of relative comparisons is known as ranking: Employees in a work group are rank ordered from the employee contributing the most to the organization down to the employee contributing the least. Another way to make relative comparisons is to use the method of paired comparisons. An example of paired comparisons is shown in Table 4.4.

With this procedure, each employee is compared to every other employee. If the employee is a better performer than another employee, then the better employee earns a checkmark.

Table 4.4
Paired Comparisons Method of Rating

	(1)	(2)	(3)	(4)	(5)	Total
(1) Goldie G.		X	X	X	X	4
(2) Mark Y.			X	X	X	3
(3) Denise W.				X	X	2
(4) Dave B.					X	1
(5) Phil Y.						0

A relative order is established based on the number of check-marks a particular employee receives. The more checkmarks, the higher the rank.

Results of one national survey by the Bureau of National Affairs (1983) showed that relative comparisons are not used nearly as frequently as absolute comparisons for performance appraisal. However, relative comparisons may actually be used more frequently than indicated in this survey. You would expect ranking to be a very common practice in small organizations (e.g., corner grocery store), where resources are not available to develop absolute standards. Had these types of organizations been included in the survey, the results may have shown relative comparisons used as frequently as absolute comparisons.

An obvious advantage of relative comparisons is that, like traits, they can be quickly and easily constructed for at least a small number of jobs. Also, the rating task may be easier with relative comparisons because the rater is only expected to indicate who is better not how much is one person better than another.

However, simplicity may also bring problems as well. A disadvantage of relative comparisons is that rank orderings made by different raters may not be comparable. For example, the difference in the performance levels of the first and second ranked employees by rater A may be different than the difference in performance levels of the first and second ranked employees for rater B. This is problematic when a common performance metric is needed to allocate merit increases across work groups.

A second disadvantage is that it is difficult to establish a relationship between pay and performance for purposes of employee motivation. Relative comparisons do not make it clear *why* one person is rated above another. Hence, it is difficult for employees to know what aspects of their performance they need to improve. A third disadvantage arises when there are severe, overall performance problems in an organization. In such cases, relative ranking may actually conceal poorly performing individuals. The employer may be ranking employees along the lines of "the best of the worst," which may overlook the fact that the performance of the entire work group is unacceptable. A relative ranking, in and of itself, tells us little about the contribution of a particular employee to the organization.

Choosing a Performance Standard

Choosing which measure(s) of performance to use in evaluating employees for purposes of merit pay is difficult. In making this choice, several factors must be considered. One obvious factor is the strengths and weaknesses of each standard just described. Depending on circumstances (e.g., limited resources), some arguments may be more compelling than others (Keely, 1975).

A second factor to consider is whether standards can be substituted for one another. Sometimes you hear the argument that standards, whether traits, behaviors, results or rankings, all basically measure the same thing. Hence, in choosing a standard for merit pay decisions, one need only look for the most convenient standard or one that is easiest to come by in an organization. However, a recent study casts serious doubt on this assertion. R. Heneman (1986) found that, across 23 studies of performance, there was only a low to moderate correlation between behaviors and results. While you would logically expect standards to be related to one another, in fact, the magnitude of the relationship does not appear to be strong enough to substitute them for one another.

A third factor to consider is that, given measures are not interchangeable, a "mix" of standards may be better than just one. It is unlikely that any organization values only one type of employee contribution to the organization. So it does not make sense to think about one "best" standard for performance measurement. Instead, multiple types of performance standards probably should be used with the "mix" dependent on the strategic mission of the firm.

A good example of this mix can be seen at General Electric and Westinghouse (Stonich, 1984). In mature business units within these companies, where the emphasis is on maintaining the current position in the industry, results-oriented performance measures such as profit, cash flow, and market share are used. On the other hand, in high-growth business units within these companies, behavior-oriented measures of performance are needed to measure the effectiveness of long-term goals such as effective research and development and the creation of new marketing opportunities.

In conclusion, while it does not appear that there is one best measure of performance to use for merit pay decisions, a "multiple" measurement strategy probably produces the best results. And, as discussed, there are a number of factors that can be considered in deciding which measure(s) to use. Moreover, as discussed later in this chapter, there are also indicators that can be used to assess the adequacy of the performance standards that have been selected. A preferred strategy for selecting performance standards might therefore be one of reasoned selection followed by an empirical evaluation of the standards selected.

Controversial Measures of Performance for Merit Pay

Along with the general issues just reviewed, some very specific issues need to be addressed as well. These issues center around the question of what actually constitutes performance under a merit pay plan. Heated conversations in the halls of many organizations point to the controversy surrounding how organizations define individual contributions. Unfortunately, little research has been conducted to guide decision makers. Nevertheless, these issues need to be considered and dealt with if a merit pay plan is to be effective.

Campbell (1990) clearly articulates the need for a model defining employee performance that is relevant to organizational effectiveness. In this section, we look at these controversial issues in performance measurement for purposes of merit pay.

Promotions

It is no surprise that people in organizations usually receive a pay increase in conjunction with an upward promotion. What is less clear, however, is *why* people receive a pay increase for a promotion. Is the pay increase due to the acquisition of new skills, an increase in job responsibilities, good performance in the previous position, or some combination of these factors? If a pay increase for a promotion is granted at the same time as a merit increase, the employee will not be able to figure out which of these factors are being reinforced, and which are most likely to contribute to subsequent raises.

In one study of a large manufacturer, performance, promotions, and salary increases were shown to be related to one another (Medoff & Abraham, 1981). This suggests that performance may be used to make both promotional and merit pay decisions. Certainly, it may be desirable to reward employees for both promotions and merit. It may not be seen that way to employees, however, if only *one* merit pay increase is given to reward *both* promotion and merit. If only one rather than two pay increases are granted, then promotions may be a controversial measure of performance because a promotional increase is viewed by employees as a substitute for rather than an addition to merit pay.

Seniority

Organizations seem to differ in how they treat seniority, or length of service with an organization, in merit pay decisions. In some studies there is no observed relationship between merit pay and seniority, in other studies there is a positive relationship, and in others a negative relationship (R. Heneman, 1990). Regardless of whether or how seniority is used in merit pay, it invites controversy.

If seniority *is* used, at least in part, to determine merit increases, it is controversial. The use of seniority runs contrary to the evidence presented by some empirical research on the relationship between traditional measures of performance and seniority. In a study of two large manufacturing organizations, Medoff and Abraham (1980) found little evidence of a positive or negative relationship between performance and seniority. In reviewing a number of studies that focused on the relationship between seniority and performance, Gordon and Johnson (1982) again found no evidence to support a positive or negative relationship. In short, the data do not support old arguments that senior employees are either *more* or *less* productive.

If merit pay *is* given on seniority, the organization may fail to contain compensation costs. More senior employees tend to be at higher levels in the pay grade. If they *all* get higher increases, overall merit increases may exceed the maximum level permissible under company policy for that pay range (discussed in Chapter 5).

On the other hand, it may not be prudent to totally *avoid* using seniority in merit pay decisions. As pointed out by Mitchell (1989), implicit contract theory (covered in Chapter 2) suggests one reason why employers may want to consider seniority.

Employers providing smaller pay increases to less senior employees could motivate these employees to remain with the firm by holding out the "carrot" of more substantial pay increases later.

Merit increases can be considered "prizes," and relative comparisons help employees gauge how successful they need to be to secure a valued merit increase. Tournament models of competitive pay situations (Lazear & Rosen, 1981) suggest that relative comparisons are considered by employees in determining the level of effort to expend at work. Employees assess the performance of others in order to determine their chances of capturing a tournament prize.

Recent research by Schmidt, Hunter, Outerbridege, and Goff (1988) may help to end the equivocation as to whether seniority should or should not be used. Using a large military data set and a sensitive measure of seniority based on months rather than years, they found that several different measures of job performance are indeed positively related to seniority for the first 12 months or so on the job. From that point on, up to the five-year mark, there is little change in performance due to seniority. These data suggest that seniority be considered for relatively new employees as a measure of performance. This concept is also consistent with the common practice of paying new employees according to seniority, until they reach the average salary in the market. From then on, they are paid according to traditional performance ratings, without regard to seniority.

Market Worth

Sometimes merit increases do not simply reflect an individual's contribution to the organization, but indicate the individual's worth on the outside market as well. Examples of this practice come from both research and the field. Landau and Leventhal (1976) found in a laboratory study that larger merit increases were granted to employees with more attractive job offers in the external labor market. In 1981, both Ford Motor Company and General Motors Corporation gave merit pay raises to salaried employees to try to retain the services of good performers who were leaving for better paying jobs in other industries (*Monthly Labor Review,* 104, 1981).

For some jobs there is a certain logic to basing pay increases on the employee's worth in the external market, because it is difficult to separate an individual's contribution inside the organization from his or her contribution outside the organization. An example here might be scientists or professors whose research has generally equal value across the labor market. Along these lines, Hansen (1989) distinguishes between internally determined and externally determined merit for professors. The stature of a university is enhanced by having professors provide good service to the university (typically in the form of teaching and service) and by having professor's contributions (typically research) valued by other institutions as well. Internal merit pay could be provided in the former case while external merit pay could be provided in the latter case. This strategy could be accomplished by soliciting information on a professor's performance from sources, both internal and external. This is a common practice in promotion and tenure decisions at universities and could be extended to merit increase decisions as well in other organizational environments.

However, basing merit increases on the market, or market adjustments as they are sometimes called, also has its problems. One problem is that market value may be determined by forces outside the control of employees. For example, a professor of engineering may have great market value today because of the shortfall in the engineering labor supply rather than because of his or her performance. In fact, there are few people being graduated with Ph.D.s in engineering. Given the scarcity of engineers with doctorates, their worth on the market is high. Some may argue that market adjustments are unfair because they do not reflect actual performance but forces that cannot be controlled in the outside labor market.

One practice that lies between the extremes of including or not including market adjustments as a part of merit pay plans is to provide market adjustments only to good performers. Both Ford and General Motors did this when merit increases were granted in 1981. They wanted to retain the services of the good performers not necessarily the poor performers. Hence, they only granted merit increases to good performers. But, it may have been that because the poor performers were not marketable, they stayed anyway. So, the automakers may have ended up retaining both the poor and good performers. This was obviously a better situation, though, than being stuck with just poor performers.

Organizational Citizenship Behavior

Organ (1988) has argued that an important contribution some employees make to organizations is organizational citizenship behavior. This type of behavior includes activities above and beyond those normally required by the organization. Examples include altruism (e.g., covering for a sick coworker), conscientiousness (e.g., keeping a clean work station), and courtesy (e.g., providing people with information in advance).

A debatable question is whether organizational citizenship behavior should be rewarded in merit pay systems. Although not calling these contributions organizational citizenship behavior, Patten (1977) argued that these behaviors should be rewarded with merit pay as they contribute greatly to the success of organizations. On the other hand, it might be argued that since these behaviors are not, by definition, required by the organization, it would be unfair to monetarily reward those who voluntarily engage in these activities.

Typical Versus Maximum Performance

Performance levels of employees are usually not constant over time (e.g., Rothe, 1946). Instead, performance varies over time. One way to think of this variance in performance is in terms of typical and maximum performance (Sackett, Zedeck, & Fogli, 1988). Typical performance takes place when individuals are not being evaluated, not attempting to work as hard as they can, for extended periods of time. Maximum performance takes place when individuals are being evaluated, working as hard as they can, for short periods of time. The research on this distinction indicates that supervisors attend more to maximum than typical performance (DiNisi, Cafferty, & Meglino, 1984) and that supervisory ratings are more closely related to maximum than typical performance (Sackett et al., 1988).

This line of research raises the policy issue of which level(s) of performance *should* be rewarded with merit pay? It would appear, based on this research, that *maximum* performance is being rewarded more than typical performance. In some jobs, this may be appropriate. For example, a sponsor of a professional bowler may be most concerned with maximum performance during a nationally televised event. In other jobs, typical performance may be of greater importance. An example here might be a nurse in a long-term health care facility, where the issues are more about patient care over extended periods of time, without much direct supervision.

The point is that maximum performance receives more rating attention than average, consistent, and regular performance. This imbalance is also most likely reflected in merit pay decisions, as pay increases are based on ratings. This practice may or may not coincide with the intended policy of merit pay in a particular organization. Therefore, the issue needs to be carefully considered. If the intent of merit pay is to reward typical performance, performance reviews should be conducted more than once a year so that a representative sample of total performance can be obtained for merit decisions. Other administrative practices such as diary keeping, described later in this chapter, should also be followed to ensure that typical performance is being evaluated.

Job Level

R. Heneman (1990) reported, in a review of the literature on merit pay, that typically the relationship between job level and size of merit pay increase is a positive one. For example, Gerhart and Milkovich (1987) found that larger merit increases were granted to employees in higher rather than lower level positions for a large manufacturing company. Certainly, this relationship is reasonable if job level is related to merit increase dollars. You would also expect larger absolute increases in merit pay for high-level jobs because the base salary is larger in these high-level jobs. Even if a high- and low-level job receive the same percentage merit increase, the total amount for each differs because the absolute amount is a percentage of base salary.

The relationship between job level and the amount of merit increase is shown in Table 4.5. While both the production manager and production associate receive a six percent merit increase, the absolute amount of the increase is larger for the manager ($2,100) than for the associate ($1,200), because of the higher base pay level of the manager's job ($35,000) versus the associate's job ($20,000). In other words, the same percentage increase applied to two job levels will always result in a larger absolute increase for the job with the higher pay level.

The relationship between job level and merit may be troublesome when merit pay decisions are made in the form of a

Table 4.5

Comparison of Percentage and Absolute Merit Increases by Job Level

Title	Job Level	Per- formance	Current Salary	Increase	Merit Pay Amount of Increase	New Salary
Production Manager	6	5	35,000	6%	2100	37,100
Production Associate	3	5	20,000	6%	1200	21,200

percentage increase rather than in the form of absolute merit dollars. This would be depicted in Table 4.5 if the percentage increase was, say, eight percent rather than the six percent shown for the production manager. A relationship between job level and percentage increase suggests that job level is being used as a measure of performance, with higher level jobs receiving larger percentage merit increases.

Whether this practice is desirable depends on other human resource practices. A positive relationship between job level and merit may be desirable if the better performers are promoted. Since most promotion systems are less than perfect, however, this assumption is a controversial one. A positive relationship may not be desirable if people already receive adequate pay for the level of job they hold. The level of job is sometimes used to determine the base wage or salary, using a procedure known as job evaluation, which is described in Chapter 5. A positive relationship between job level and merit pay may not be desirable in this situation because people would be paid for job level twice—once for merit pay and once based on job evaluation.

Immediate Versus Distant Past Performance

A question that arises in the administration of a merit pay plan is how far back in time should the employer go to reward performance? Based on the limited empirical research, it seems that allocators should look at performance over multiple merit pay periods. Birnbaum (1983) reported that, for samples of professors and students, allocators tended to look at the amount recipients were underpaid in the past in determining current merit increases. This may have been done by allocators to restore perceptions of equity for the recipient. (See Chapter 2 for a review of equity theory.)

By considering performance prior to the current merit pay period, the allocator can resolve previous inequities in merit increase decisions. But, when distant rather than immediate performance is considered, it may just as likely create equity problems as solve them. In effect, performance may be double counted. An employee may receive an increase for the same episode of good performance in two pay periods. An inequity may be created if other employees only receive one merit increase for the same level of performance.

One way this situation could be handled would be to offer "equity" adjustments on a very limited basis, under a policy that takes into account exceptional circumstances. Exceptional circumstances could include, for example, a monumental feat performed by an employee two merit pay periods ago that was inadequately compensated at the time because of a limited merit pay budget. Such an approach, however, could invite bargaining behaviors by the allocators and recipients. Hence, an equity adjustment should only be made under exceptional circumstances that have been documented and approved.

Policy Guidelines for Controversial Performance Measures

As shown in the preceding section on controversial measures of performance, it is not always clear which measures of performance are appropriate for merit pay decisions. Additional research is needed to guide decision makers as to which criteria to use. Given the controversial nature of some criteria, it appears that not only is further discussion of the issues critical, but it is incumbent on policy makers to communicate the resulting decisions. If an organization has not clearly communicated its position on these controversial issues, the organization may encounter unanticipated outcomes with a merit system. As shown by reinforcement theory (reviewed in Chapter 2), organizations are likely to encounter different outcomes depending on which measures of performance lead to rewards. Also, feelings of inequity (discussed in Chapter 2) may result if employees consider these controversial measures as inputs while the organization does not.

Adequacy of Performance Measures

Fortunately for decision makers in organizations, the process of performance measurement is not without criteria to evaluate the adequacy of the measures that are developed. While judgments are, of course, required in deciding which measures to use, these judgments can be guided by a number of indicators of adequacy, discussed in this section. These indicators concern the validity or extent to which performance standards measure what they purport to measure. Indicators of or approaches to assessing validity at various levels of performance measurement are shown in Figure 4.1.

Figure 4.1 is a guide for the discussion of the adequacy of performance measures. Each indicator provides an important and unique piece of information for deciding which performance standards to use. In line with current thinking on criterion and validity issues (Binning & Barrett, 1989; Landy, 1986; James, 1973), it is argued here that multiple indicators need to be used to make inferences about the validity or adequacy of performance measures.

Content Validity

One indicator of the adequacy of performance measures is known as content validity. As shown in Figure 4.1, content validity refers to the job relatedness of performance standards, or the extent to which performance standards are related to the actual job. A numerical estimate of content validity can be generated using formulas by Aiken (1980) and Lawshe (1975), which rely on judgments of the job relatedness of performance standards by subject-matter experts. An excellent example of both Aiken's and Lawshe's procedures is found in Distefano, Pryer, and Erffmeyer (1983). These authors developed a behavioral rating scale for psychiatric aides in psychiatric hospitals. Job experts generated behavior-based performance standards.

Figure 4.1
*Indicators of Validity at Various Levels
of Performance Measurement*

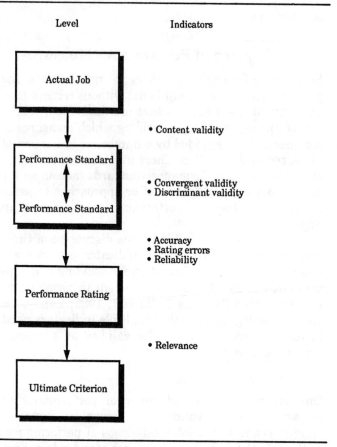

Level   Indicators

Actual Job

• Content validity

Performance Standard

• Convergent validity
• Discriminant validity

Performance Standard

• Accuracy
• Rating errors
• Reliability

Performance Rating

• Relevance

Ultimate Criterion

In turn, another group of job experts rated aides using these standards. These ratings were then used to calculate the degree to which these standards were job-related using the Lawshe (1975) and Aiken (1980) formulas.

To illustrate the importance of content validity, you need only envision a situation where performance standards are not job related. Under such a system, employees are likely to feel that their duties on the job are inconsequential, and perform accordingly. Merit pay may, in turn, reinforce non-job related behaviors, such as political behaviors intended only to garnish a larger pay raise.

Convergent and Discriminant Validity

Another two indicators, convergent and discriminant validity, have to do with the relationship among performance standards as shown in Figure 4.1. These indicators are used to show the degree to which performance standards are measuring the same construct. A construct is a summary label attached to a category of employee performance. Convergent validity refers to the degree to which performance standards, judged to be similar to one another, are indeed correlated with one another. A correlation shows the strength of the relationship between performance standards. If performance standards are measuring the same construct, they should be highly correlated with one another. Discriminant validity refers to the degree to which performance standards, judged to be dissimilar to one another, are indeed not correlated with one another. If performance standards are measuring the same construct, then they should not correlate with dissimilar standards. In short, similar measures of performance should be more strongly correlated to one another than dissimilar measures of performance.

One empirical procedure to test for convergent and discriminant validity is the multitrait-multimethod matrix developed by Campbell and Fiske (1959). Refinements to the original procedure can be found in Schmitt and Stults (1986). An excellent example of the statistics involved with this procedure as it relates to performance standards is found in Kavanaugh, Mackinney, and Wolins (1971).

A descriptive rather than statistical example may make the concepts of convergent and discriminant validity more clear. For example, service supervisors in a state government are responsible for managing vocational rehabilitation counselors and their own caseload of clients (Moore & R. Heneman, 1983). Two standards by which supervisors are held accountable for the management aspects of their job are performance planning and performance problem solving. If these two standards, and others like them, do indeed measure management, they should be correlated with one another. If they are correlated, then this is evidence for the convergent validity of the management aspect of the work. It would also be expected that these two standards would not be as strongly related to how well the service supervisors provide services to their own individual clients. After all, the handling of clients involves a different set of activities than the management of subordinates. The extent to which performance planning and performance problem solving are more strongly correlated with one another than they are with how well the supervisors provide services to their clients is evidence for the discriminant validity of the management aspect of work.

The importance of establishing the convergent and discriminant validity of ratings is also highlighted by Kavanaugh et al. (1971). Convergent and discriminate validity enables organizations to be efficient in the development of performance standards. In terms of time and money, it is more efficient for an organization to use fewer than more standards to measure performance. That is, of course, assuming the same performance constructs can be measured using fewer standards. Tests for convergent and discriminant validity help assess to what degree this assumption is a reasonable one.

Reliability

At a general level, reliability refers to the consistency of ratings. As shown in Figure 4.1, ratings are the actual values assigned to performance standards by evaluators reviewing employee performance. Consistency can be thought of in terms of time, raters, and performance standards. Depending on which perspective you take regarding consistency, that perspective will define the form of reliability that should be calculated.

There are three forms of reliability. *Test-retest reliability* looks at the stability of ratings over time. To examine stability, ratings in one time period are correlated with ratings in another time period, given by the same set of raters. *Interrater reliability* refers to the consistency of ratings across different raters. It is assessed by calculating the correlation between ratings of different raters who are evaluating the same employee and using the same performance standards. *Internal consistency reliability* is a measure of the degree to which measures of the same performance standard are correlated with one another. The formulas needed to calculate these forms of reliability can be found in any test construction text (e.g., Ghiselli, Campbell, & Zedeck, 1981).

The importance of reliability to the merit pay process can be examined in at least two ways. First, the reliability of the performance measure used for merit pay is the upper boundary or limit to the strength of the relationship between performance ratings and merit increases (Rothstein, 1990). Second, the less consistent you are in measuring performance, the less likelihood you have of linking pay increases to performance. If employees are unsure as to how you measured their performance, how can you expect them to see any relationship between their pay and performance? This question is the heart of the notion of reliability as an "upper bound." It should be noted, however, that the magnitude of the impact of reliability on the actual relationship between pay and performance may not be very substantial when the reliability of performance measures varies by a small amount (Schwab & Olson, 1990).

Even though the impact of reliability on the actual pay-for-performance relationship may not be that strong, there is a second and perhaps more compelling reason for ensuring reliability. If ratings are not reliable in a merit pay plan, or not perceived as reliable, it is unlikely that employees are going to accept the decisions being made. Employees are likely to reject a merit pay plan when merit increases depend more on the timing of ratings, the rater being used, or the standard being used, than upon the actual performance level of the employee. As shown by Folger and Konovsky (1989) and discussed in Chapter 6, procedures as well as outcomes are important to employee acceptance of a merit pay plan. Reliability is one important component of the procedures used in determining merit pay.

Accuracy

As shown in Figure 4.1, another indicator of the adequacy of performance measures is the accuracy with which ratings are made of performance. Accuracy refers to the relationship between *ratings* of employee performance and *actual,* correct, or "true" employee performance (R. Heneman, Wexley, & Moore, 1987). The stronger the relationship between ratings and true performance, the greater the accuracy. Because accuracy implies some true or correct measure of performance, there is considerable controversy as to how to best assess accuracy (Kruglanski, 1989; Padgett & Ilgen, 1989; Sulsky & Balzer, 1988). Currently, the most accepted method of assessing accuracy seems to be using ratings by "experts" who view the videotaped performance of a sample of employees in simulated or actual work settings. These ratings from experts become true scores and are then used to gauge the accuracy of other's ratings of the same videotaped performances.

Although problematic to assess, the concept of accuracy is certainly an important one when it comes to the adequacy of performance measures. If performance ratings are not accurate in a merit pay plan, pay increases may be allocated to the wrong employees (Ball & R. Heneman, 1990). That is, employees incorrectly rated as good performers may receive large pay increases, while employees incorrectly rated as poor performers may receive small increases. The accuracy of raters' decisions may need to be assessed from time to time using expert ratings to prevent incorrect decisions.

Rating Errors

Like reliability and accuracy, rating errors also have to do with ratings of performance standards as shown in Figure 4.1. In the discussion of reliability, consistency in ratings was portrayed as a desirable property of performance measures. This is true, however, only up to a point. If consistent ratings are granted in the face of true performance that is inconsistent, there may be a rating error. For example, a manager may rate an employee as excellent for three consecutive years. But actual employee performance may have been excellent for two of the three years and average for one year. In this case there was an error committed because while the ratings were consistent, actual employee performance was inconsistent. Major rating errors include halo, leniency, and central tendency. The absence of these rating errors is sometimes used to assess the adequacy of performance measures. Each of these rating errors will be described below.

Halo error takes place when a rater generalizes from one aspect of an employee's performance to other aspects of an employee's performance without regard for the true or actual level of employee performance. Examples could include rating professors good in teaching because they are good in research, or rating supervisors good in management duties because they are good in the technical duties of their job. Sometimes this pattern of ratings does not turn out to be an error (Nathan & Tippins, 1990). Some people do indeed perform at the same level in other aspects of their work. However, this pattern of rating can also be an error. People good at research are not necessarily good at teaching, and people good at technical work are not necessarily good at management.

Another rating error, known as *leniency error,* is a specific type of halo error. Positive leniency takes place when employees are rated high on one or more aspects of their performance, while negative leniency takes place when employees are rated low on one or more aspects of their performance. In both cases, these patterns of ratings are errors if they run contrary to the pattern of ratings of true performance. One possible reason for these errors is that they may allow raters to justify a large merit increase for themselves. If a rater commits positive leniency error, the rater can tell the boss what a good job he or she has done at managing his or her subordinates. If a rater commits negative leniency, the rater can use poor performing subordinates as an excuse for his or her poor performance.

Along with leniency, *central tendency* is another specific type of halo error. When central tendency error takes place, employees are rated average on one or more aspects of their performance. In a sense, this is a play-it-safe approach for raters. It is difficult to be accused of favoritism under this scenario. It is an error, however, if true employee performance is not average.

While it may be easy to see why these errors occur, the explanations do not minimize the problems that rating errors cause with merit pay. Examples of these problems abound in organizations. Accusations of favoritism and discrimination take place when leniency error is present. Good performers feel cheated when the supervisor commits central tendency error. Managers are upset with other managers who commit positive leniency error and, as a result, get a larger share of the merit budget than those who did not commit the error. These examples point to the importance of diagnosis and correction of rating errors.

To have a high degree of certainty that the rating patterns just described are rating errors rather than ratings of actual employee performance, it is essential to calculate these errors relative to true scores (Pulakos, Schmitt, & Ostroff, 1986). However, true scores are often difficult if not impossible to develop (R. Heneman, Wexley, & Moore, 1987). Consequently, inferences need to be made, in the absence of true scores, as to the degree of rating errors actually present. For example, you might infer that positive leniency is at work when the rater gives high ratings to all aspects of an employee's performance. This inference might be further strengthened if there is evidence that the rater not only rates all aspects of one employee's performance high, but also rates all aspects of *all* employees' performance high. While you may encounter a work group where all members perform well at all aspects of their jobs, a more likely scenario is that some people perform better than others and that each person performs some aspects of their job better than other aspects. When inferences such as these can be safely made, it is possible to calculate rating errors without true scores. Formulas to calculate rating errors without true scores can be found in Saal, Downey, and Lahey (1980).

An important function of the human resource department is to call such erroneous rating patterns to the attention of line managers. Performance appraisals should be collected and reviewed by the human resource department. If troublesome patterns are detected, documentation and/or an explanation may be solicited to show that the pattern of ratings is not an error. If rating errors are revealed, the problem can be referred to the raters' supervisors for corrective action.

Relevance

The concept of relevance, as shown in Figure 4.1, refers to the relationship between performance ratings and some measure of an ultimate criterion (Thorndike, 1949). The ultimate criterion is the final or ultimate goal of the organization in terms of individual job performance. It is a more distant and abstract standard than traits, behaviors, and results, which are more immediate and measurable. It may be, for example, the overall contribution of the organization to the product or service market that the organization competes in.

Relevance is usually less than perfect because of two factors known as deficiency and contamination (Brogden & Taylor, 1950). *Deficiency* refers to variance in the ultimate criterion that is not captured in the performance ratings. Ratings may not capture all of the ultimate criterion because raters may, for example, have limited opportunity to observe employee performance. As an illustration, supervisors often have a large number of employees reporting to them and, as a result, have limited opportunity to observe the performance of any one employee.

Contamination refers to variance in performance ratings that is unrelated to the ultimate criterion. Ratings may be contaminated, for example, when they capture aspects of the performance outside the control of the individual employee. In an outside sales position, the number of sales made may be more closely linked to the state of the economy than to the effort of the salesperson. As would be predicted from expectancy theory (reviewed in Chapter 2), pay is unlikely to motivate performance when performance is not under the control of the employee.

The relationship between the concepts of relevance, contamination, and deficiency are shown in Figure 4.2. As illustrated in this figure, the level of relevance for performance ratings depends on the amount of contamination and deficiency in ratings. There is a greater level of relevance possible when there is less deficiency and less contamination.

An additional example may help to clarify the concepts of contamination and deficiency. The National Football League (NFL) uses a passing rating system to evaluate the passing performance of quarterbacks in the NFL (Ordine, 1990). Passing

Figure 4.2
The Relevance of Performance Ratings

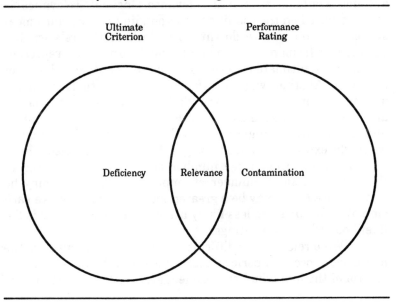

performance is assessed using four categories: completion percentage, touchdown percentage, interception percentage, and average gain per attempt. A rating for each category and an overall rating is determined by comparing a quarterback's performance to statistics of quarterback performance in the NFL and the old American Football League (AFL) from 1960 to 1971.

This rating system for quarterbacks is highly controversial and disliked by some quarterbacks because incentive bonuses are frequently based on these ratings (Ordine, 1990). Complaints about the system center around the concepts of contamination and deficiency. Some think that the ratings are unfair because the ratings are contaminated by the play of other players on the team. You would expect that the ratings would be higher for a quarterback with a high-performing offensive line than a quarterback with a low-performing offensive line. Others think that the ratings are unfair because they are a deficient measure of the total contribution of the quarterback to the performance of the team. Missing from the calculations are contributions other than passing, such as rushing yardage and play-calling ability.

Relevance is a difficult, if not impossible, concept to measure due to the abstract and distant nature of the ultimate criterion. Hence, unlike the other indicators reviewed, formulas are not available to assess relevance. Instead, relevance is inferred based on the conditions surrounding performance measurement. One way to do this is to look at the relationship between performance ratings and some intermediate representation of the ultimate criterion such as the strategic mission of the firm. Another way to infer relevance is to look for an absence of conditions that are likely to lead to contamination and deficiency in ratings. The less present are contamination and deficiency, the higher the level of relevance. For example, we might expect relevance to be greater when supervisors have a small rather than large number of employees reporting to them. With a small number of employees, deficiency may be less because there may be a greater opportunity to observe each employee. In turn, the less likely is deficiency, the greater is the likelihood of relevant ratings.

While relevance is difficult to assess, it is essential to the merit pay process. If performance is viewed as being outside the control of the individual or not adequately reflecting actual contribution to the organization, then, as discussed in Chapter 2, it is doubtful that employees will be able to make the desired link between pay and performance.

Selecting an Indicator to Evaluate Performance Standards

Multiple indicators are needed to evaluate the validity or the adequacy of performance standards. Each of the indicators provides a unique bit of information about the adequacy of performance measures. To put it another way, there is no one best way to assess the adequacy of performance measures. Also, the research evidence indicates that indicators are not substitutes for one another. For example, it has been shown across many studies that the magnitude of the relationship between halo error and rating accuracy is modest (Murphy & Balzer, 1989). Even if halo error is reduced, accuracy is not always improved. Even the relationship among alternative measures of the same indicator may be modest. Pulakos et al. (1986) found this to be the case for alternative measures of halo error, while Murphy, Garcia, Keskar, Martin, and Balzer (1982) found it also to be the case for alternative measures of rating accuracy. So, different ways to measure the same indicator of validity may lead to different results.

The Upper Boundary of Performance Rating Validity

To interpret the results of studies designed to assess the adequacy of performance standards, it is useful to know what the upper bound, or maximum possible level, of validity is for performance ratings. Several attempts have been made to estimate the upper bound of performance rating validity using some of the alternative indicators of validity just reviewed. Even though different methodologies were used, the results were very similar and suggest that the upper bound of validity for performance ratings is about .60, with a value of 0 representing no validity and a value of 1.00 representing perfect validity. What this value of .60 indicates is that about 36 percent of the variability in the indicators being used to assess validity is due to performance ratings. Although it is a judgment call, a value of .60 is a respectable level in human resource research. Also, this value of .60 is very comparable to the validity of more objective performance indicators such as output (R. Heneman, 1986). Although this value is respectable, it is the highest value that can be expected. It can be lower and, even at its highest value, it suggests that about 64 percent of the variability in standards being used to assess validity are due to factors other than performance ratings. What this means is that most measures of performance are less-than-perfect representations of the employee's ultimate performance contribution to the organization.

In one of the studies, interrater reliability, convergent validity, and rating errors were assessed in near-perfect laboratory conditions (Borman, 1978). These conditions consisted of raters who were very knowledgeable about the jobs rated, had ample opportunity to observe performance, and used a well-developed rating scale. In another study, there were near-perfect field conditions (Weekley & Gier, 1989) to assess reliability, convergent validity, and discriminant validity. These conditions were found in a world-class figure-skating event where the judges were very experienced, well trained, and had excellent observational opportunities. A large-scale investigation by Rothstein (1990) for 9,975 ratees in 79 organizations examined the interrater reliability of a well-developed rating scale. King, Hunter, and Schmidt (1980) conducted a review of several studies concerned with the reliability of single raters. As can be seen from these brief descriptions, a variety of different methodologies were used and, as previously noted, similar results were obtained. When a variety of different methods yield the same results, considerable confidence can be placed in the results (Jick, 1979).

Methods to Improve the Validity of Performance Standards

Although it may not be possible to develop performance standards with perfect validity for merit increase decisions, it is possible to take some steps that have been shown to be related to increases in the indicators of validity. These steps, which will now be reviewed, have to do with how the standards are used as well as how they are developed. The way in which standards are used is as, or more, important than the standards themselves (Landy & Farr, 1980).

The steps shown here should also make it clear that the performance appraisal process is not without costs. Efficiency wage theory (described in Chapter 2) suggests that there are administrative expenses when an organization attempts to monitor employee performance. These costs include the time and money needed to ensure that adequate performance measurement is taking place. In considering whether to use merit pay, an eye must be kept on anticipated costs as well as anticipated productivity returns.

Ties to the Strategic Mission

One way to improve upon the relevance of ratings is to link performance standards and ratings to the strategic mission of the organization. The mission of the organization refers to a philosophical statement by upper level decision makers concerning the strategic direction of the organization. Schneier (1989a) provides an excellent example from National Car Rental of how a mission statement can be translated into results and behavior-oriented measures of performance. This example is shown in Figure 4.3.

In many organizations, a formal document known as a mission statement states what the mission of the organization is. It can be used to ground performance standards in the business of the organization and can also be used to make raters aware of desired end results. Henderson (1980) provides step-by-step instructions on how to do this, and these instructions are summarized in Figure 4.4. Case study examples of where procedures such as these have been followed can be found in Schneier's (1989a,b) description of Pratt and Whitney, and Hurwich's (1986) description of Towers, Perrin, Forster, and Crosby.

Job Analysis

A review of both textbooks and court cases in performance appraisal indicates that it is essential for performance standards to be based on job analysis for validity to be improved (Bernardin & Klatt, 1985). Unfortunately, this prescription appears to be followed by only 37 percent of the organizations in a survey of American Society for Personnel Administration members by Bernardin and Klatt (1985).

Job analysis refers to procedures used to come up with a systematic description of the duties and requirements of a job. One method of job analysis that job analysts believe to be very effective in establishing performance standards (Levine, Ash, Hall, & Sistrunk, 1983) is the critical-incident technique (Flanagan, 1954). With this approach, job experts are asked to generate lists of highly effective and ineffective behaviors observed in the past. In turn, these behaviors, or incidents, are used to develop behavior-based measures of performance, such as the frequency-of-behavior scale shown in this chapter, behavioral observation scales (Latham & Wexley, 1981), and behaviorally anchored rating scales (Smith & Kendall, 1963). Hence, performance standards based on the critical-incident technique are very job related and may be more likely to lead to more accurate (Osburn, Timmreck, & Bigby, 1981) and reliable (Borman & Dunnette, 1975) ratings than are non-job-related performance standards.

Multiple Raters

A common prescription in performance appraisal is to use multiple raters, and this prescription appears to be used by organizations to a moderate degree (Bernardin & Klatt, 1985). Typically, the immediate supervisor is the only rater. Others can, however, be used to generate ratings including peers, incumbents, subordinates, customers, and clients.

The reason that multiple raters are recommended is that multiple rating may yield a more complete picture of actual employee performance. Each rater should have a unique perspective on the performance of the rated employee. By using multiple raters, any deficiency in ratings by one rater may be compensated for by the perspective of another rater. Overall, multiple raters should lead to more relevant ratings.

Figure 4.3 (opposite)
Strategic Performance Management: Linking Strategy to Performance Management and Recognition/Rewards (PMRR) Systems

Source: Schneier (1989a). Reprinted with permission.

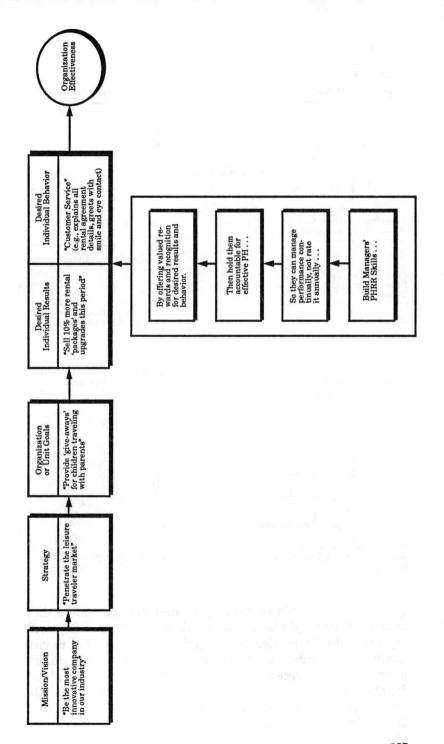

Mission/Vision	Strategy	Organization or Unit Goals	Desired Individual Results	Desired Individual Behavior
"Be the most innovative company in our industry"	"Penetrate the leisure traveler market"	"Provide 'give-aways' for children traveling with parents"	"Sell 10% more rental 'packages' and upgrades this period"	"Customer Service" (e.g., explains all rental agreement details, greets with smile and eye contact)

Organization Effectiveness

By offering valued rewards and recognition for desired results and behavior.

Then hold them accountable for effective PH...

So they can manage performance continually, not rate it annually...

Build Managers' PHRR Skills...

Figure 4.4
Tying Organizational Mission to Work Force Productivity

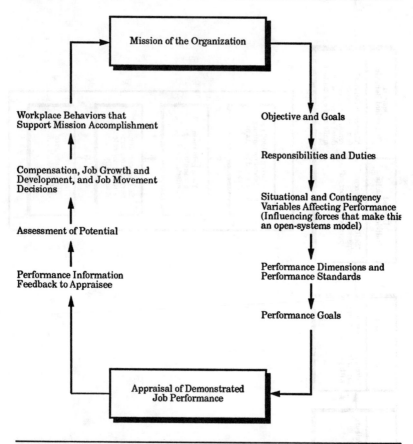

Source: Richard Henderson, *Performance Appraisal: Theory to Practice,* ©
1980, p. 26. Reprinted by permission of Prentice Hall, Englewood Cliffs, NJ.

While multiple raters may be desirable to remove deficiencies, they may also create problems when used for merit
pay purposes. In particular, multiple raters may lead to contamination in ratings. For example, incumbents may inflate
their ratings to receive a larger merit increase. Peers may
deflate their ratings of incumbent performance to prevent the
incumbent from getting a larger increase than they would.
These distortions would seem to be more likely in a competitive

reward situation (e.g., fixed merit budget) in which one person's gain is another person's loss.

Given the potential problems with multiple raters and merit pay, multiple raters should *not* be used for merit pay purposes. However, these same parties that are sometimes used to produce multiple ratings might be used as sources of information if the process is managed carefully. The immediate supervisor could use performance incidents that come to his or her attention from other parties. To use these pieces of information, the following conditions are necessary. First, performance-related observations rather than judgments by other parties should be used. The supervisor, rather than other parties, should make the overall judgment of performance and corresponding merit. Second, information collected by the supervisor from other parties should be kept confidential. Third, information should be used only from those parties who are knowledgeable about the incumbent's job and have the opportunity to observe the incumbent perform the job.

In short, multiple raters do not appear to be appropriate for merit pay decisions. On the other hand, it would be naive to think that merit allocators do not draw upon the opinions of others. A compromise position would be to use other parties as sources of observation rather than judgments. This recommendation is a very tentative one, however, as there is no empirical research regarding multiple raters and merit pay.

Participation in Scale Development

The importance of getting those parties who are affected by performance ratings involved in the development of performance standards has been shown in three studies. Friedman and Cornelius (1976) found that when raters participated in the development of performance standards, the resulting ratings had less halo error and more convergent validity than did the ratings of raters who did not participate in scale development. Silverman and Wexley (1984) reported that ratees involved in the development of performance standards were more satisfied with the appraisal and more willing to improve than were ratees not involved in the development of performance standards. Balkin and Gomez-Mejia (1990) found that participation in scale development by ratees was correlated with perceptions of the overall effectiveness of the pay system.

Taken together, these studies indicate that both raters and ratees should participate in the development of performance standards for merit pay. A recent national survey by Bretz and Milkovich (1989) suggests that while this is being done for upper level jobs, in lower level jobs employees are infrequently used in developing performance standards. Based on the research, however, it would seem that organizations should consider inviting greater employee participation in scale development for lower level jobs as well as upper level jobs.

It should be noted that participation is not for everyone. Those involved must have the skills and motivation to develop meaningful performance standards (Lawler, 1981). The organization may need to train both managers and subordinates on how to develop performance standards. Also, turnover has to be low for participation to make sense. If employees are frequently leaving the organization, the participation process may need to be repeated with new employees. This would be a costly procedure for organizations to follow on a repeated basis.

The steps that can be taken in a participative approach to scale development are illustrated in Figure 4.5 and contrasted with a nonparticipative approach. In very large organizations, it may not be feasible to have all employees involved in the development of performance standards. However, participation may still be possible by using task forces composed of representatives of both raters and ratees. Examples of the use of task forces in developing performance standards at Pratt and Whitney, Blue Cross, and Quanex Corporation can be found in Schneier (1989b), Cowan (1978), and Goodale and Mouser (1981) respectively.

It may also make sense to get customers involved in developing performance standards. I recently made this recommendation to a small manufacturing firm. The mission statement of this firm clearly stated that the firm was to place a premium on responsiveness to customers' needs. To back this vision up, I suggested that customers be involved in establishing standards of performance for such things as quality and delivery time. This approach is consistent with the increased emphasis on quality service found in many organizations.

Rating Format

Over the years, there has been considerable controversy about the superiority of various rating formats or scales relative to the

Figure 4.5
Nonparticipative and Participative Approaches to Developing Performance Standards

Nonparticipative Approach

1. Supervisor gathers data on the performance measures.

2. Supervisor completes the performance appraisal forms.

3. Supervisor shows completed appraisal to immediate boss and gains concurrence that it has been completed in acceptable form.

4. Supervisor presents completed performance appraisal to subordinate and asks subordinate to react and sign.

5. Appraisal is entered into information system and predetermined consequences result.

Participative Approach

1. Supervisor and subordinate separately gather data on the appraisal measures.

2. Superior and subordinate meet to compare the data they have collected.

3. Superior and subordinate jointly agree on a tentative set of results for the subordinate's appraisal.

4. The tentative appraisal is shown to supervisor's boss, who reacts to it.

5. Appraisal result is communicated to the subordinate.

6. Appraisal results are put in the information system and appropriate action is taken.

Source: Adapted from Mohrman, Resnick-West, and Lawler (1989). Reprinted with permission.

indicators of adequate performance standards. A prime example is the ongoing debate on the virtues of behavioral observation scales versus behavioral expectation scales. Dossett (1989) provides a review of this debate, and the most current data having a bearing on these arguments.

Unfortunately, there are no data on the adequacy of various formats when it comes to merit pay appraisal. Given the somewhat mixed results on the adequacy of various formats used for purposes other than merit pay (Landy & Farr, 1980), you would expect differences between different formats used for merit pay. Organizations may wish to conduct empirical studies to explore the adequacy of alternative formats in developing merit pay plans. Banks and Roberson (1985) provide a good set of guidelines on how performance appraisal formats should be developed.

Rater Training

A well-documented method of improving the validity of ratings is to train raters. Smith (1986) provides a review of 24 studies that looked at the effectiveness of alternative rater training programs. His review suggests that the effectiveness of rater training programs varies by method of presentation and content being presented. In terms of method of presentation, the more active raters are in training, the better the outcomes. Hence, giving raters the opportunity to discuss issues and to participate in practice and feedback sessions during training resulted in fewer rating errors and more accuracy than did training presented in a lecture format.

In terms of the content presented, it appears that emphasis must be placed on both the observation and judgment of performance (R. Heneman, 1988). As shown in the Smith (1986) review, training that emphasizes the observation of performance, by having raters become familiar with the actual performance standards used, results in more accurate ratings. Training that emphasizes performance-related judgments by training raters to minimize ratings errors is related to a reduction in rating errors. Because both rating errors and accuracy are important indicators of validity, the content of training programs should emphasize both observation and judgment.

Several surveys of employer practices have been conducted, which shed some light on the degree to which these research findings are being followed by organizations. On a positive note, it appears that more organizations are providing rater training if you compare earlier (Bureau of National Affairs, 1983; Bernardin & Klatt, 1985) to later surveys (Bretz & Milkovich, 1989; Hall, Posner, & Harder, 1989). On a negative note, the content of these programs does not appear to have changed much. Emphasis continues to be more on how to fill out forms than on how to observe and judge employee performance (Bretz & Milkovich, 1989; Bureau of National Affairs, 1983; Downs & Moscinsky, 1979; Hall, Posner, & Harder, 1989). Data have not yet been collected on the processes used to present rater training programs in the surveyed organizations.

Administrative Practices

Administrative practices, such as how and when ratings are conducted, influence the adequacy of performance measures. It seems that often what is required by the organization is in conflict with the capabilities of the rater to "mentally process" performance information. As a result, the accuracy of ratings is diminished. Therefore, to increase the accuracy of ratings, required administrative practices should be made consistent with the mental processes of the raters.

Time Delay in Ratings.   One specific application of this general statement has to do with the timing of ratings. According to one national survey, 85 percent of U.S. organizations only conduct ratings once a year (Bureau of National Affairs, 1983). One implication of this finding is that a considerable period of time passes between the observation and rating of employee performance. Raters are, in effect, being asked to evaluate performance that took place up to 12 months earlier. Given the time delay in ratings, considerable demands are made upon the memory capabilities of raters. Given less-than-perfect memories, less-than-perfect ratings should be expected as well. A study by R. Heneman and Wexley (1983) suggests that this speculation is indeed the case. They reported that the longer the delay between the observation and rating of performance, the less accurate were the ratings. This decrease in accuracy took place after a mere three-week delay in ratings. Imagine the potential decline in accuracy after 12 months! These data suggest that ratings need to be made more frequently than once a year. Ratings should be made at least twice a year and, preferably, every quarter.

Amount of Information Observed.   Many, if not most, supervisors have limited opportunity to observe employee performance. This limited opportunity is a result of large spans of control, physical distance from the ratee, and responsibilities not requiring interaction with the ratee. In any event, what this means is that the rater is making a summary judgment of employee performance on the basis of a limited sample of the employee's total performance. You would expect, and it has been empirically verified, that ratings would be more accurate the greater the amount of observation time (R. Heneman & Wexley, 1983). Also, greater opportunity to observe is associated with higher levels of interrater reliability (Rothstein, 1990).

Hence, arranging work conditions to facilitate the observation of employee performance is recommended. For example, the observations of peers could be used if a supervisor has a large number of people reporting to him or her thereby limiting the opportunity to observe. In large consulting firms, partners are sometimes asked to evaluate the performance of associates who spend large amounts of time working at client organizations. But, the partners have limited opportunity to observe the actual performance of associates. In these cases, it would be better to ask the client organization to evaluate the associates, as the client has had more opportunity to observe them.

Diary Keeping. Time and other resource constraints may make it impossible for organizations to require anything but limited observation of employees and once-a-year ratings. But even under these less-than-favorable conditions, organizations can still attempt to make administrative practices consistent with the rater's mental abilities by requiring diary keeping. By carefully recording employee performance, the rater is relying more on documentation and less on memory when rating performance. Moreover, a diary can be used to impose some structure on a large amount of performance information that may seem scattered. With structure, the information may be easier to recall.

DeNisi, Robbins, and Cafferty (1989) conducted a study to look at the effects of diary keeping. They found that raters who kept a diary were more accurate in their ratings than were raters who did not keep a diary. Also, they found that raters who organized their diary by the ratee, rather than by the task being performed by ratees, were more accurate. Finally, they found that raters preferred to organize their diaries by ratees rather than by tasks. These findings clearly point to the utility of diary keeping in performance measurement. While it is naive to expect raters to keep extremely detailed diaries given their busy schedules, it should be a required practice that raters document the critical episodes of employee performance.

Social Comparisons

Two studies showed that indicators of the convergent validities of ratings were increased by providing raters with comparative performance information on other subordinates. R. Heneman (1986) reported stronger correlations between ratings and objective measures of performance, while Farh and Dobbins (1989) reported stronger correlations between self and supervisory ratings, when relative comparisons rather than absolute comparisons were made. The results of these two studies suggest that the convergent validity of ratings is increased when relative rather than absolute comparisons are made in performance ratings.

There are several reasons why ratings may be more valid with relative rather than absolute comparisons. First, individuals typically seek out comparative information about the performance of others when making performance judgments. The sought-after information provides a context or point of reference for the ratings to be made (Farh & Dobbins, 1989). Second, relative comparisons may be a less complex rating task for the rater. It may be easier to compare ratees to one another than it is to compare ratees to a poorly defined anchor on a rating scale (R. Heneman, 1986).

Although relative comparisons are used very infrequently, as previously discussed, perhaps greater use of relative comparisons should be made as they have been shown to improve the convergent validity of ratings. Given the limited research, it is not suggested that relative comparisons be used to replace absolute comparisons. However, the data do seem strong enough to warrant relative comparisons as a supplement to absolute comparisons.

Rater Motivation

The discussion of ways to increase the validity of ratings thus far has focused on ways to improve the rater's skills, or on ways to arrange working conditions to promote the rater's ability to mentally process performance information. Another way to improve the validity of ratings, which may be as good as or better than focusing on the rater's skills and abilities, is to increase the rater's motivation to make valid ratings (Murphy & Cleveland, 1991). Unfortunately, very little research has been conducted along these lines.

The importance of rater motivation in the validity of ratings is perhaps best illustrated in a study by Napier and Latham (1986). They found that raters did not see any personal consequences for the ratings they assigned, such as appreciation from the boss, a pay raise, or a promotion. Although the studies were conducted with small samples of employees, the results were consistent for two different industries (newsprint and banking) and methods of research (interviews and question-naires). Based on these results, the authors suggest that we may be very naive to expect valid ratings in the absence of any moti-vating outcomes for those conducting the ratings. One way to motivate raters is to hold them accountable for their ratings. Methods to hold raters accountable for performance ratings and merit increase decisions are discussed in Chapter 6.

Statistical Control of Halo

One approach that appears to have great promise as a way to improve the validity of ratings is to statistically control halo error. Under this approach time and other resources are not devoted to minimizing rating errors. Instead, rating errors are allowed to occur and be statistically partialed out from the rat-ings. You might expect that this procedure would yield ratings free from error at a reduced cost to the organization, as a statis-tical manipulation is used rather than more costly interventions such as rater training programs. A good example is a study by Landy, Vance, Barnes-Farwell, and Steele (1980) in which they reported greater discriminant validity after statistically partial-ing out halo error.

The major problem with this approach is that it assumes halo is an error rather than true employee performance (e.g., Hulin, 1982). There may, in fact, be work situations where uni-form ratings of employee performance does and should take place, because it reflects true performance. In some settings, the same abilities are required to perform different aspects or dimensions of the job (Cooper, 1981). Given the difficulty of sep-arating out valid from invalid halo in ratings, this procedure has not received widespread acceptance and use.

One interesting approach to the statistical control of halo has been offered by Bartlett (1983). Under his procedure, he is very explicit as to what constitutes valid and invalid halo. He then uses a special rating technique, known as "forced choice," to remove invalid halo from overall ratings. Just as important as the procedure that he offers is the explicitness with which he treats halo. If you use the statistical control of halo, you must be explicit as to what constitutes halo error to provide logical justification for its removal.

Summary of Major Points

1. *The importance of performance measurement.* The first and foremost step in the development of a merit pay plan is the adequate measurement of performance. Theory, research, and practice indicate that it is not possible to have an effective merit pay plan if performance is not adequately measured. This is true regardless of the desirability and feasibility of merit pay.

2. *A variety of performance measures can be used.* These measures include traits, behaviors, results, rankings, and paired comparisons. Each approach has distinct advantages and disadvantages. These sets of performance standards should not be treated as substitutes for one another. No one approach is clearly superior to another for all considerations. A preferred strategy for selecting which standards to use includes reasoned selection followed by an empirical evaluation of the standards selected.

3. *Controversial measures of performance.* Some specific measures of employee performance are very controversial and need to be carefully considered before being used for merit pay. These measures include promotions, seniority, organizational citizenship behavior, maximum versus typical performance, and job level.

4. *Adequacy of performance measures.* The adequacy of performance measures refers to the concept of validity or the extent to which performance standards measure what they purport to measure. Validity is assessed with a number of indicators including content validity,

convergent validity, discriminant validity, accuracy, rating errors, reliability, and relevance. These indicators are not substitutes for one another, and each indicator provides a unique source of information from which to make inferences about validity.

5. *Methods to improve the validity of ratings.* The validity of ratings can be improved by how performance standards are developed and how the standards are used. Validity appears to be greater when the following conditions are present: Ratings are tied to the strategic mission of the firm, performance standards and ratings are based on job analysis, multiple sources of performance information are used, raters and ratees participate in the development of performance standards, rater training is provided, rating formats that are based on test construction principles are used, the delay between observation and ratings is minimized, the opportunity for the rater to observe is maximized, the rater keeps a diary organized by ratee, social comparison information is provided to the rater, raters are held accountable for their ratings, and the statistical control of halo is only used under well-defined conditions.

Conclusions

The most difficult aspect of developing a merit pay plan is creating a valid way to measure performance. If a valid method of measuring performance is not developed, it is doubtful that employees will see the link between their pay and performance. And, in turn, if employees do not see the link between their pay and performance, merit pay, as shown in Chapter 2, will not lead to improved performance.

A central theme in this chapter is that there is no one best way to measure performance, to assess validity, or to improve upon the validity of performance measures. A variety of guidelines have been offered as to the development of performance standards, the assessment of validity, and ways to improve validity. While there is no one best way, some guidelines to measuring performance appear to be more promising than others when it comes to using performance measurement for purposes of merit pay. In particular, three guidelines stand out. At a minimum, the following three guidelines need to be followed.

First, controversial measures of performance need to be clearly defined and communicated to employees. It must be clear to employees what the organizational policy is regarding how merit pay will be linked to promotions, seniority, organizational citizenship behavior, maximum versus typical performance, and job level. If these factors are not explicitly treated by the organization, even the most sophisticated rating scales may fail for merit pay decisions. If the employee hears that pay is based strictly on performance, but sees that merit increases are based on other factors that may or may not be related to performance (as defined in the rating scale), then the scales and merit pay plan will fail.

Second, no matter which performance standards are selected, an empirical study should have been conducted on the validity of these standards. As shown in this chapter, with the exception of accuracy, which requires a true score, and relevance, which requires an ultimate criterion, there are a number of straightforward indicators that can be used to assess the validity of performance standards.

Third, the validity of ratings appears to be heavily contingent on the acceptability of the standards to the affected parties. To enhance the acceptability of standards, both raters and ratees should be involved in developing standards, the rating task should be made consistent with the ways in which raters mentally process performance information, raters should be trained and held accountable for their ratings, and the system of performance measurement should be related to the job.

If the standards used to assess performance are well defined, show evidence of validity, and are acceptable to the affected parties, then there should be a strong relationship (both actual and perceived) between merit increases and performance ratings. If these three guidelines are not followed, then judgments regarding performance may be inconsistent with judgments about merit increases. Obviously, this inconsistency will create dysfunctional consequences if pay is to be linked to performance under a stated merit pay plan.

In short, a great deal of effort has been spent on trying to find the one best way to measure performance. A great deal of journal space has been devoted to comparing alternative rating formats, and organizations frequently change their methods used to assess performance. Unfortunately, these lines of inquiry have failed to produce the one best way to measure performance. A better use of resources is to develop measures of performance with clearly defined standards, with known validity properties, and which are acceptable to the affected parties. Hence, greater attention needs to be given to discussing the desired status of controversial performance measures for particular organizations and to the acceptability of performance standards to the affected parties than has been done in the past.

Some may argue that the development of standards with known validity properties is not "practical" for organizations. Nothing could be further from the truth. As shown in this chapter, the procedures used to develop standards with reasonable levels of validity make good "business sense." Many organizations, for example, are looking for a way to achieve greater adherence to their strategic plans. One way to do so is to use the mission statement in the development of performance standards so that behaviors consistent with the strategic plans will be rewarded.

The standards, in and of themselves, are also important for business purposes. The obvious argument is that standards must be measuring what they purport to measure for actual performance to be linked to merit pay. A less obvious, but perhaps more important, argument is that for performance standards to be accepted and acted upon, the standards must be seen as reasonable ones by the affected parties. Standards are much more likely to be acceptable to managers and employees when the standards themselves have adequate validity properties. Again, sound measurement is a very "practical" consideration.

5

Establishing Pay Increases

This chapter discusses how pay increases can be tied to performance once adequate measures of performance have been developed. Establishing pay increases is the second step in the development and administration of a merit pay plan. To establish pay increases based on performance, two major activities must take place. First, a policy, or set of guidelines, must be developed regarding pay increases and their relationship to performance. Second, this policy needs to be introduced and implemented in the organization. Both topics will be covered in this chapter.

Creating a Merit Pay Policy

In creating a merit pay policy, attention must be given to the size, form, and timing of pay increases that will be linked to various levels of performance. The size, form, and timing of pay allocated to merit increases depends on many factors, including the budget and pay structure. Before considering these issues, the concept of "just-noticeable differences" (JND), which is the frame of reference for a merit pay policy, is discussed.

Just-Noticeable Differences

A just-noticeable difference (JND) refers to the minimum pay increase that employees would perceive as "making a difference" with regard to their attitudes and behaviors (H. Heneman & Ellis, 1982). This concept has also been referred to as a "just meaningful difference" (Zedeck & Smith, 1968) and a "smallest meaningful pay increase" (Krefting & Mahoney, 1977). Regardless of how labeled, the concept of JND is an important one in merit pay as it may mediate the relationship between merit pay and subsequent performance as shown in Figure 5.1. What this means is that a JND is the psychological state that translates merit increases into subsequent performance. If merit increases are not large enough to have a JND, they may not produce increases in future performance. Hence, one critical goal in establishing pay increases is to create a JND. Another goal, of course, is to minimize cost, as described throughout the book.

A common question is how large a merit increase is required for the increase to have a JND? There is no precise numerical value that can answer this question. Rather, the amount of increase likely to cause a JND appears to depend on the person and situation. Research has shown that a smaller pay increase is likely to produce a JND when employees are in lower rather than higher level jobs (Zedeck & Smith, 1968); have lower rather than higher earnings (Hinrichs, 1969); anticipate a low rather than high cost of living (Krefting & Mahoney, 1977); anticipate great difficulty in attaining a new job; have a small rather than large current wage; anticipate a small rather than large pay increase; and work a long rather than a short work week (H. Heneman & Ellis, 1982).

When determining what size increase is needed to create a JND, three other factors need to be kept in mind. First, simply increasing the amount of money allocated to merit increases does not necessarily produce a JND. A recent study by Rambo and Pinto (1989) showed that there is not a one-for-one return in the form of a JND, for each dollar spent on increases. Instead, they

Figure 5.1
The Role of Just-Noticeable Differences in the Merit Pay Process

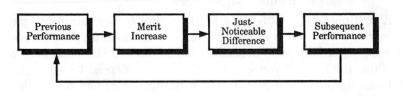

found diminishing marginal returns on each additional dollar allocated. That is, each additional merit increase dollar resulted in smaller increases in JND.

Second, the amount of influence that characteristics of the employee and situation have on JNDs may depend on the attitudes of employees. In two studies, it was shown that the ability of person (i.e., employee) and situation variables to predict JNDs depends on attitudes toward rewards (Krefting & Mahoney, 1977; Varadarajan & Futrell, 1984). For those who value pay for its purchasing power, or the amount of goods and services that can be bought, JND seems to be best predicted by the cost of living. For those who value pay as a form of organizational recognition, JND seems to be best predicted by the size of the anticipated pay increase (Krefting, Newman, & Krzystofiak, 1987).

Third, equity considerations need to be kept in mind as well. (See Chapter 2 for a review of equity theory.) For pay to have a just-noticeable difference, the employee must see the size of the increase as meaningful in a relative sense as well as in an absolute sense. Equity theory (Adams, 1965) suggests that the employee must regard his or her own ratio of merit pay to performance as roughly equivalent to the ratio for other comparably performing people in the organization.

Actual Size of Merit Increases

Given the variability in JNDs, it is not surprising to find variability in the actual size of merit increases that are allocated. To give the reader an idea of the magnitude of merit increases, the results of a recent survey by Sibson and Company (1989) are shown in Table 5.1. Similar surveys are reported by the Conference Board (1984) and the Personnel Policies Forum (1981).

The *variability* of merit increases can be seen in surveys by Peck (1984) and Teel (1986). The large-scale survey by Peck (1984) indicated that the average point spread between low and high merit increases was 9.3 percent. The average merit increase was 8.8 percent with a range from 5 percent to 14.3 percent. The difference between the low and average increase was 3.8 percentage points while the difference between the average and high increase was 5.5 percentage points. This variability seems consistent with the research on JNDs as people with higher performance levels

Table 5.1
Comparison of 1988 and Projected 1989 Merit Increases by Employee, Industry, and Geographic Category

By Employee Category

Employee Category	1988 Actual	Months Since Preceding Increases	1989 Plans	Anticipated Months to 1989 Increases
Hourly Nonexempt	4.9%	12	4.8%	12
Salaried Nonexempt	5.0	12	5.0	12
Exempt	5.2	12	5.2	12
Officer/Executive	5.8	12	5.5	12
All Employees	5.3	12	5.2	12

By Industry Category

Industry Category	1988 Actual				1989 Plans			
	Hourly Nonexempt	Salaried Nonexempt	Exempt	Officer/ Executive	All Employees	Hourly Nonexempt	Salaried Nonexempt	Exempt	Officer/ Executive	All Employees
Durable Goods Mfg.	4.3%	4.5%	4.8%	5.3%	5.0%	3.9%	4.7%	4.9%	5.1%	4.9%
Non-Durable Goods Mfg.	4.2	4.8	5.1	5.8	5.0	4.5	5.0	5.2	5.6	5.1
Financial Institutions	5.0	5.1	5.5	6.0	5.6	5.1	5.2	5.4	5.7	5.4

Insurance	5.6	5.7	6.0	6.5	6.0	5.3	5.4	5.7	6.0	5.7
High Technology	4.8	4.8	5.1	5.3	4.9	4.8	5.0	5.1	5.1	4.9
Services	4.9	4.8	5.0	5.6	5.0	4.7	4.9	5.0	5.5	5.1
Cons. Brand./Home Prods.	4.6	5.0	5.5	6.4	5.4	5.0	5.1	5.3	5.6	5.3
Retail/Wholesale	5.0	5.1	5.2	6.2	5.3	4.8	4.9	5.1	5.6	5.2
Energy	3.8	4.3	4.2	4.6	4.4	3.8	4.3	4.6	4.9	4.6
Comm. & Publishing*	5.0	5.2	5.5	5.4	5.4	4.8	4.9	5.0	5.4	5.0
Utilities	4.2	4.3	4.5	5.6	4.5	4.1	4.4	4.7	5.1	4.6
Conglomerates	4.9	4.7	5.0	5.7	5.2	5.0	5.1	5.2	5.7	5.4
Other	4.8	5.0	5.2	5.7	5.2	5.3	5.2	5.3	5.6	5.4

By Geographic Region

Geographic Region										
Northeast	5.3	5.4	5.6	6.1	5.7	5.2	5.3	5.5	5.7	5.5
Southeast	4.9	5.0	5.2	5.8	5.2	4.8	4.8	5.0	5.4	5.0
North Central	4.6	4.6	5.0	5.8	5.0	4.5	4.7	5.0	5.5	5.0
South Central	4.3	4.6	4.7	5.1	4.7	4.4	4.8	5.0	5.1	4.9
West	4.8	4.9	5.1	5.5	5.1	4.9	5.0	5.1	5.4	5.0

Source: Reprinted with permission of Sibson & Co., Inc., Princeton, NJ (*Compensation Planning Survey*, 1989).

*Based on a limited sample

and correspondingly higher pay levels receive larger increases than those with lower performance and pay levels. As previously discussed, a smaller increase is needed to create a JND for those with lower pay levels.

While there does appear to be some variability in increases across organizations, the amount of variability is not large. Teel (1986) reports that for the majority (76 percent) of employees in 16 organizations, raises only varied by plus or minus 2 percent around the average. What this means is that the difference in merit pay increase between the best and worst performer is only 2 percent! Under these circumstances, it is doubtful that poor performers will be motivated to improve or that good performers will continue their high levels of performance. Although this study is based on a very small sample and should be treated with caution, it nevertheless highlights the importance of creating a sound set of merit pay policies and guidelines. Without a sound policy, it is doubtful that there will be much, if any, differentiation in pay among levels of performance. And for reasons described in greater detail in Chapter 2, it is doubtful that employees will be motivated to improve subsequent performance under such circumstances.

Form of Merit Increases

In addition to determining the size of merit increases, consideration must also be given to the form that merit increases will take. Two notable features taken from current practice need to be discussed here: the type of increase and the permanence of the increase.

Type of Merit Increase.

In virtually all organizations, merit pay comes in the form of direct pay. That is, merit pay represents an increase in wage or salary, which shows up in the employee's paycheck. Recently, however, there has been talk of allocating indirect pay or employee benefits on the basis of performance. Brunker (1982) appears to have first advocated the use of benefits as a type of merit pay.

A Houston-based organization, CRS Sirrine, Inc., has put a performance-based benefits plan into place for its 3,000 employees in architecture, engineering, and construction (*Compensation and Benefits Manager's Report,* 3 (20), 1989). Under the plan, the organization contributes to employees' health plan costs only if employees' performance ratings are adequate. Employees with less than adequate ratings must pay the full cost of their health care until their performance reaches an adequate level. Reasons for undertaking this plan included a desire to strengthen the pay-for-performance philosophy by linking all types of pay to performance and to get employees to view benefits as a reward for performance rather than an entitlement based on membership in the organization. The plan has been in effect for two years, but the company has yet to realize any cost savings with the plan.

An obvious advantage of benefits over pay increases for purposes of merit pay is the tax savings for the employee. Under present tax laws, direct pay increases are treated as taxable income, but most benefits are not treated as taxable income. Hence, if benefits are used for merit increases, the reward may not be taxed. A potential, yet solvable, problem with performance-based benefits is that some benefits (e.g., social security) are legally mandated for all employees regardless of performance. Hence, legally mandated benefits would have to be excluded from the plan. Another problem may be that if the amount of benefits granted is based on performance, some employees could be left defenseless in the face of a catastrophic illness. This may create pressure on the supervisor to evaluate employees as average or better even if actual performance does not warrant such ratings. A way around this problem may be to make employer contributions, rather than the amount of benefits, contingent on performance. In short, performance-based benefits represent a new direction in merit pay. Organizations considering such a plan need to pay careful attention to current tax laws (Brunker, 1982).

Permanence of the Increase. A merit increase can become a permanent addition to base pay. For example, an employee who receives a 6 percent increase in pay would continue to receive that 6 percent increase as long as they remain with the organization under a *traditional merit pay plan*. Merit pay *is* traditionally granted on a permanent basis. A recent survey by Wyatt Company (1987) indicated that about 78 percent of U.S. organizations have such a traditional merit pay plan. A permanent increase, if costed out over time, represents a very large reward for future increased and sustained performance. If employees perceive the total value of the merit increase over time, they may see the increase as very large and be very motivated.

The traditional merit plan has also been criticized for a number of reasons. First, the costs associated with permanent increases can be huge. Minken (1988) offered an example of the mathematics involved. Under a traditional plan, an employee earning $30,000 a year who gets a 5 percent merit increase would receive a $1,500 (.05 × $30,000) raise in year one, and a $1,575 (.05 × $31,500) raise in year two—for a *total* merit increase over two years of $3,075. Had this same employee not received a permanent increase, he or she would have received $1,500 in year one, another $1,500 in year two, with a total of $3,000 for the two years. While a total payout difference of $75 ($3,075 minus $3,000), between a permanent and nonpermanent increase, may not seem large, consider that an employer may have thousands of employees working for an extended number of years.

A second problem with traditional merit pay plans is that they may lessen the strength of the perceived pay-for-performance relationship. As noted by Belcher (1980), traditional merit pay plans pay not only for performance but for membership in the organization as well. The longer an employee is with the organization, the larger the merit increase becomes in any one year. Over time, the size of the increase is compounded by the increase built into the base salary. Whether this correlation between seniority and pay is desirable or not depends on your view of seniority as a measure of performance (see the discussion in Chapter 4).

A third problem with traditional merit plans is that the statistical effects of a permanent increase may result in the relative pay status of employees being unalterable. In an interesting study, Haire, Ghisseli, and Gordon (1967) found that if there is a strong correlation between pay level and increase, as one would expect with a permanent increase, the rank ordering of the lowest to highest paid employees would continue to remain the same, regardless of changes in employee performance. To the extent that merit pay possesses status properties as well as consumption properties (Frank, 1984), merit increases *may* produce an unalterable status hierarchy that may be unacceptable to many employees.

A fourth problem with a permanent increase is the potential for a decrease in the actual relationship between pay and performance. The magnitude of the relationship may decrease because, as time goes on, pay increases will become compounded more by the passage of time than actual performance. This appears to be only a potential problem, as a recent study by Schwab and Olson (1990) found that the permanence of merit increases had little impact on the actual relationship between pay and performance. However, as noted by the authors, these results occurred in a situation where the "maximums" (reviewed at the end of this chapter) paid by the organization were increased to keep up with pay increases in the market. Had these adjustments not been made or been done less frequently, the impact of the permanence of the increase may have been more pronounced. The actual pay-for-performance relationship would have been weakened because long-tenured employees would no longer be eligible for pay increases, having reached the maximum allowable rate of pay.

An alternative to the traditional merit pay plan exists and is known as *lump-sum bonuses* (Overstreet, 1985; Minken, 1988). Under this form of merit increase, the increase received is not permanent, but instead is a one-time increase that is not rolled over into base pay. As shown in Figure 5.2, there are a variety of lump-sum merit pay plans. Many organizations, including AETNA, B.F. Goodrich, Timex, and Westinghouse, now have lump-sum merit plans (Kanter, 1987).

Lump-sum plans seem to have been developed in response to the criticisms of traditional merit plans. By not making merit pay a permanent addition to base pay, costs can be minimized and the pay-for-performance relationship may be strengthened. Also, benefit costs may be reduced as benefit amounts are sometimes linked to the base pay amounts (Minken, 1988). Under a lump-sum plan, base pay is not increased with a merit increase and, hence, the amount of benefits may remain the same. Another potential advantage with lump-sum plans has to do with tax savings (1983). Under the salary advance plan shown in Figure 5.2, any employee could choose to distribute increases over two years rather than receive the increase in one year. Tax savings would be greater if pay were deferred to a second year in which the marginal tax rate is lower.

Although lump-sum merit pay plans seem to offer some advantages over traditional pay plans, there is, unfortunately, no research that has verified these advantages. The limited evidence

Figure 5.2
Lump-sum Merit Plans

No-strings approach.   Employees are given the option to receive the increase in the traditional manner or to take the total amount in a lump-sum. Employees who take the lump-sum option are under no obligation to repay an unearned portion should they leave the company for any reason.

Salary-advance approach.   Employees who elect to receive a lump-sum increase must sign a contract obligating them to return the unearned portion should they leave the company. Installments are possible under this approach as well.

Earned-out approach.   Lump-sum increase is paid in advance, but is excluded from pension plans, profit sharing, and other benefit programs until the increase has been earned out over the future period by the lump-sum amount.

Source: Small Business Reports, June 1983. Published by the American Management Association, Monterey, CA. Reprinted with permission.

on frequency of use indicates that only about 14 percent of U.S. organizations use lump-sum merit plans; about 7 percent have studied or tested lump-sum merit plans; and about 1.4 percent have used but terminated lump-sum plans (Wyatt Company, 1987). There is an obvious need for evaluative research on lump-sum merit plans. It could be argued, for example, that cost savings associated with a lump-sum plan are offset by decreased motivation due to a reduction in the total value of a merit increase to the employee.

Timing Considerations

In most organizations, merit increases, as well as other increases such as cost-of-living, are allocated once a year (Wyatt Company, 1987). An issue that arises is when during the year should the annual merit review take place? Two different approaches seem to exist in practice, each of which has its advantages and disadvantages.

One approach is to have a *common review date* for all merit increase decisions. One advantage to this approach is that the amount of paperwork may be decreased over having different review dates for different employees. A second advantage may be that relative performance information is more readily available to allocators and covers the same time period for each employee. This may be desirable for enhancing the accuracy of performance ratings (as discussed in Chapter 4). A disadvantage to this approach is that allocators may have a large number of decisions to reach during a short period of time. Also, depending on the size of the merit budget, this approach may put a large monetary burden on the organization once a year rather than spreading it out over the entire year.

A second approach is to use each *employee's anniversary date*. With this approach, employees are reviewed on the day they began work with the organization. By having, in effect, staggered review dates over the course of the year, the review burden placed on the allocators and the monetary burden placed on the organization is spread out over the year. However, additional paperwork may be required in the form of reminders to allocators, and relative performance information may not be current or readily available.

The decision as to which approach to use may be dictated by current circumstances. If relative comparisons are used as a method of performance appraisal, and departments "compete" for budget money, then a common review date is needed. By having a common review date, employees and departments are compared to one another over the same time period. If absolute comparisons are used for performance appraisal, and there are fixed raise amounts to which all departments must adhere, then using service dates of employees could be a better approach if the performance standards and raise guidelines remain constant over time.

In terms of actual practice, a recent survey by Bretz and Milkovich (1989) indicates that a common review date is used more frequently than an anniversary review date. Merit increases were granted on common review dates in 58 percent of the organizations, on the employee's anniversary date in 27 percent of the organizations, and on a rolling date based on some factor other than the employee's anniversary date in 15 percent of the organizations.

Another timing issue that arises in merit pay policy is whether the period between merit increases should be constant or variable. In some organizations, the time that elapses between merit reviews is not uniform for all employees. Instead, the time between reviews depends on performance. The better an employee's performance under this arrangement, the more frequently he or she is reviewed for another pay raise. (For an example, see the discussion of guidecharts later in this chapter.)

From a motivational perspective, it has been argued that this approach is problematic (Mohrman et al., 1989). If the review dates for poor performers are stretched out, there is little incentive for them to improve. From a budgeting perspective, however, it has been argued that variable review periods based on performance are advantageous (Farmer, 1978). By paying below-average performers less frequently, more money is available for better performers.

Budgeting Issues

The budgeting process behind merit pay increases is not well described or researched (R. Heneman, 1990). Nevertheless, it is a topic of crucial importance for establishing merit increases. The importance of financial considerations is clearly spelled out in economic theory (as reviewed in Chapter 2) and is a continuing theme of the book. The limited information available on budgets is reviewed here. Readers interested in case study examples of the merit pay budgeting process can look at descriptions of Armstrong Cork (Farmer, 1978), a private-sector organization, and a review of practices by various public-sector organizations (Van Adelsberg, 1978). Consideration will be given in this section to budgeting models that can be used and issues that arise in the use of these models.

Before describing some of these more formal budgeting procedures and issues, it should also be noted that many informal, yet important, practices also accompany merit pay budgeting. For example, a great deal of "horsetrading" can go on with merit pay budgets. A new manager may see, for example, that when he or she requests and argues for a $12,000 budget for merit increases in the next year, he or she receives a $6,000 budget. It doesn't take a new manager very many budgeting periods to realize that to be assured of the $12,000 budget he or she needs, the manager will need to submit a proposed merit increase budget of $24,000. The point here is that many rituals and other informal behaviors accompany merit budgeting and may be just as influential in determining the ultimate size of the budget as formal dollar-and-cents considerations.

Uniform Versus Flexible Budgets. It appears that in the majority (67 percent) of U.S. organizations, merit pay budgets are allocated as a uniform percentage of payroll (Peck, 1984). What this means is that a uniform percent of the total payroll is allocated to each business unit in the organization for merit increases. No allowance is made for differences in costs or revenues associated with personnel in each business unit. Alternatively, flexible budgets make allowances for differences in costs and revenues for each unit.

The frequent practice of uniform budgets is potentially problematic (Brennan, 1985; R. Heneman, 1990). If one business unit is very profitable because of employee efforts and another unit is not, when pay increases monies are allocated on a uniform basis, pay-for-performance perceptions may be low for the more profitable unit. As a result of the budgeting process, money is, in a sense, being taken away from the more profitable unit to pay for the less profitable unit. Given this potential problem with uniform budgets, some organizations use more flexible budgets, which take into account differences between business units. The risk of using flexible budget models is, of course, the chance of creating perceived inequities across business units.

Top-Down Versus Bottom-Up Models. Distinctions between business units that can be used in flexible budgets can be "top-down," "bottom-up," or some combination of the two (Rock, 1988). A top-down approach is based on a valuation of cash generation received by capital markets. Business units that generate greater revenues receive a larger merit budget. In the public sector, cash generation may be supplemented with funds not only generated by capital markets, but by the legislature as well. Lawther et al. (1989) reported that many states receive merit budgets solely on the basis of legislative funds.

A bottom-up approach is based on management projections of cash uses and sources. An example is the setting of merit budgets on the basis of anticipated comparative salary ratios. According to the Peck (1984) survey, about 13 percent of U.S. organizations grant merit budgets on the basis of comparative salary ratios, with business units with larger comparative salary ratios receiving larger budgets. Another example comes from the public sector. Merit increases for state employees in Alabama, Idaho, Minnesota, Montana, Nebraska, and Texas are funded by turnover, retirement, and open positions in the state (Lawther et al., 1989). Savings from these sources are used to fund merit increases.

Fay (in press) provides an excellent description and evaluation of top-down and bottom-up budgeting procedures. He concludes that a bottom-up procedure is superior to a top-down approach for a variety of reasons. Among them is the consideration given in the bottom-up procedure to changes in cash-flow and human resource requirements over the budgeted time period. Under a top-down approach, changes in these variables are not taken into consideration. Also, a bottom-up approach facilitates the strategic planning process by involving business unit managers in the budgeting process. Under a top-down approach, budgets are established by the finance department in conjunction with the compensation department. Such an approach may not take into consideration the strategic direction of individual business units.

While a bottom-up procedure appears to be desirable from both time and managerial perspectives, Fay notes that this procedure is not without costs. In particular, if an organization is to be successful with a bottom-up model, it is essential that it has the information-processing capabilities required to make changes in resource requirements over time. By having a human-resource information system on computer, the line manager can see the impact of salary decisions under various sets of circumstances. Along with a human-resource information system, it is also essential that line managers be trained in the salary and budgeting process as it relates to strategic planning. The human resource department can be helpful in this training as well as in auditing the results of the budgeting process.

Overall Size of Budget. Regardless of the procedure used to allocate budgets among business units, consideration also needs to be given to the *overall* size of the budget. The Peck (1984) survey suggested that while the financial performance of the organization is important, the competitiveness of the organization in terms of pay is even more important in setting merit pay budgets. This can be seen in Table 5.2. These figures are quite consistent with economic theory (reviewed in Chapter 2). As would be expected under the theory of marginal revenue product, employers seem to base merit budgets on financial considerations concerning the

Table 5.2
Considerations in Establishing Merit Increase Budgets

Factors	Number of Mentions	Average Rank*
External Pay Relationships	503	1.9
Company Financial Results	471	2.6
Company Financial Prospects	452	2.9
Internal Pay Relationships	419	3.7
Cost-of-Living Changes	420	4.3
Ability to Hire	386	4.7

Source: Peck (1984). Reprinted with permission.

*1 = most important

price of the product. Also, as would be expected from efficiency wage theory, employers also base merit budgets on labor market considerations.

Gross Versus Net Costs. There is confusion as to the actual costs involved in developing, using, and reporting merit pay budgets. According to Mitchell (1989) this confusion comes from a failure to distinguish between gross and net costs. He provides an example to show how easily actual costs can be over-stated by failing to subtract turnover savings from gross merit costs in getting to net or actual merit increase costs. In his example, four employees are granted a $1.00 merit increase. Another employee retires and saves the firm $14.00, while a new employee replaces the retired employee at a cost of $10.00. The gross cost of merit pay in this situation is $4.00, as four employees each receive a $1.00 merit increase. The net cost, however, is zero because of the turnover savings of $14 – $10 = $4. When the turnover savings of $4 is subtracted from the gross cost of $4, the net cost is zero. As can be seen from this simple example, care must be taken in specifying gross versus net costs in budgeting procedures. It should also be noted that an argument can be made against subtracting out turnover savings that are not directly attributable to the merit pay plan.

Pay Structure Issues

A pay structure is an organizational policy that specifies the rates that can be paid to employees holding jobs of varying worth to the organization. An example of a pay structure is shown in Figure 5.3. Each box in this figure depicts the rates of pay that can be allocated to individuals who hold a particular job. To simplify the discussion, each box represents one job. However, each box could be viewed as representing a collection of jobs of similar worth to the organization. Such a collection is known as a pay grade. For example, an individual in entry-level job A can be paid anywhere from $14,000 to $20,000 per year. Rates of pay are similarly shown for individuals in jobs B, C, and D. The rates of pay specified for each job in a pay structure

Figure 5.3
Example of a Pay Structure

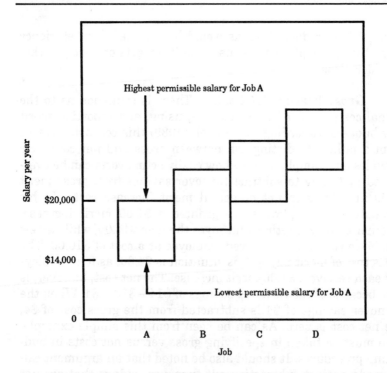

are determined by two procedures known as job evaluation and salary surveys. Both of these procedures are described in detail in Milkovich and Newman (1987).

Job Evaluation. Job evaluation is a procedure undertaken by the organization to determine the worth of jobs to the organization. Some jobs are graded or evaluated higher than other jobs because they have more of certain characteristics believed to be of value to the organization. For example, in Figure 5.3, Job B may be evaluated higher than Job A because more independent judgment is required by the job holder and because the duties of the job are more complex. Jobs evaluated as having greater worth or value have corresponding rates of pay that are, on average, greater. So, for example, in Figure 5.3, the rates of pay for Job B tend to be greater than the rates of pay for Job A. By paying people on the basis of the relative worth of the job, the organization is attempting to create a pay system that is equitable. (See Chapter 2 for a discussion of equity theory.)

Salary Surveys. A salary survey is a procedure used to evaluate the worth of jobs in the marketplace. This procedure helps the organization to establish pay rate levels that are assigned to evaluated jobs. In Figure 5.3, for example, the starting salary for a person in Job A is $14,000 because this is the amount that is being paid as a starting salary in the marketplace for entry-level workers in Job A. Pay rates are made competitive with the market to attract, retain, and maintain a quality work force. To conduct a salary survey, organizations solicit pay data for jobs similar to theirs from other organizations providing similar products or services in similar geographic areas. There is an incentive for organizations to release their pay data to other organizations: They are usually promised a copy of the results of the survey by the organization conducting the survey. In turn, they can use these results to make the rates of pay for their own jobs competitive with the market.

In summary, pay structures establish the rates of pay for employees based on the value of the jobs they hold. The value of a job is established by a job evaluation and salary survey. Pay structures, like budgets, set boundaries, or limits, on merit increases. Merit increases for an individual employee must not exceed the salary parameters for his or her job as defined by the pay structure. Pay structures can be further explained by looking at certain characteristics of the structures. Characteristics that are likely to have an influence on merit pay increases are described in detail below.

Pay Ranges.   It is possible for a pay structure to be more simple than the one in Figure 5.3. In a single-rate structure, for example, there is one rate of pay for each job rather than a range of rates, as shown in Figure 5.3. So, under a single-rate plan, a person in Job A could only receive a particular rate, say $17,000, rather than being assigned a rate somewhere between $14,000 and $20,000. The advantage of paying a single rate is that such a structure is straightforward to communicate and easy to administer. The problem with single rates, however, is that they fail to account for differences among employees in their contribution to the organization. For example, under a single-rate structure, both a well-performing and poor-performing employee in Job A would receive a salary of $17,000 per year. Applying any of the motivational theories discussed in Chapter 2, this arrangement is likely to put a damper on employee motivation.

Because single-rate structures can be problematic, many organizations provide a range of pay levels for people working at a particular job. As in Figure 5.3, a range of pay levels are granted, depending on the individual contribution of the job holder. For example, as in Figure 5.3, an average-performing employee in Job A may receive a salary of $17,000 a year, while an excellent-performing employee may receive $20,000. When a range of rates is used, pay is more clearly linked to performance, which, in turn, should motivate employees.

A more detailed treatment of a specific pay range is shown in Figure 5.4. This figure shows the range of pay for people holding a specific job. For the sake of illustration, the salaries correspond to the range of salaries for Job A in Figure 5.3. Of course, there are also ranges of salaries for Jobs B, C, and D.

A pay range is defined by three values: the minimum, midpoint, and maximum. The *minimum* is the lowest rate paid to a job holder and may correspond to a starting salary for a person with no previous experience. The *maximum* is the largest amount that can be paid to an individual in this job. The maximum

Figure 5.4
Example of a Pay Range

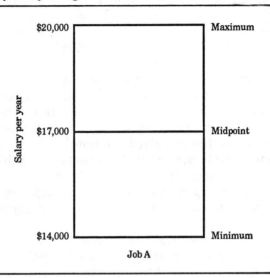

represents the most the job is worth to the organization regardless of the job incumbent. The *midpoint* represents the desired average that the organization wishes to pay for a particular job. The midpoint can, but does not have to be, set at the market average, as identified in a salary survey. An organization may choose to set the midpoint above or below the market average to either lead or lag the competition. The supervisor uses this range of values in deciding how much his or her subordinates are to receive. Allowances can be made for differences in performance levels of employees holding the same job. Typically, more senior and better performing employees are between the midpoint and maximum salaries, and less senior and poor-performing employees are between the midpoint and minimum.

Adjustments are periodically made to pay ranges by organizations. These adjustments are usually in the form of increases to the minimums, midpoints, and maximums. Increases are usually made in response to many factors, including rising costs of goods and services, rising pay levels in the market, increases in the minimum wage required by law, and large numbers of employees reaching the maximum of their pay ranges. Care must be taken by employers in making these adjustments so that employees do not become confused as to why their pay is increasing. If employees do not know whether they received a pay increase for performance or for cost-of-living, for example, they will be unable to make the link between pay and performance. As shown in Chapter 2, merit pay is unlikely to be motivational when pay is not linked to performance. This means that organizations need to carefully communicate to employees on what basis they are receiving additions to their pay. Once again, the perceived relationship between pay and performance is as important as the actual relationship between pay and performance. In short, adjustments in pay level for reasons other than performance should be kept separate from merit increases to manage the perception that pay is linked to performance.

Both the maximum and the spread between the minimum and maximum have implications for merit pay. The maximum obviously sets an upper boundary to the size of the merit increase. An increase cannot be so large as to put an employee's pay over the maximum allowed by policy. The size of the spread between the minimum and maximum may also have an influence on performance levels. Obviously, the greater the spread between the minimum and maximum, the larger the potential spread of salary increases. Kopelman and Reinharth (1982) found in a study of white-collar employees in a large financial institution that the greater the range of salary increases awarded, the better the business unit performance. A survey by the Bureau of Labor Statistics indicates that for white-collar occupations, the most likely occupations to have merit pay plans, the average spread between the minimum and maximum is about 50 percent (Personiak, 1984).

Comparative Salary Ratios. Along with the boundaries of the pay structure, another variable that may influence employees' merit increases is position within the pay range. The position of an employee within the pay range can be defined with a comparative salary ratio, or compa-ratio as it is sometimes called. A compa-ratio is simply the pay level for an employee divided by the midpoint or average pay level desired by the organization for employees in the pay range. An example of the calculation of a compa-ratio is as follows:

Employee ID	Current Salary	Salary Range Midpoint	Compa-ratio
1439	21,000	25,000	.84

It is a common policy in organizations to grant larger merit increases to those with lower compa-ratios. The reason for this policy is to ensure adherence to the desired policy of paying at the budgeted midpoint. Individuals with a compa-ratio greater than one are granted smaller increases to slow down their ascent from the midpoint and to prevent them from exceeding the maximum. Individuals with a compa-ratio less than one are granted larger increases to hasten their progression to the pay midpoint and to prevent them from falling below the minimum. What this means, is that individuals with identical performance ratings may receive different merit increases depending on their position in the pay range. While this type of policy may be desirable from the standpoint of minimizing costs, it may conflict with the goal of motivating subsequent performance. In recognition of this tradeoff, some organizations have implemented lump-sum merit increases, where the merit increase is not permanent, to control costs. The increase is not made contingent upon the compa-ratio so as to motivate performance (Sullivan, 1989).

Locked or Fixed-Step Systems. In some organizations, primarily in the public sector, a fixed or locked-step approach to pay ranges is taken (Van Adelsberg, 1978). What this means is that the progression of employees' pay increases within a pay range is based on a series of steps or defined increments. Under such a plan, each level, or step, of performance corresponds to a particular merit increase amount. Hence, the size of a merit increase is locked or fixed for each level or performance rating. For example, a rating of three might correspond to an increase of five percent. This approach is in contrast to other merit pay plans where a range of pay increases is possible for a particular level of performance rating. For example, a rating of three might correspond to an increase anywhere from four to six percent.

An obvious advantage to a fixed or locked-step system is that it is a simple plan to follow and administer. Allocators are only required to evaluate the level of performance. The increase associated with the level of performance is automatically determined. On the other hand, this approach may be problematic from a motivational standpoint. It may be possible to more accurately match pay and performance when there is a range of values that can be allocated. Also, allocators may be more motivated to use merit pay the more discretion they have in allocating pay increases. Merit pay is an important source of authority for supervisors in managing employee performance. The potential downside to this greater amount of discretion, however, is the possibility of creating inequities in pay increases.

Forced Distributions. To control the amount of money allocated to merit increases, forced distributions are sometimes used for performance ratings. A forced distribution requires that a predetermined percentage of employees be rated at various levels of performance. This forced distribution of performance ratings in turn leads to a forced distribution of merit increases within pay ranges. An example of a forced distribution comes from the merit pay guidelines at Research-Cottrell, Inc., (Smith, O'Dowd, & Christ, 1987) and is shown in Table 5.3. At first glance, the actual frequency with which forced distributions are

Table 5.3
Example of a Forced Distribution at Research-Cottrell, Inc.

Rating	Description	Percent of Employees
5	Clearly outstanding	10
4	Above expectations	45
3	Fully satisfactory	40
2	Needs improvement	5
1	Unsatisfactory	0

Source: Smith et al., "Pay for Performance—One Company's Experience." Reprinted, by permission of the publisher, from *Compensation and Benefits Review,* May/June 1987, © 1987 American Management Association, New York. All rights reserved.

used appears low. Peck (1984) reported that 10 percent of the surveyed organizations formally use forced distributions. However, this figure may be too low. Peck (1984) further reported that an additional 37 percent of the surveyed organizations informally use forced distribution. Bretz and Milkovich (1989) reported that 27 percent of the Fortune 100 used forced distributions for professionals.

Forced distributions seem to be used in response to the positive leniency error (discussed in Chapter 4) found in some organizations. Ratings are sometimes skewed to the positive extreme, which, in turn, creates cost pressures due to the corresponding large number of large merit increases granted (Smith et al., 1986). A further rationale for forced distribution is the argument that true performance is normally distributed along a bell-shaped curve. Hence, actual ratings should be normally distributed to capture true performance.

These arguments for the practice of forced distributions have met some conceptual and empirical counterarguments that question even the informal use of forced distributions. Mohrman et al. (1989) pointed out that the assumption of performance being normally distributed only holds for a large population of employees. In most merit pay situations, allocators are dealing with a small number of employees. Moreover, these employees have been influenced by other human resource interventions (e.g., selection and training), which may skew true as well as actual performance in a positive (or negative) direction. McBriarty (1988) presented an interesting case study on the use of forced distributions in the U.S. Air Force. Based on the results of some 200 interviews with participants in this system, McBriarty concluded that the system led to decreased motivation as well as increased turnover, competition among subordinates, and conflict between subordinates and supervisors.

Overall, it is recommended that forced distributions not be used. However, although problematic, the goal of cost minimization may drive some employers to use forced distributions. If a forced distribution is necessary, the guidelines set forth by Mohrman et al. (1989) may be reasonable. A forced distribution should only be used when absolute rather than relative ratings are used, when work groups are at least 50 members in size, and when only a few categories are "forced" on the allocator with the bulk of employees being rated in the middle category.

Range Penetration. In addition to *current* position within the pay range, the desired *future* position within the pay range can also be considered. It is possible to provide allocators with mathematical formulas showing the recipient's position in the pay range over time (Basnight, 1980; Moran, 1986; Seithal & Emans, 1983; Stokes, 1981). Position in range is predicted on the basis of various assumptions regarding expected performance levels, range widths, and changes in the pay structure, among other things. These formulas can be used to ensure that an actual merit increase in one year will *not* lead to an employee exceeding the maximum in future years. Also, the formulas can be used to develop merit pay guidelines so that certain combinations of merit increases over time do not exceed the maximum.

This process of basing merit increases on anticipated range penetration as well as actual performance makes some sense from a cost containment perspective. It is most likely to be used when organizations have limited promotion opportunities and want to ensure that adequate performers receive a pay increase each year. From a motivational perspective, however, it seems to be a less effective procedure. As discussed in Chapter 2, when pay is *not* contingent on performance, it is unlikely to motivate future performance.

Guidecharts

A summary statement of organizational policy regarding merit pay is sometimes known as a merit pay guidechart. A guidechart details the amount and timing of merit increases for various levels of performance at various locations in the pay grade. In a sense, a merit pay guidechart is an operational statement of an organization's pay-for-performance theory or policy. It spells out the contingency between pay and performance in specific terms.

Merit pay guidecharts range from the simple to the complex, depending on the number of variables on which pay is made contingent. A simple merit pay guidechart is shown in Table 5.4 in which pay is made contingent solely on performance; the better the performance, the larger the increase. According to reinforcement theory (see Chapter 2), such a policy is likely to motivate improved performance. Also, this policy is consistent with the theme of doing more with less. It is less expensive to give large increases to good performers and no increases to poor performers than it is to give large increases to

Table 5.4
Simple Merit Guidechart

	Performance Rating			
Unsatisfactory	Needs Improvement	Fully Satisfactory	Above Expectations	Clearly Outstanding
(1)	(2)	(3)	(4)	(5)
0%	2%	7%	8%	9%

both good and poor performers. Merit is usually in the form of a percentage increase in base salary rather than in the form of an absolute increase, for purposes of equity. If an absolute increase amount had been used in Table 5.4, then the percentage increase for high salary employees would have been less than the percentage increase for low salary employees, even though the performance levels of high and low salary employees were the same. Under this absolute increase scenario, employees probably would perceive inequity. (See chapter 2 for a review of equity theory.)

It should also be noted, in Table 5.4, that to emphasize the importance of good performance, anything less than adequate performance is usually given a zero percent increase. In some organizations, a nominal increase instead of no increase may be granted, to retain employees. This practice of giving a nominal increase to poor performers is a curious one, because it appears that the organization wants to retain rather than lose poor performers! Although negative increases or reductions in salary have been advocated (e.g., Silverman, 1981) for less than adequate performers, this seldom seems to be done in practice.

A more complex guidechart is shown in Table 5.5. It is more complex in three ways. First, a range of merit increases is offered rather than a single value for each level of performance. This is done to more closely link pay to performance and to give allocators more discretion in the process. Note also that the salary increase ranges do not overlap, to prevent perceptions of inequity. Second, increases depend upon position in the pay range as well as performance. Employees in higher quartiles receive smaller increases than employees in lower quartiles to prevent those in higher quartiles from exceeding the maximum. Third, the timing of increases varies. Better performers are rewarded more frequently than are poorer performers.

Table 5.5
Complex Merit Guidechart

Position in Range	Performance Rating				
	Unsatisfactory (1)	Needs Improvement (2)	Fully Satisfactory (3)	Above Expectations (4)	Clearly Outstanding (5)
4th Quartile	0%	0%	3–5% 15–18 months	5–7% 12–15 months	7–9% 9–12 months
3rd Quartile	0%	0–3% 15–18 months	5–7% 12–15 months	7–9% 9–12 months	9–11% 9–12 months
2nd Quartile	0%	0–3% 12–15 months	7–9% 9–12 months	9–11% 9–12 months	11–13% 6–9 months
1st Quartile	0%	0–5% 9–12 months	9–11% 9–12 months	11–13% 6–9 months	13–15% 6–9 months

A different task confronted by the millions of managers who are required to use complex guidecharts is deciding the specific percentage increase to grant to subordinates when a range of values is possible. For example, using Table 5.5, if a manager has a fully satisfactory performing subordinate in the second quartile of the pay range, the manager can grant that subordinate a seven to nine percent merit increase. Which increase to give—seven, eight, nine percent, or some value in between—is a tough decision.

It seems likely that when managers need to make decisions at the margin, they look at some of the controversial measures of performance described in Chapter 4. That is, they look at factors like seniority, promotability, and market value. For example, a manager may be more likely to grant a nine percent instead of a seven percent increase when the fully satisfactory employee has been on the job a short period of time, is seen as being promotable, and has talents that are in demand in the labor market. Factors such as these should be considered on the margin when they are related to the business mission of the organization, are clearly communicated to employees, and do not violate the laws and regulations discussed in Chapter 6.

There is almost no research on employees reactions to merit guidecharts. In one study in a transit agency by Hills, Scott, and Markham (1988), all people paid on the basis of guidecharts were satisfied with their pay except for those in the highest quartile with the lowest performance ratings. You would also expect to find that reactions to guidecharts would depend on social comparisons made. In two studies, it has been shown that reactions to pay vary according to the selection of comparison other (H. Heneman, Schwab, Standal, & Peterson, 1979; Scholl, Cooper, & McKenna, 1987). It might, therefore, be expected that reactions to guidecharts depend upon the comparisons employees make between the guidechart they operate under and the guidecharts that the comparison others they have selected are believed work under. For example, a seven percent increase for excellent performance may be upsetting in the absence of information about merit increases in other organizations. The same seven percent increase may lead to being pleased rather than upset when it is known that in other similar organizations a four percent increase is granted for excellent performance.

Allocator Selection

A final policy issue that arises is who should be making merit increase decisions? In the majority of cases, the individual allocating merit increases is the recipient's immediate supervisor, who makes the decision in conjunction with the business unit head and personnel manager (Wyatt Company, 1987). This most-often followed policy makes sense in that performance information is available through the immediate supervisor, as discussed in Chapter 4. Budget information is perhaps best known by the business unit head, and the personnel manager can ensure consistency across business units. This approach is consistent with the traditional model of management in which managers are responsible for the performance of their subordinates and are given discretion within limits to manage their subordinates.

As traditional models of management change, however, so too may those involved in merit allocation decisions. An example is work settings where individuals perform in a more autonomous fashion with less immediate supervision. In these situations, organizations may have to draw upon allocators other than immediate supervisors. These could include peer nominations for merit increases in public school systems, team leaders as allocators in matrix organizations, host-company supervisors as allocators for outside consultants, managing partners as allocators in law and accounting firms, and ratings of behaviors rather than results for CEOs by their board of directors. Changes in the nature of work are having an impact on traditional merit pay systems (Gabor, 1989).

Implementing a Merit Pay Policy

It is unlikely that a well-designed merit pay policy will lead to desired outcomes, such as improved performance, in and of itself. In other words, a well-designed policy is a necessary but not sufficient condition for a merit pay plan to work (R. Heneman, 1984b). Attention must also be given to factors that facilitate the introduction and implementation of a merit pay plan. Although there is not much research on factors that facilitate this process, several factors based on theory and case study reports are presented here. These factors that facilitate the implementation of a merit pay plan include the timing of plan introduction, upper level support, participation in plan development, and employee trust.

Timing of Plan Introduction

A merit pay plan can be introduced in two ways: either as a lead or a lag system (Lawler, 1981). What this means is that a merit plan can be used either to bring about a change in the organization (lead system) or to reinforce other changes being made in the organization (lag system). There could, of course, be parallel change, where merit pay is introduced at the same time as another change in the organization. As pointed out by Lawler (1981), such an attempt is likely to produce chaos because of the drain on organizational resources and the difficulty of meshing the two changes. A good example of these difficulties is pointed out by two reports that examined the simultaneous implementation of both a new performance appraisal system and merit pay system in the federal government (R. Heneman, 1990; U.S. Congress, 1981).

Merit Pay as a Lag System. Under many circumstances, it would seem that merit pay should be introduced as a lag system. As described in Chapter 2, merit pay possesses strong motivational properties, which can be used to reinforce desired changes in the organization. Reports by Patten (1976) and the Florida Power Corporation (1985) show how merit pay can be used to reinforce a desired change. Patten shows how merit pay was used to support the introduction of an MBO program for sales personnel. This method of management was reinforced by merit increases that were made contingent on the successful completion of agreed-upon objectives established by the employee and his or her supervisor. At Florida Power Corporation, merit pay was used to reinforce behaviors back on the job that employees learned in a new management development program. Successfully completing learning objectives from the development seminar back on the job was coupled with a merit increase.

Given the motivational properties of merit pay, it might seem that merit pay should be used solely as a lag system. This does not, however, seem to be the case. It merit pay is introduced following the implementation of another program with perceived negative properties, merit pay may be viewed or used in a negative fashion as well. Pagano (1985) reported on employees' reactions to a merit pay plan introduced after a reduction in force in a

U.S. government agency. Rather than using merit pay for its intended purpose (i.e., rewarding past performance to motivate future performance), merit pay was used instead to retain staff members from a reduction in force. In short, merit pay, as a lag system, can be a very powerful intervention in organizations. Therefore, care must be exercised to ensure that it is used to reinforce desirable rather than undesirable behaviors.

Merit Pay as a Lead System. Merit pay can also be used as a lead system with the intent of bringing about a change in the organization, rather than simply reinforcing some other change that has been implemented. One advantage to introducing merit pay as a lead system is that it shows the organization is committed to meaningful change (Lawler, 1981). A merit pay system may show employees that the organization is serious about change because resources are being devoted to change. This situation can be contrasted with one where resources are not devoted to change, and employees therefore view any change as merely cosmetic.

A good example of merit pay as a lead system comes from the Evanston, Illinois school district (Cohen & Murnane, 1980). Merit pay was introduced as a lead system to demonstrate the school district's commitment to improved performance in the classroom. Comments by Evanston school teachers indicated that merit pay as a lead system did result in more teacher commitment to quality education. However, it did not necessarily result in improved teaching performance. Many teachers viewed merit awards as a vote of confidence by the community for quality education rather than viewing these awards as an incentive to improve teacher performance.

The Evanston example indicates that merit pay as a lead system may not always produce the intended results. To achieve the intended results, those managing the merit process must carefully monitor users' reactions. Also, as pointed out by Lawler (1981), for a merit pay plan to work as a lead system, there often needs to be dissatisfaction with current conditions in the organization. If dissatisfaction is not present, employees may not be receptive to a change in the pay system.

Upper Level Support
Another factor that may contribute to the successful implementation of a merit pay plan is upper level support in the organiza-

tion. Upper level support can consist of at least three features. The first feature is the linking of the merit pay plan to the strategic mission of the organization. By tying these two systems together, the message is communicated that merit pay is an integral component of the business mission of the organization rather than a tangential system. An example of this feature can be observed at Pratt and Whitney (Schneier, 1989). Here, the performance standards on which merit increases are based are tied explicitly to the business goals of the organization.

A second feature that may demonstrate upper level support is endorsement of the plan by the top decision makers in the organization. This is one of several factors attributed to the success of merit pay for managers in New York City (Allan & Rosenberg, 1986). Perhaps the best way for upper level decision makers to demonstrate support is to participate in the process. That is, if merit pay is to be used, it should apply to all levels of the organization, not just to the lower levels. This participative approach is one of the reasons given for the successful implementation of a merit pay plan at Pratt and Whitney (Schneier, 1989a). The reason this support is vital to the successful implementation of a merit pay plan is that it communicates the importance of performance for employees at all levels of the organization.

A third feature is the use of performance-contingent rewards as a method of leadership by upper levels of the organization (Hinkin, Podsakoff, & Schriesheim, 1987). What this entails is making sure that not only are rewards based on merit for upper level managers, but that upper level managers apply this same philosophy to their subordinates. Pay as well as other nonmonetary rewards, such as recognition, need to be made contingent upon successful performance. A merit pay plan should be more acceptable to employees when *all* rewards are made contingent upon performance for *all* employees than when merit pay is the *only* reward contingent on performance and when this contingency applies to only *some* employees.

Participation in Plan Development

Both theory and research seem to indicate that the successful implementation of a merit pay plan involves participation in the development of the pay plan by the parties who will be affected. Drawing upon motivational theory, Lawler (1981) suggested that participating in the development of a merit pay plan leads to the strengthening of pay-for-performance perceptions. The reasons for this strengthening of the pay-for-performance relationship is that, by participating in the development of a merit pay plan, employees have more knowledge about the plan, are more committed to the plan, feel that they have some control over the plan, and trust the system (Lawler, 1981). A proposed model of participation is shown in Figure 5.5.

Support for this model comes from two very interesting studies conducted with custodial workers by Lawler and his colleagues (Lawler & Hackman, 1969; Schefflen, Lawler, & Hackman, 1971). In the first study, comparisons were made among workers who developed their own bonus plan for good attendance, workers who received a bonus for good attendance based on a plan imposed by management, and workers who did not

Figure 5.5
The Effects of Participation on Perceptions of Pay

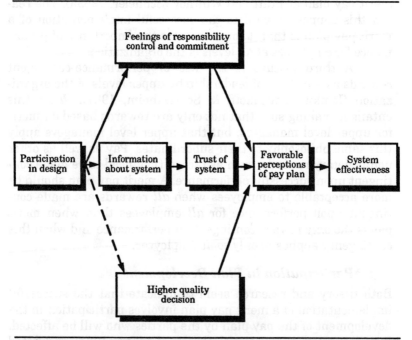

Source: From Lawler (1981), *Pay and Organization Development,* © 1981 Addison-Wesley Publishing Co., Inc., Figure 4.1. Reprinted with permission.

receive a bonus for good attendance. A significant improvement in attendance only occurred for the group that participated in developing the bonus plan. In the second study, it was shown that this improved attendance record was carried over into the next year even for custodians in the group that did not develop the original plan. These positive results were attributed by the authors to the increased commitment, knowledge, and trust of employees who participated in the development of the bonus plan. These are the variables shown in Figure 5.5 to explain the favorable effects of participation in pay plan development.

Three empirical studies also provide support for participation in the implementation of merit pay plans. One of the studies was conducted in a small manufacturing plant in Ohio (Jenkins & Lawler, 1981; Lawler, 1981). In this study, attitudes and behaviors were compared before and after implementation of the merit pay plan. After participative implementation of the plan, there were significant improvements in turnover, job satisfaction, and pay satisfaction. A second study was conducted in a public utility company (Bullock, 1983). Again, reactions were measured before and after the plan was implemented. The results indicated that participation in the development of the plan led to strengthened pay-for-performance perceptions, commitment, and job satisfaction. Pay satisfaction was not, however, increased. A third study was conducted in the city government of Biloxi, Mississippi (Gabris & Mitchell, 1988; Gabris, Mitchell, & McLemore, 1985). Pay fairness was measured only after the implementation of the plan, and it was found that while the high performers believed the system was fair, low performers were less inclined to believe the plan was fair.

All three of these studies provide some support for participation in the implementation of merit pay plans. Some confidence can be placed in the generalizability of these findings, as the studies took place in very diverse settings. On the other hand, some caution should be exercised in the interpretation of these findings as there were no control groups. (See Chapter 7 for a discussion of the importance of control groups.) Without a control group, it is difficult to know if the observed changes were due to participation or some other factor.

The form that participation took in the three studies was very similar. A committee, council, or task force was established in each location. These task forces were composed of members from a representative sample of the work force. Also, these task forces consisted of both employee and management representatives. In all three cases, the groups developed the actual merit pay plan that was used. From the reported characteristics of these groups, it seems that, for a merit pay plan to be successfully implemented, all of the parties who will be affected by the plan must have a voice in its development through a chosen representative.

While participation can have some very desirable results it will not work in all situations. This was pointed out to me recently in a project that I was involved in with a Japanese parts manufacturer in the United States. The Japanese managers in this organization felt that participation is appropriate when it comes to technical matters, such as how parts are produced. They did not, however, feel that participation is appropriate in managerial decisions concerning how performance is measured, evaluated, and rewarded. Once again, as noted in Chapter 4, participation may or may not be acceptable to the affected parties. This issue clearly needs to be addressed in the administration of merit pay plans.

Employee Trust

A very difficult-to-define, but apparently important concept in the implementation of merit pay plans is employee trust (Lawler, 1971; Patten, 1976). Trust, as it relates to merit pay, seems to refer to a belief that management has developed and adheres to a fair set of performance standards used to grant merit increases. A recent study by Vest, Hills, and Scott (1989) demonstrated the importance of trust. A significant positive relationship between trust and pay-for-performance perceptions was reported for a sample of employees in a transit authority. The more trust, the stronger the belief that pay was related to performance.

The importance of developing an agreed-upon and adhered to set of performance standards for merit increases also comes from a recent report about merit pay practices at the Dayton-Hudson Corporation (Schwadel, 1990). According to this news report, sales personnel were disgruntled with the performance standards as well as other facets of the merit pay plan. For example, the longer the time on the job, the higher the sales quotas under the plan. If the quotas were not attained, employees were fired. You would expect employee trust to be low in a situation where the better you perform, the more likely you are to lose your job!

Trust also has to do with participation in pay plan development and the degree to which merit decisions are kept confidential. (See the discussion of pay secrecy in Chapter 6.) Some organizations encourage employee participation in the setting of performance standards but limit employee access to salary information. Employees will question the motives of management when they are asked to develop standards that will influence the size of their pay increase, but are not allowed to know how their performance actually influenced the size of their pay increase. If participation is used, then there must be some openness concerning how merit increase decisions are reached.

Summary of Major Points

1. *Just-Noticeable Differences.* Merit increases do not automatically influence subsequent employee performance. For a merit increase to influence subsequent performance, it must be large enough in magnitude to create a just noticeable difference to the employee.

2. *Size of Merit Increases.* There is no ideal size for a merit increase. The size of the increase likely to create a JND depends on the characteristics of the person and situation, including the job, performance, and earnings level.

3. *Lump-Sum Merit Increases.* Under a lump-sum merit pay plan, a merit increase is not rolled over into the base salary of the employee. Instead, the merit increase is a one-time award. Although not well researched, a lump-sum plan seems to be less costly to the organization and more likely to tie pay to performance over the long term.

4. *Common Review Date.* In recent times, some organizations have made a practice of reviewing merit increases for all employees on a common date. This practice seems to lessen the paperwork burden, but may impose time pressures on the allocator and cost pressures on the organization.

5. *Merit Pay Budgets.* Establishing merit increases depends, in part, on the budget for merit pay. The most common practice, allocating merit pay budgets as a uniform percentage of payroll, appears to be problematic as attention is not given to differences in business unit performance. Flexible budgeting procedures, such as top-down and bottom-up procedures that recognize differences in subunit performance, should be used more often.

6. *Pay-Structure Considerations.* Establishing merit pay increases also depends on characteristics of the pay structure. To control costs and keep employees within the existing pay structures, organizations sometimes give consideration to rate ranges, maximums, comparative salary ratios, forced distributions, and range penetration in determining merit increases. These other considerations may, however, detract from the purpose of merit pay, which is to motivate subsequent performance.

7. *Guidecharts.* A guidechart is the formal policy statement issued by an organization regarding merit pay. A guidechart details the amount and timing of merit increases for various levels of performance at various locations in the pay range.

8. *Policy Versus Implementation.* A well-developed merit pay policy is important. Although necessary, it is not a sufficient condition for a merit pay plan to lead to desired outcomes, such as improved performance. For a merit pay plan to contribute to desired outcomes, management must also focus on the implementation of the plan.

9. *Implementation Steps.* Considering the results of a number of case studies, it seems that merit pay plans are more successful when the plan is not implemented simultaneously with other large-scale organizational changes. There also needs to be upper level support for the merit pay plan, employee participation in the development of the plan (all those affected), and employee trust in the standards that are used to determine merit increases.

Conclusions

As noted in the first chapter, merit pay is an attempt by organizations to get more for less. The goal is to get more performance for less money. To do so, attention must be paid to both motivational and financial considerations. Motivational considerations help us guide reward systems toward greater performance. Financial considerations help us minimize the costs associated with reward systems. Attention must be given to *both* motivational and financial considerations because the goals of improved performance may conflict with the goals of minimizing costs. Too often, it seems attention is given to one but not to the other. As a result, merit pay plans are developed that are likely to motivate improved performance, but are too costly to implement. Also, merit plans are developed that cost very little to implement, but are unlikely to motivate improved performance. In either event, when motivation and finances are considered independent of one another, a merit pay plan is unlikely to produce desired results.

In developing a merit pay plan, attention must be given to both the creation and implementation of a policy or intended statement about the relationship between performance ratings and pay increases. One promising development in merit pay policy is the creation of lump-sum merit plans. Compared to more traditional merit pay plans, lump-sum plans seem to strike a better balance between the goals of performance maximization and cost minimization. Under a lump-sum plan, pay increases are not permanently rolled over into base salary as is done in traditional merit pay plans. Hence, pay is "earned as you go" rather than granted for the duration of your entire career—on the basis of performance in one rating period.

This promising feature does *not* mean that organizations should rush into using a lump-sum plan. Organizations with preexisting, traditional merit pay plans need to exercise extreme caution in shifting to a lump-sum plan. The shift to a lump-sum plan may clash with the culture of the organization. For example, as a result of years of experience with a traditional merit plan, employees may believe they are entitled to an annual merit increase that rolls over into their base salary. A rapid shift to a lump-sum plan may shatter beliefs and lead to disruptive work behaviors.

Even organizations implementing a merit pay plan for the first time need to proceed slowly with lump-sum arrangements. When a lump-sum plan is implemented, the initial reactions of employees may be favorable. Who wouldn't be pleased with the possibility of a large cash bonus at the end of the year? However, these favorable reactions may not last very long when employees find that their monthly paychecks do not keep their incomes at acceptable levels, or when they find that their neighbors keep merit increases as a permanent addition to their salaries. A lump-sum plan simply will not work if it is used as a substitute for a well-developed total compensation system that provides adequate levels of income in the form of salaries, incentives, and benefits.

As with lump-sum plans, a note of caution should be added vis-a-vis employee participation in merit plan development. Two warnings are warranted. First, participation requires a certain level of expertise. For example, a merit pay plan must be integrated with other components of a total compensation system, such as salaries and benefits. This integration requires knowledge of pay systems. As a result, a leader knowledgeable in compensation matters should facilitate the participatory process, and employees involved in the development of merit pay plans should receive training in compensation matters.

A major factor in the successful implementation of merit pay plans is employee participation. Participation in the implementation of merit pay plans is *in addition* to the participation that is recommended in the development of performance standards (see Chapter 4). Employee participation in the implementation of merit pay plans has both theoretical and empirical support. Research shows that participation works well when a task force of elected employees is used in an advisory capacity to help implement a merit pay plan. Such participation is likely to foster more favorable attitudes toward merit pay and commitment to the merit pay plan.

Second, participation requires a willingness to become involved in the development of a merit pay plan. Some employees may not see participation as desirable. While these employees may want to share in merit pay increases, they may not want to participate in determining the procedures to be used to link pay to performance. As a result, participation in merit pay plan development should be voluntary.

6

Merit Pay Administration

Over the years, several authors have called attention to the importance of the administration of merit pay plans (Hamner, 1975; Berger & Schwab, 1980; R. Heneman, 1984b). Some merit pay plans are not very effective, even though they are eloquently designed, because they are poorly administered. In this chapter, attention is given to issues that must be considered to properly administer a merit pay plan. These issues center around what the organization does or can do to ensure that the merit pay policy is actually carried out as intended in practice.

Procedural Justice

An important new area of investigation for organizational researchers is known as procedural justice. This concept refers to the perceived fairness of decisions made about employees in organizations. It will be shown in this section that procedural justice has important implications for merit pay administration.

Theory

Greenberg (1986, 1987a, 1987b) made an important distinction, for purposes of merit pay administration, between distributive and procedural justice. Distributive justice, as it relates to merit pay, refers to the perceived fairness of merit increases allocated. That is, distributive justice focuses on the perceived fairness of the amount allocated for various performance inputs. Procedural justice, on the other hand, refers to the perceived fairness of the procedures used to determine merit increases. That is, procedural justice looks at the procedures organizations undertake to ensure a link between pay and performance.

Much of what has been covered in the book thus far relates primarily to distributive rather than procedural justice. For example, Chapter 5 discusses setting policy on the amount to be allocated in merit increase decisions. Greenberg's distinction suggests that attention should also be given to issues related to procedural justice.

Importance

Two surveys illustrate the importance of procedural justice to merit pay. First, Hyde (1988) found, for a large sample of federal managers, that while 90 percent were in favor of pay for performance, 74 percent of these managers felt that the present merit pay system was unfair. Second, Bretz and Milkovich (1989) reported that, for a study of Fortune 100 companies, the most important issues organizations faced regarding their performance appraisal systems were issues of fairness in how the systems were used. Both these studies suggest that concern is as likely or more likely to be expressed over procedural as over distributive justice issues.

Rules

Based on the work of Leventhal et al. (1976), Miceli and Lane (1990) provide an excellent summary of rules to follow to attain perceptions of procedural justice. These rules and their potential applications to merit pay are shown in Table 6.1.

Research

Several empirical studies have been conducted that give further insight into the issues of procedural justice as they relate to performance appraisal and compensation in general, and to merit pay in particular. Each of these studies will be briefly reviewed. The studies provide some general support for the rules shown in Table 6.1. Also, these studies are suggestive of additional rules that might enhance perceptions of procedural justice.

Greenberg (1986) looked at the determinants of perceived fairness of performance evaluations. He asked mid-level managers, by way of an open-ended questionnaire, to describe determinants of fair or unfair appraisals. He found that several of the determinants related to procedural justice. These determinants

Table 6.1
Procedural Justice Rules Applied to Merit Pay

Rule	Description	Application
Consistency	Procedures for allocation should be consistent across persons and over time.	Reliable and valid measures of performance are used to make merit decisions.
Bias Suppression	Bias should be suppressed.	Rater training is provided to eliminate rating errors.
Accuracy	Decisions must be based on accurate information.	Allocators are held accountable for their decisions.
Correctability	Decisions should be correctable.	Merit pay decisions can be appealed.
Representation	The allocation process must represent the concerns of all recipients.	Employee participation takes place in the development of a merit pay plan.
Ethics	Participants should comply with ethical standards.	Laws and regulations are followed.

Source: Leventhal, Karuza, & Fry (1980); Miceli & Lane (1991). Reprinted with permission.

were: soliciting input prior to evaluation and using it, engaging in two-way communication during the appraisal interview, providing the opportunity to challenge or rebut the evaluation, the rater being familiar with the ratee's work, and consistently applying performance standards. These factors seem very consistent with the rules in Table 6.1.

Folger and Konovsky (1989) examined distributive and procedural justice as they relate to pay decisions for employees in a manufacturing plant. They found that procedural justice could be summarized in terms of how feedback was presented to the employee, the planning of the performance and salary increase review, recourse available to the employee in response to appraisal, and frequency of performance observation by the supervisor. These procedural factors were more strongly related to organizational commitment than were measures of distributive justice. Although related to pay satisfaction, procedural justice items were not as strongly related to pay satisfaction as were perceptions of distributive justice. An important implication of this study is that organizations and individuals can and should take a proactive stance toward procedural justice. This is reflected in the results of Folger and Konovsky (1989) for the planning aspect of procedural justice, and is consistent with Greenberg's (1987a) observation that procedural justice can vary from reactive to proactive.

In a study of managers, Dyer and Theriault (1976) looked at the perceived adequacy of pay system administration. The results indicated that the perceived adequacy of pay system administration provided an explanation of pay satisfaction above and beyond the explanation offered by characteristics of the job and person alone. The perceived adequacy of pay system administration appears to be very closely related to the concept of procedural justice. It is defined by employee understanding of the pay criteria, superiors' influence over pay decisions, superiors' accuracy in work assessments, and the congruence between the employee and superiors' preferences for pay criteria. Subsequent studies of the perceived adequacy of pay system administration have also shown this concept to be related to pay satisfaction (Weiner, 1980; Miceli & Near, 1988). One interesting aspect of this concept is that it requires the clear communication of rules and procedures of the merit pay system. To do so, training seems appropriate for both allocators and recipients of merit pay.

In addition to providing some support for the perceived adequacy of pay system administration, Miceli and Near (1988) also formulated and tested another variable believed to be a part of the procedural justice concept. This variable was the perceived adequacy of merit funding. As expected, this variable was positively related to pay satisfaction for executives in the sample. Unexpectedly, this variable was negatively related to pay satisfaction for middle managers in the sample. Hence, there was some support for the perceived adequacy of merit funding. The reason why adequacy of merit funding may be related to pay satisfaction is because employees are more likely to be satisfied when they believe that the merit budget is large enough to reward all employees deserving of a merit increase (Miceli & Lane, 1990; Miceli & Near, 1988).

The most recent study on procedural justice and merit pay was conducted by Mulvey (1991). He examined the reactions of employees to pay outcomes and procedures in eight midwest service organizations with merit pay plans. In particular, he looked at the extent to which satisfaction with pay depends on procedural justice. His findings indicated that pay satisfaction is likely to be higher when employees believe they have the opportunity to appeal and modify pay decisions, and when pay decisions are clearly communicated and justified to employees.

Although there has only been a limited amount of research conducted on procedural justice as it relates to merit pay, it does have promise as a very fruitful area for future inquiry (R. Heneman, 1990). The research to date has been supportive of the theory, which has important implications for the administration of merit pay as shown in Table 6.1. It should be noted, however, that the research has primarily been descriptive and has related procedural justice to attitudes such as pay satisfaction. Additional well-designed studies that relate procedural justice to behaviors such as performance are needed. This is an area of merit pay research to monitor closely in the future.

Appeals Procedure

The importance of setting up an appeals procedure for employees who have a concern about their merit increase is clearly shown by the correctability rule in Table 6.1. The correctability rule suggests that for there to be perceptions of procedural justice, merit decisions must be correctable if needed. An appeals procedure can be instituted to determine if corrections are needed and how to go about making them.

Having an appeals procedure for performance appraisal review appears to be a common practice. Two national surveys (Bretz & Milkovich, 1989; Bureau of National Affairs, 1983) showed that about 55 percent of U.S. organizations have an informal procedure, about 30 percent have a formal procedure, and only about 15 percent have no procedure. As noted by Bretz and Milkovich (1989), this is an area where practice appears to be ahead of the research.

The extent to which merit increase decisions are appealed is not known. As noted by Perry and Pearce (1985) in their evaluation of the federal government's experience with merit pay, an appeals system for performance appraisal does not guarantee the adequate resolution of concerns over merit increase decisions. Merit increases do not necessarily correspond to performance ratings even when an appeals procedure is in place. As an example, Perry and Pearce (1985) reported that in some federal agencies the payroll system, which is on computer, had to be reprogrammed to ensure that unsatisfactory performers did not receive merit increases!

This discussion of the federal government's experience with merit pay suggests that an appeals procedure is needed for merit pay as well as for performance appraisal decisions. Folger and Konovsky (1989) generated a list of characteristics, based on the procedural justice literature, which seem to be desirable features of an appeals procedure for merit pay decisions. Moreover, these features were found by the authors to be positively related to pay satisfaction, organizational commitment, and trust in supervision. These characteristics are listed in Figure 6.1.

Merit Pay Communications

Another issue of importance in the administration of merit pay is the communication of merit pay information. Marriott (1962) reported that one of the biggest complaints about merit pay by factory employees was the "lack of information and understanding" about merit pay. This lack of understanding may in turn diminish perceptions of procedural justice (Dyer & Theriault,

Figure 6.1

*Desirable Characteristics of an Appeals Procedure
for Merit Pay Decisions*

---

1. Can find out why you got the size of raise you did.
2. Can make an appeal about the size of a raise.
3. Can express your feelings to your supervisor about your salary decision.
4. Can discuss with your supervisor how your performance was evaluated.
5. Can develop with your supervisor an action plan for future performance.

Source: Folger & Konovsky (1989). Reprinted with permission.

1976; Miceli & Lane, 1990; Miceli & Near, 1988). It also may diminish employee motivation, as there may be misunderstandings concerning pay and performance links (Stiglitz, 1987). From the perspective of expectancy theory (see Chapter 2 for a review), instrumentality perceptions are likely to be strengthened when the link between pay and performance is clearly communicated.

Some of the realities associated with communicating merit pay decisions are shown in Figure 6.2. As can be seen from the advice offered by Scheele (1991) to employees on how to get a merit increase, employees are not always passive recipients of merit increases once a year. They may, from time to time, ask or even demand a merit increase. Employees are proactive and, at a minimum, want to know why they did or did not receive a certain merit increase. Given the importance of merit pay communications, a number of issues that bear on this topic are covered here, including interactional justice, perceived accuracy of performance feedback, pay secrecy, split systems versus combined reviews, and the communication medium.

Interactional Justice

A recent paper by Greenberg and McCarty (1990) reviewed the concept of interactional justice as it relates to pay. Interactional justice is the perceived fairness in the way in which pay is communicated. Based on the social psychology literature, it seems

Figure 6.2
How to Get the Raise You Want

HOW TO GET
THE RAISE YOU WANT
(no matter what the boss says at first)

You're about to ask your boss for a 15 percent raise. The two of you have a good rapport, but the company is facing a tight economy, and getting this kind of increase is going to be tough.

Prepare two charts. The first should outline whatever improvements you've made while on the job: money you've saved, training procedures you've instituted, and so forth. The second compares your responsibilities with those of your peers in the firm. Now you are ready to state your case assertively.

YOU It's time for my salary review, and this year I feel comfortable asking for a substantial increase. The specific number I have in mind is 15 percent.

BOSS Whoa! You know there's no way I can give you a raise like that at this point.

YOU Why not?

BOSS Quite simply, your work load doesn't warrant that dramatic an increase.

YOU Why not?

BOSS You're certainly worth it, but you know there's a ceiling on raises.

YOU What? You gave Bob a raise, and his work isn't any better than mine!

BOSS What Bob makes is irrelevant. I've said everything I have to say on the matter. Thank you.

GRADE: F. It's tough to stay cool in an unfair situation, but getting angry gets you nowhere in negotiations.

YOU Really? Let me give you my perspective on why I think it does. [You now cover the material you've prepared.]
I believe I'm at least twice as valuable to the firm as when I arrived three years ago, but I'm only asking for a 15 percent raise. Let's talk about this again next week, OK?

GRADE: A. Forceful, yet not confrontational. If you're well prepared, you won't let your boss's diversionary tactic throw you. Give him enough time to think it over, but be specific about when you'll check back.

YOU I'm surprised. What makes you say that?

GRADE: C. The response is nonthreatening but will inevitably lead the conversation astray as you battle a barrage of complaints, accusations and criticisms.

YOU Yes, I know that, but I have a good basis for asking for this increase. The company's lean operations have made my position more demanding than ever, and I've met those demands. I think you'll see from my list I have here of the efficiencies I've instituted that I've saved the company a substantial amount of money.

GRADE: C+. Demonstrating money saved is a sound strategy, but only if backed up by a strong close: a reiteration of the request for a specific dollar figure.

BOSS If I give you *that* kind of increase, it will use up my entire budget for departmental raises.

YOU Yes, I know that. So can I have your promise that when the firm is in better shape, I'll be the first to get a raise?

BOSS Sure, no problem. You'll be at the front of the line. I'll get back to you when the time comes.

GRADE: C. You've given your boss an easy out, and he's taken it. By not setting a time frame for action, you've let him off the hook-possibly forever.

YOU Well, how about reconsidering the raise question in three months then, and in the meantime coming up with some things that don't count as salary? Lots of our clients belong to the Nirvana Club-how about picking up my membership there? Or what about my car and parking fees?

BOSS That stuff costs us money, too, you know. And besides, it will upset everyone else if you get special privileges.

YOU What I'm asking for is reasonable. It's just an alternative form of compensation. And, of course, I would treat it confidentially. I want to stay here, but I need to know my accomplishments are recognized.

GRADE: B. This is a good fallback position. Just don't resort to it unless you are sure that your initial request for a cash raise is futile.

BOSS I understand what you're saying, and I agree you deserve something now. Let me see what I can do about getting your dues paid at the club. And I'll look into a car allowance.

YOU Thanks. OK if I check back with you on this next week?

YOU Not necessarily. I've thought of a way for us both to win. How about if I postpone my 15 percent raise for now if I can get 20 percent when the ceiling is removed in a few months? In the meantime, acknowledge my work with a token that doesn't count as salary. Let me have a one-time bonus of $4,000. That seems fair under the circumstances, doesn't it?

GRADE: A. You've made it clear by making a concession that you're willing to be a team player, but you've also stood by your demand for what you're worth-now or later.

BOSS OK, let me think it over.

YOU Thanks. OK if I check back with you next Monday?

Source: Scheele (1991). Copyright © 1991 by WWT partnership. Reprinted with permission.

that two factors contribute to interactional justice (Greenberg & McCarty, 1990).

First, pay decisions need to be adequately explained. For example, allocators can and should provide an explanation of the rationale for a particular merit pay increase. In addition to providing a rationale, Greenberg and McCarty (1990) point out that the explanation must be viewed as logical and sincere by the recipients.

Second, information must be communicated in a sensitive manner. In terms of merit pay, allocators need to be courteous, honest, timely, and respectful of the rights of the merit pay recipient when they communicate merit pay decisions.

Perceived Accuracy of Performance Feedback

One factor that may influence the recipient's willingness to accept and act upon performance feedback is the perceived accuracy of the performance feedback (Ilgen, Fisher, & Taylor, 1979). A study by Landy, Barnes, and Murphy (1978) showed, for a sample of professional and managerial employees in a large manufacturing organization, that the perceived accuracy of performance information was greater when performance evaluations were frequent, goals were identified to eliminate performance deficiencies, and the supervisor was knowledgeable about the subordinate's job and performance. When these steps are taken in communicating merit pay decisions, employee perceptions of the accuracy of merit decisions should similarly be increased. In turn, with this perceived accuracy comes a greater likelihood that employees will not only accept decisions but be willing to *act* on the decisions because, as suggested in Table 6.1, accuracy is an important component of procedural justice.

The results of the Landy et al. (1978) study indicate that the credibility of the source of merit pay communication is an important factor, as well as how pay information is communicated. Allocator credibility is enhanced when the allocator is timely in merit communications, knowledgeable about the true performance of the individual, and sensitive to the recipient's needs to maintain and improve current performance.

Pay Secrecy

Pay systems can range from being "open" to "closed." Under an open pay system, virtually everything regarding pay levels and increases is known to employees. An example would be some land grant universities where employee salaries must be made public, and, therefore, each employee knows the salaries of other employees in the organization. At the other extreme is the closed system under which pay information is kept totally confidential by the organization. In some organizations, the individual employee's pay level and increase are made known only to that individual.

Empirical research on pay secrecy has been reviewed by several authors (H. Heneman, 1985; Lawler, 1972 & 1981; Leventhal, 1976). In general, the research seems to indicate that pay secrecy is likely to produce a greater differentiation in performance ratings and merit increases by allocators. That is, there are larger differences in the performance ratings and merit increases between high and low performers when pay is closed rather than open (Peters & Atkin, 1980; Leventhal, Michaels, & Sanford, 1972). Under open systems, allocators may be fearful of creating interpersonal conflict among employees by differentiating too much (Leventhal et al., 1972; Leventhal, 1976). From a motivational perspective, a "secret" merit pay plan is desirable as it makes it possible to create a stronger link between pay and performance through greater reward differentiation.

The research on the impact of pay secrecy on employee satisfaction is less clear. Lawler (1972 & 1981) argued that empirical studies indicate that employees are more satisfied with open than closed pay plans. Perhaps employees overestimate the pay of other employees under a closed system. H. Heneman (1985) argued that the evidence is more mixed and pointed to several studies where pay secrecy had no impact on pay satisfaction (e.g., Fossum, 1976).

Given the strong possibility that pay secrecy is likely to improve employee motivation and the somewhat less likely outcome that pay secrecy will diminish pay satisfaction, you would expect to find that merit pay systems tend to be more closed than open. It would seem (although no data are available) that many organizations "hedge their bets" when it comes to pay secrecy and merit increases by being more closed than open, but not totally closed. Under this partially closed system, an individual employee's merit increase is known only to that employee. The employee is also told the range of increases granted to others but not the actual amounts. This approach allows employees to better view their position within the merit pay plan.

A better approach than the "hedge your bet" approach may be to take a contingency point of view in determining the amount of information to be released under a merit pay plan. This approach is based on the results of more recent research on pay secrecy. Konrad and Pfeffer (1990) provided evidence that some close-knit work groups may favor rather than oppose reward-based differentiations among group members. Hence, the degree of openness may depend on the social norms of the group. The degree of openness may also depend on the needs of the allocator. Bartol and Martin (1989) found that open pay systems may be needed when the allocator is highly dependent on the recipient, so that the recipient can verify the amount received relative to other recipients. Balkin and Gomez-Mejia (1990) found that open pay systems were judged to be more effective than closed systems in organizations whose business strategies favored the growth of a single product line, rather than the maintenance of a diversified product line. The former firms were more likely than the latter firms to use innovative approaches to pay like open systems rather than more traditional pay practices like closed systems. Finally, the impact of openness seems to be more pronounced in nonunionized than unionized organizations. Kleiner and Boullion (1988) reported that openness was related to a reduction in cash flow and profitability in nonunion firms. This reduction was not present in unionized organizations.

The contingency view indicates that openness is more likely to work when satisfaction is more of a concern than is motivation, when the supervisor is dependent on his or her subordinates, when the social norms of the group support openness, when the organization has innovative pay practices, and when the organization is unionized. It should be noted that this perspective is based on research that looks at the impact of pay on the individual employee. When a broader perspective is taken, as with the Kleiner and Boullion (1988) study, the overall influence of the degree of openness on measures of organizational effectiveness is not large. Hence, in administering merit pay plans, managers must direct attention to a variety of other issues beyond the openness of the pay plan.

Split Roles Versus Combined Reviews

Back in the 1960s, a series of significant studies was conducted at the General Electric Company (Meyer, Kay, & French, 1965). One of the important outcomes of these studies was the suggested use of split roles in performance reviews. With split roles, the developmental function of performance appraisal is separated from the administrative decision making function of appraisal. Two reasons were offered for this split (Prince & Lawler, 1986). First, if the two functions of appraisal are combined, the supervisor is required to be a helper and judge at the same time. Second, self-appraisals, if used, are likely to be more positive than supervisory appraisals, and subordinates are likely to become defensive when supervisors justify their salary actions.

This logic of split roles has led to the use of two separate performance review sessions by some organizations. One session is to discuss performance for purposes of development, and the other session is to communicate salary increase actions on the basis of performance. In at least one industry, high technology, the practice of split roles has become very common. A survey by Hall, Posner, and Harder (1989) suggested that about two-thirds of the industry now uses split roles in performance appraisal.

Current research has not shown the superiority of split roles over combined reviews. If anything, the data seem to indicate that there may be more desirable outcomes with combined reviews (Lawler, Mohrman, & Resnick, 1984; Giles & Mossholder, 1990; Prince & Lawler; Dorfman, Stephen, & Loveland, 1986). Interestingly, Lawler et al. (1984) returned to General Electric and found that employees were not supportive of split roles. The authors found that employees wanted pay discussed in their performance reviews and felt that this was not done enough. Two other studies showed that a discussion of salary did lead to increased satisfaction, but did not produce a change in motivation or performance (Dorfman et al., 1986; Prince & Lawler, 1986). Prince and Lawler found that employee participation and involvement in performance planning subsequently increased when salary was discussed in the development review. Giles and Mossholder (1990) reported increased employee satisfaction in the performance appraisal system when a discussion of salary was included in the performance review.

The current research casts serious doubts on assertions that the split role method is superior to a combined review. This conclusion is not entirely unexpected. Reinforcement theory (discussed in Chapter 2) clearly shows the futility of measuring performance at one point in time and granting rewards at another point in time. Before a definitive statement can be made as to the superiority of one method over another, a better test of the models should be run, in which split roles and combined reviews are directly compared to one another. A direct comparison of the two has not been made in the current studies. In the meantime, until direct comparisons are made, Prince and Lawler's (1986) recommendation that a discussion of salary *not* be outlawed in developmental appraisal meetings seems reasonable.

Two practical issues arise in putting either split role reviews or combined reviews into practice. First, if performance reviews are split, the door is opened to the possibility that an employee will receive conflicting performance reviews. An employee's performance may be rated as acceptable for purposes of the developmental review, but rated unacceptable in terms of a merit increase. How could this happen? The supervisor conducting the reviews may find it more expedient or more comfortable to tell the employee that his or her performance is acceptable than to spend the time and emotional energy to try to redirect unacceptable performance. However, at the end of the fiscal year, under the pressure of a merit budget, the supervisor may be forced to tell the employee the real story; namely that his or her performance is unacceptable. The point is that the split review system, if used, needs to be closely monitored to make sure that conflicting decisions are not reached. Better yet is the use of a combined review, which should lessen the chances of conflicting assessments of performance.

Second, when using a combined review, some experience problems with too much discussion of the merit increase amount at the expense of a discussion of the performance that led to the merit increase. Recently, I did some training of first-level supervisors in an organization where combined reviews were seen by the supervisors as a problem. The supervisors were required by policy to use a one-page form with performance ratings at the top and middle of the form, and the size of the percentage increase at the bottom of the form.

During discussions of performance and merit pay at the annual review, employees focused attention solely on the bottom of the page. It was nearly impossible for the supervisors to direct the employees' attention to the behaviors at the middle and top of the form. To deal with this situation, we agreed on the following solution. In the long run, an attempt would be made to change the policy of the organization so that a new form would be created with the merit increase information on a separate page. In the short term, supervisors would put a blank sheet of paper over the form during the discussion, moving it down the page on a line-by-line basis to focus the discussion on each aspect of performance before getting to the size of the merit increase.

Communication Medium

A variety of different mediums or vehicles are used to communicate pay information in organizations. Sibson and Company (1988) reported, in a national survey of organizations, the following percentage of organizations that use the following mediums: one-on-one meetings (66 percent), group meetings (59 percent), company newsletters (32 percent), brochures/pamphlets (26 percent), and the grapevine (20 percent). With one important exception, no research has been conducted on the effectiveness of these mediums.

The one exception is a merit pay newsletter that was developed, evaluated, and is used at McDonnell Aircraft Company (Handshear, 1988 & 1989). An example of this newsletter, which is issued on a periodic basis to all McDonnell supervisors, is shown in Figure 6.3. To evaluate the effectiveness of the newsletter, a survey was conducted of users inside McDonnell Aircraft Company, and a survey was also conducted of American Compensation Association compensation professionals' reactions to it. Both surveys indicated a positive overall reaction to the newsletter (Handshear, 1988 & 1989). Among other things, the surveys indicated that the most frequent use of the newsletter was to "explain issues to subordinates" and that additional detail was sought by readers on merit pay guidelines. As a result of these positive evaluations, the newsletter continues to be used and has been expanded to include other compensation topics as well (Handshear, 1989).

Figure 6.3
Sample Merit Pay Newsletter from McDonnell Douglas Corporation

MCAIR COMPENSATION (DEPT 067) NEWSLETTER
10 A-H SUPERVISION FOR ROUTING TO SALARIED EMPLOYEES
04 SEP 87

The first issue of MERIT REVIEW NEWS outlined the major decisions and objectives of the merit review process. The intent of this issue is to give you general information about each of these decisions prior to publication of the actual 1987-88 review guidelines.

MERIT REVIEW BUDGET

The merit review budget provides a pool of money which is distributed as merit or promotion increases to employees from December 1987 to November 1988. The budget is the primary vehicle by which we administer our compensation costs and reinforce our "Pay for Performance" philosophy.

It is easy to "Pay for Performance" and administer a merit budget if you have unlimited funds. However, while MCAIR has many valuable assets—the talents of our employees, technology, successful programs—the company has to operate in a financially responsible manner that will ensure our continued success and the future security of our employees. That is why the budget amount must represent a balance between "what we would like to pay," "what the market is paying" and "what we can afford to pay."

In achieving this balance, many internal and external factors are analyzed in arriving at a merit review budget amount. These factors include: MCAIR rates of pay compared to similar jobs in the relevant market place (aerospace and local salary survey data); internal pay relationships (average salary growth for different employee groups); guidelines resulting from recent audits conducted by our customer; aerospace and local merit budgets; and the projected change in the consumer price index.

(continued)

Figure 6.3 *(continued)*

DIVISIONAL ALLOCATION

Once Corporate Office decides MCAIR's budget, the MCAIR Executive Team determines each division's allocation. The allocation is decided through the participative process discussed in our 28 August NEWSLETTER with each division's/program's needs taken into consideration. Divisional allocations may vary based upon the number of employees in critical skill jobs within a division. MCAIR defines critical skill jobs as those for which we face keen competition in recruiting, or for which there is a scarcity due to an increased internal need as the result of our programs.

RATE RANGE MOVEMENT

Rate ranges provide a minimum and maximum rate of pay for each job. Our rate range structures reflect the internal value of our jobs as well as their external market value. Rate ranges make possible different pay rates, based on performance and experience, for individuals in the same job classification. In establishing and moving the rate range, it is common compensation practice to look at how the midpoint of the rate range (the middle value between the minimum and maximum) for a job compares with the average rate paid for the job in the external market. Movement of the rate ranges can be tied to internal inequities, such as a large percentage of employees near the top (maximum) or bottom (minimum) of grade, or external factors, such as market rates for jobs and our competitor's rate range movement.

GUIDELINES ON DISTRIBUTING THE MERIT REVIEW POOL

In recent years, the guidelines have played a much larger role in the review process as they have focused on how to achieve MCAIR's pay for performance objective. In general, the guidelines have tried to set parameters to help achieve fair distributions of merit funds in which top performers get significantly greater than the average increase. Guidelines are a built-in protection against a "spread the butter" or a "general wage increase" approach in which a large majority of employees receive the average increase. Consistent with this has been the message that satisfactory performance should not automatically equate to an average increase granted.

Two recent and significant changes in the guidelines have been a more balanced emphasis during the review between external and internal pay considerations and the introduction of one-time merit payments (lump sum wage payments). Last year's guidelines, for instance, identified job classifications that are "over market" based upon wage surveys and recent government audits. In addition, two years ago the use of one-time merit payments was introduced as a method to reward employees who are good performers yet whose rate of pay

(continued)

Figure 6.3 *(continued)*

exceeds the relevant market rate and/or who are at the maximum of the rate range.

PERFORMANCE BONUS BUDGET AND PLAN DESIGN

In 1983 The Performance Bonus Plan acknowledged the fact that base pay increases are not always the best vehicle to reward performance. This Plan was designed to recognize significant one-time accomplishments by our employees with a one-time award in a timely manner.

The implementation of the Plan has been evolving since 1983. We anticipate significant changes to the Plan in 1988 in order to achieve the objectives stated above. We will provide you with more information on the Performance Bonus Plan for 1988 during the week of November 30.

NEED MORE INFORMATION?

If you have questions about the merit review process, please call your division/program Employee Relations Manager or the Compensation Department (ext: 24296).

Source: McDonnell Douglas Corporation. Reprinted with permission.

Summary

In summary, an important component in the administration of merit pay plans is the communication of merit pay information. To be effective, the limited research suggests that the message needs to be consistent with interactional justice principles, and the source needs to be perceived as credible. It should also be noted that although open pay systems and split roles are sometimes advocated, there is no clear-cut superiority of these communication policies over secret pay systems and combined reviews. Finally, one promising medium used to communicate merit pay issues appears to be a well-designed newsletter.

Role of the Allocator

Another major area of concern in the administration of merit pay plans is the role of the allocator. As the one responsible for implementation of the merit pay policy, the allocator has a critical role. To ensure that allocators are carrying out the policy as it was intended, allocators must be given the knowledge, skills, and motivation to do so in an effective manner. These three areas are discussed here in turn.

Knowledge

Allocators need to be sensitized to the fact that merit decisions may be influenced by factors other than the intent of the merit pay policy. These other factors include the characteristics of both the merit pay recipient and allocator. As shown in a recent study, recipient characteristics accounted for 24 percent of the variation in merit increases, while allocator characteristics accounted for 11 percent (R. Heneman & Cohen, 1988). Some of these characteristics, which may not immediately come to the mind of the allocator, are as follows:

Impression Management. You might expect that attempts by the recipient to manage the allocator's impressions of the recipient would influence the size of the merit increase (Ferris, Russ, & Fundt, 1989). This does not, however, appear to be the case for at least one method of impression management; namely, ingratiation by the recipient. In two studies, ingratiation by the recipient did not lead to larger merit increases (Gould & Penley, 1984; Martin, 1987). A flattery tactic may have backfired because the allocators may have reasoned that they would have the support of the recipient regardless of the merit increase granted (Martin, 1987). It should be noted that ingratiation is only one of many impression management tactics (Ferris et al., 1989). Impression management techniques may have a bigger impact on the boss when the boss is dependent on the merit pay recipient. Bartol and Martin (1990) found that demands for higher pay by threat of appeal to upper level management did work when the recipient had a known and credible political connection to upper level management.

Equity Off the Job. Freedman (1978) looked at the influence of equity for recipients off the job. In particular, she found in a laboratory study that allocators granted larger pay increases to those employees whose homes had burned down than to those employees where such information was not available to the allocator!

Allocator Values, Grades, and Board Scores. Bass (1968) appears to have conducted the first study on allocator characteristics as they relate to merit pay, and the results of his study are among the most interesting of all the merit pay studies conducted. Two results are notable. First, the personal values of the allocator influenced the size of the merit increase allocated to the recipient. In particular, allocators recommended larger merit increases when the allocators held stronger social and service values than theoretical and economic values. Similarly, Vecchio and Terborg (1987) found that allocators high in moral maturity granted larger increases than those low in moral maturity. Interestingly, Wexley and Youtz (1985) found that raters with altruistic beliefs tend to be less accurate raters of performance. It may be the case that more altruistic allocators are more lenient in performance ratings, which in turn leads to larger merit increases.

Second, Bass (1968) reported that merit increases were smaller when allocators had high board scores on the Admissions Test for Graduate Schools of Business and a high undergraduate grade point average. One interpretation of these results is that allocators who have excelled in school may have higher standards of performance than those who have not excelled in school. As a result of these higher standards, allocated increases may be smaller (R. Heneman, 1990).

In- and Out-Group Membership. Preferential reward treatment is given to recipients whose relationship with the allocator can be characterized as in-group rather than out-group status (Green & Liden, 1980). In-group members have a relationship with the allocator characterized by a high degree of trust, interaction, support, and rewards, whereas out-group members have a relationship with the allocator characterized by a low degree of trust interaction, support, and rewards (Dansereau, Graen, & Haga, 1975; Dienesch & Liden, 1986). Preferential reward treatment of in-group over out-group members seems to take place regardless of true performance. R. Heneman, Greenberger, and Ananyuo (1989) reported that ineffective performance was attributed to unfavorable conditions for in-group but not out-group members. On the other hand, effective performance was attributed to the person for in-group but not out-group members.

These attributions took place even when the level of actual performance was controlled for in the study. Hence, no matter what the true level of performance, causality of performance seems to be assigned in a way to favor in-group rather than out-group members. As outlined by Bennister and Balkin (1990), compensation decisions are unlikely to be accepted and acted upon by employees if employees are not treated consistently in the assignment of performance attributions.

A word of caution is in order at this point. The allocator characteristics just reported should be treated as *suggestive* of factors other than performance used by allocators to make merit decisions. Given the research methodology used in some of these studies, the results are not always conclusive. Some of these studies used students in the role of managers. Whether students' merit decisions in a prescribed role are similar to actual managers' merit pay decisions is questionable.

Similarly, the use of "paper people" may be problematic. That is, in some of these studies the manager was asked to give merit increases to a hypothetical employee described on a sheet of paper. The extent to which this person described on paper is treated similarly to an actual employee with these characteristics is again open to question. Both of these concerns relate to the concept of external validity, which is reviewed in detail in Chapter 7. For now, it is important to simply recognize that these concerns make the results tentative and suggest areas for additional research.

Training to Improve Allocator Skills

The importance of training to the measurement of performance was discussed in Chapter 4. Training programs designed to improve the measurement of performance were also reviewed in that chapter. Training is also needed, however, to support the making of merit pay decisions after performance has been measured. According to a recent survey by the Wyatt Company (1989), lack of training was seen as the "major impediment to success in managing pay for performance." Strategies that can be used to improve the allocators' merit pay decision-making skills will be reviewed below.

As shown in a review of the empirical research by Balzer, Doherty, and O'Connor (1989), an excellent approach to the improvement of accuracy in decision making is to provide individuals with cognitive feedback or knowledge about relations among variables. Three particular forms of relations among variables discussed by Balzer et al. (1989) seem to be relevant to merit pay decisions and can be used to set the framework for a merit pay training program. The cognitive feedback upon which merit pay training is based consists of three components: guidechart orientation, policy capturing, and feedback on actual decisions.

Guidechart Orientation. One component of cognitive feedback is known as *task information*. Essentially, this refers to information cues available for decision making. In the context of merit pay, this task information is essentially the merit pay guidechart. (See Chapter 5 for a review of guidecharts.) A key element of a merit pay training program would be a discussion of the merit pay guidechart to show managers how the pay-for-performance policy is supposed to work. Also, a discussion of this policy may help to shift the frame of reference from egalitarianism (see Chapter 3 for a discussion of pay philosophies) to pay-for-performance, for those managers whose reward strategies differ from the desired policy (Kroeck, Avolio, Small, & Einstein, 1987).

Policy Capturing. A second component of feedback is called *cognitive information* and refers to individuals' judgments in relation to cues they pick up in the environment. Cognitive information is a form of feedback that can be given to managers to help them improve the decisions they are required to make. From the perspective of merit pay, this cognitive information is the *actual* allocation decisions versus those decisions *intended* by policy. One way to build this component into merit pay training is to use a research method known as policy capturing, which has been used to model the decisions used in performance appraisal (Hobson, Mendel, & Gibson, 1981) and merit pay (Sherer, Schwab, & H. Heneman, 1987).

Policy capturing can be used to provide cognitive information to managers by taking three steps. First, information potentially used to make merit pay decisions would be collected. Actual information could be obtained from personnel files, or vignettes could be used to simulate the information available for a merit pay decision. An example of simulated merit pay information is shown in Table 6.2.

Table 6.2
Merit Increase Exercise

You are a consultant who has been called in by the chairman of the board to make recommendations on handling his merit budget for 1977. The company experienced a drop in profits of 23 percent in 1975 and 10 percent in 1976 from the 1973 and 1974 levels. The company is in a cash squeeze, so the merit budget program, which had been generous in past years, is very tight this year. The chairman is concerned about the top people in the company—those who report to him and to the president (the chief operating officer).

The company has a formal job-evaluation program. Salary ranges are set by competitive survey and the salary administration structure is in good shape. Jobs were evaluated and regraded and the structure was revised only a few months ago.

The company does not have a bonus plan and is not in a position to establish one in the near future. So the salary structure is essentially a total compensation structure, which must match competition that, in some cases, uses bonuses.

The chairman has decided that he will not get a raise this year, but he wants your recommendations on which of his key executives should receive increases and on the size of those increases, considering the difficult circumstances facing the industry and the company. The economic environment is one of cautionary recovery in the midst of slowed but continuing inflation. The current unemployment rate is 7.5 percent and has ranged between seven and 7.5 percent for the past six months. The inflation rate has been eight percent for the past 12 months and the annualized rate for the recent month was 7.5 percent.

The chairman's basic objectives are to provide the maximum motivation possible through the merit program under the difficult circumstances. He does not want to lose any of his key people.

Traditionally, all top executive increases have at least exceeded the inflation rate, but that is not possible this year.

The chairman gives you an organization chart and brief data on salary grade, age, years of service with the company, years in the present job, base salary, Compa/Ratio, performance-potential-exposure rating and an indication of whether there is a qualified backup for each of the key executives. The performance rating system is a good one and ratings on all the key people were completed recently. The system uses an A-B-C-D coding. A is the highest performance rating, the highest potential rating and the highest level of exposure to the possibility of the individual's being attracted away from the company; B is a good rating and C is considered adequate. Anyone who receives a D rating must bring it up at the next rating period or face termination or demotion. The company has few special fringe benefits and is not in a position to inaugurate any new ones at this time, if any cost is involved.

There is a stock option program, but it has been relatively ineffective in recent years because of the drop in the company's stock price. Few shares are available for grant under the plan and management cannot go to the shareholders for more shares for two years. So the option program offers little opportunity for augmenting the meager merit program for this year.

The chairman informs you that the maximum amount of merit money you can spend is $85,000 (this represents 6.06 percent of the executive group payroll excluding the chairman). Finally, he tells you that no promotions or retirements are expected in this group. The only rule that you have to contend with in allotting the raises is: no increases to pay levels above the maximum of the range.

Table 6.2

Name	Title	Salary Grade	Age	Years Service	No. Of Employees Supv.	In This Job	Base Salary	Compa Ratio	Perf	Pot	Expo-Sure	Back-Up
Walnut	Chairman	20	62	24	20,000	5	210,000	105.5	—	—	—	—
Prexy	President	18	57	8	20,000	7	180,000	118.9	B	B+	B-	Yes*
Numbers	V.P. Compt	15	42	3	40	1	85,000	76.6	A	A-	A	No
Money	V.P. Treas	15	48	12	15	4	100,000	90.1	B	B-	B	No
Peoples	V.P. Pers IR	13	51	17	25	7	80,000	90.1	A	C+	B+	Yes
Press	V.P. P.R.	13	46	6	7	2	92,000	104.5	C+	C	B	Yes
Laws	V.P. Legal	14	45	5	10	5	110,000	111.1	B	B+	A-	No
Maker	V.P. Mfg	15	59	20	15	6	113,000	101.8	B	B-	B-	Yes
Sellers	V.P. Mkt	14	54	13	10	3	84,000	84.8	A	B	A-	Yes
Thinker	V.P. R&D	14	50	14	50	8	102,000	103.0	B	C	B	Yes
Nuts	GR V.P.	16	42	4	5,500	4	115,000	92.0	A	A	A	No
Bolts	GR V.P.	15	46	10	4,000	3	112,000	100.0	B+	B+	A	No
Washer	GR V.P.	16	59	19	7,400	11	130,000	104.0	B	B-	B-	No
Hooks	GR V.P.	15	49	15	2,900	8	100,000	90.0	C	C	C	Yes

Total Excluding Chairman $1,403,000

*Nuts

Source: Foster & Lynn (1978). Reprinted with permission from *HR Magazine* (formerly *Personnel Administrator*), published by the Society for Human Resource Management, Alexandria, VA.

Second, the data collected in the first step would then be analyzed, using various statistical techniques (c.f., Hobson et al., 1981), to come up with the actual weights used by managers in making actual or simulated merit pay policies. An example of the weights used by managers in making merit pay decisions is shown in Table 6.3. The larger the entry shown in each cell of

Table 6.3
Weights Used by Allocators in a Hospital[a]

Parti- cipant[b]	Perfor- mance	Ten- ure	Sal- ary	Perf. consist.	Job offer	R^2
1	18**	47**	−28**	11	53**	62
2	78**	10**	−16**	14*	14*	69
3	84**	06	00	45*	−01	92
4	62**	28*	−11	37**	−05	62
5	86**	08	−30**	−08	02	86
6	74**	09	−13	04	−01	58
7	96**	−07	00	03	−01	93
8	77**	−01	−10	36*	03	74
9	65**	16**	−11**	53**	23**	80
10	63**	09*	−04	00	62**	79
11	92**	06	−09**	−23**	05	91
$\bar{r}^2$	57	03	02	08	04	

Source: Sherer, Schwab, & H. Heneman (1987). Reprinted with permission.

Note: Participant refers to the allocator. Performance consistency refers to the stability of performance over time. Job offer refers to an offer of a job with another company at a higher salary.

[a] Decimals omitted
[b] $n = 96$ for each participant
* $p < .05$ ** $p < .01$

Table 6.3, the greater the weight placed on that variable by the managers in making merit pay decisions.

Third, managers would be given feedback by other managers and trainers on the extent to which their decisions (shown by actual weights) correspond to the weights specified in desired organizational policy. Discussion could take place regarding methods to use to ensure that decisions are as closely in line with desired merit pay policy as possible.

Feedback on Actual Merit Decisions. A third component of feedback is based on the concept known as *functional validity information.* This information consists of the relations among decisions and outcomes. In terms of merit pay, it refers to the link between merit increases allocated and subsequent performance by the recipients. This information should also be provided in merit pay training.

Functional validity can be assessed only after enough time has passed to accurately evaluate changes in performance resulting from merit increases. Once these data have been collected, however, an additional training session should be held to give allocators feedback on the outcomes of their decisions. This feedback would effectively reinforce the guidechart orientation and policy capturing phases of training as well as lead to discussion on additional ways to tie performance to pay.

Increasing Motivation of the Allocator

In Chapter 4, it was recommended that there be consequences for the rater to improve the validity of ratings. Similarly, there need to be consequences for allocators to motivate them to make their merit pay decisions consistent with merit pay policy. One consequence for the allocator would be accountability for merit pay decisions.

Accountability can be enforced by insisting that allocators provide face-to-face feedback on merit pay decisions to the recipients. In and of itself, this strategy is probably not very effective. Klimoski and Inks (1990) found that raters tended to inflate their ratings when they had to give face-to-face feedback as compared to when ratings were kept anonymous or no feedback was provided. More effective ways to hold raters accountable may be those outlined below.

First, the signature of the allocator's immediate supervisor can be required as an approval of the ratings given by the allocator. The human resource department can ensure that approval signatures are made prior to the distribution of merit increases. A signature of approval by immediate supervisors increases the accountability of allocators for their merit pay decisions.

Second, organizations can evaluate allocators on the basis of how well they conduct merit pay reviews. That is, allocator performance becomes a standard of performance used to evaluate the allocator. According to a survey of Fortune 100 firms by Bretz and Milkovich (1989), only about 22 percent of these firms take such an approach for performance appraisal. The number is probably even less for merit pay.

Although not frequently practiced, there are two excellent case study examples where allocators are rated on how well they conduct merit reviews. This practice is undertaken in the city of Scottsdale, Arizona (*Management Review, 73* (10), 1984) and at Pratt and Whitney (Schneier, 1989b). To facilitate the process, standards for conducting merit reviews have been developed at Pratt and Whitney and are shown in Figure 6.4. These are the standards that allocators are rated against in their own annual reviews.

Third, allocator decisions can be audited or reviewed by a third party such as the human resource department. This practice is also followed by the city of Scottsdale (*Management Review, 73* (10), 1984). An empirical study by Rozelle and Baxter (1984) indicated that when ratings are reviewed by a committee, the reliability of these ratings is increased. Hence, there is some empirical support for this practice.

Fourth, recipients can appeal allocators' decisions to a third party (e.g., human resource department) to increase allocator accountability. This is yet another practice followed by the city of Scottsdale. Although it seems that this practice, like face-to-face feedback, could lead to inflated ratings, other procedures designed to hold raters accountable would suppress this effect. That is, inflated rating would be detected in the review of the allocator's performance as an allocator. Considering this, it may be desirable to use all three forms of accountability, as is the practice in Scottsdale.

Figure 6.4
Merit Pay Standards for Allocators at Pratt and Whitney

Exceptional Manager

Is a leader in drawing high performance from employees and recognizing them for it. Is aware of each employee's level of contribution and supports continued growth through many forms of recognition.

Fully Competent Manager

Assesses accurately the accomplishments of employees, differentiates between performance levels, and communicates candidly regarding performance. Makes compensation decisions that reflect clear distinctions between levels of performance achieved. Spends time in the work area interacting with employees, inquiring about day-to-day activities, and providing specific, timely performance feedback. Effectively uses formal and informal recognition actions. Maintains group performance. When warranted, takes appropriate action with poor performers through corrective action plans, firing employee when necessary.

Developing Manager

Is becoming more aware of the importance of employee recognition and feedback, and is increasing in ability to be involved in the accomplishments of employees on a regular basis.

Source: Schneier, "Capitalizing on Performance Management, Recognition, and Rewards Systems." Reprinted, by permission of the publisher, from *Compensation and Benefits Review,* March/April 1989, © 1989 American Management Association, New York. All rights reserved.

Laws and Regulations

Back in 1985 and 1986, General Motors Corporation shifted its compensation arrangement from automatic cost-of-living adjustments to merit pay for its roughly 125,000 employees (Kanter, 1987; Schlesinger, 1988). Since this time, the merit pay plan has received considerable attention in the popular press due to a class-action discrimination suit filed against General Motors by four black salaried employees on behalf of 10,000 such employees in Michigan, Ohio, and Indiana (*The Ohio State Lantern,* June 26, 1989). The dispute arose over allegations concerning the performance appraisal system used for salary increase and promotion decisions (Vines, 1989). General Motors did not admit any discrimination and reach a preliminary agreement out of court (Molloy, 1989). The estimated cost of the settlement ranges from three (Vines, 1989) to 40 (*The Ohio State Lantern*, June 26, 1989) million dollars. Included in the settlement are adjustments in pay for current and former employees (Molloy, 1989) and a computer-based monitoring system (Vines, 1989; *The Ohio State Lantern*, June 26, 1989).

This is just one example of the increased litigation that is likely in the area of merit pay. The potential for litigation should serve as an important reminder to employers to comply with relevant laws and regulations. Relevant laws and regulations include Title VII of the 1964 Civil Rights Act, the Equal Pay Act, Age Discrimination in Employment Act, National Labor Relations Act, and the Merit Pay Reform Act. Each of these acts will be briefly reviewed.

Title VII of the 1964 Civil Rights Act

This act prohibits discrimination in virtually all personnel decisions, including merit pay, on the basis of race, sex, color, religion, and national origin. The act is enforced by the Equal Employment Opportunity Commission. Very comprehensive reviews of Title VII, as it relates to court cases involving performance appraisal decisions, have been conducted (e.g., Nathan & Cascio, 1986). Reviews of Title VII as it relates to merit pay decisions have also been conducted but are more limited because of the smaller number of cases reviewed (Martin, Bartol, & Levine, 1987; Sovereign, 1989). Although the reviews are somewhat limited, the results of the merit pay cases are consistent with the larger number of performance appraisal cases.

These three reviews suggest that a number of actions could be taken by employers to defend their merit pay practices from allegations of discrimination. These actions are as follows:

- Performance standards should be based on a thorough job analysis. These standards also should be updated to reflect changes in job content. The use of traits as performance standards is discouraged as it is difficult to show the job relatedness of these standards.

- There should be a demonstrable relationship between pay increases and performance levels. Otherwise, the plan may not be seen as a bonafide merit pay plan.
- The merit pay plan should be clearly communicated to all employees. Information should be provided for both allocators and recipients. This information should be made available *before* the merit pay review.
- Care must be taken to ensure that bias is not present in performance ratings or merit increases. Rater and merit pay training should be provided to allocators. An appeals procedure should be made available to recipients.

It should be noted that the law is not written to require the above actions but to prohibit discrimination. These actions are simply employer practices found in written summaries of court cases. These practices seemed to be persuasive in courts as evidence that the employer did not discriminate.

Very little empirical research has been conducted on discrimination in merit pay decisions. The limited amount of research has been reviewed by R. Heneman (1990). He reports that there is almost no evidence of a relationship between protected-class status and merit pay decisions. The absence of a relationship between protected-class status and merit pay decisions in the reported research implies that no discrimination is in evidence.

Equal Pay Act

The Equal Pay Act prohibits discrimination on the basis of gender in pay decisions. Men and women must be paid the same for jobs requiring "substantially similar" skill, effort, responsibility, and working conditions. Pay differentials between men and women are permissible for men and women performing the same job if the differential is due to seniority, merit, production, or any factor other than sex. As with Title VII, the Equal Employment Opportunity Commission is the enforcement agency for the Equal Pay Act.

The Act suggests that different pay increases are permissible for men and women performing the same job if a bona fide merit pay plan is in place and where there is a demonstrable relationship between pay increases and performance. Along with this demonstrable relationship, there should be no relationship between merit increases and gender. The limited research on this subject provides no evidence of a relationship between gender and merit increase (R. Heneman, 1990).

Age Discrimination in Employment Act

This Act prohibits discrimination on the basis of age. In essence, the statute makes age a protected class along with sex, race, color, religion, and national origin. The act provides protection to those over age 40 and is enforced by the Equal Employment Opportunity Commission.

Almost no research has been conducted on age effects in merit pay. In one study, however, R. Heneman and Cohen (1988) reported that older employees received smaller merit increases. Given the aging population in the U.S., you can expect to see increasing litigation in this area. It is an area where employers need to pay strict attention in auditing merit pay plans for compliance to laws and regulations.

National Labor Relations Act

Under the National Labor Relations Act, employees granted the right to form and join labor unions. The act is enforced by the National Labor Relations Board (NLRB). Once a labor union is legally recognized, management must bargain with labor over wages, hours, and working conditions. One aspect of wages that may be a negotiable issue is the use of merit pay. One aspect of working conditions is employee participation in the development of a merit pay plan. Merit pay is found in some, but not very many, unionized organizations (as explained in Chapter 3). In unionized settings where merit pay is present, the collective bargaining agreement between labor and management may spell out the conditions of the merit pay plan as well as grievance procedures for employees who do not feel the plan is being administered according to the contract (Elkouri & Elkouri, 1973; Milkovich & Newman, 1987).

Under the grievance procedure, disputed merit increases are sometimes reviewed by an independent arbitrator when labor and management cannot come to an agreement. In general, merit pay decisions are not subject to successful challenge unless they are shown to be unfair, arbitrary, or discriminatory (Elkouri & Elkouri, 1973). When so charged, managements' defense is, in general, to show that the decisions are reasonable, demonstrable, and objective (Elkouri & Elkouri, 1973). Given the fact that arbitrators can only make judgments under the merit procedures previously agreed upon by labor and management, at least one arbitrator urges the parties to develop a detailed set of procedures in advance of plan usage (Barkin, 1970).

Merit Pay Reform Act

The Civil Service Reform Act of 1978 covers most employees working in the federal government. Chapter 4 of the Act established a merit pay plan that was required for some federal government supervisors and managers. In essence, the Act shifted pay increases from a seniority basis to a performance basis as well. The Act went into effect in 1981. In 1983, the Act was changed to the Merit Pay Reform Act. This new Act revised the merit pay procedures from the Civil Service Reform Act, because of the disastrous results of the original plan in the early 1980s (Holliman, 1983).

The considerable details of the required regulations of the Merit Pay Reform Act will not be reviewed here. The Act expired in 1987, was "sunsetted" until the end of 1989, and is currently being reviewed as to what form, if any, merit pay should take in the future of the federal government (Ilgen, *Personal Communication,* 1990). The most recent development in this area was a report issued by the National Research Council (1990) and requested by the federal Office of Personnel Management. It was conducted by a blue-ribbon commission known as the Committee on Performance Appraisal for Merit Pay and will be used for discussion at the congressional hearings on the reauthorization of the federal merit pay system.

The report consists of a selected review of the literature on merit pay and performance appraisal, along with a set of policy recommendations for the federal government. Policy recommendations include the following:

- A well-developed performance appraisal system will not automatically lead to desired merit pay outcomes.
- The context in which performance ratings take place must be considered. For example, there must be

incentives for managers to do what is expected with performance appraisals.

- Appraisals and merit pay decisions should be decentralized within a centralized set of policy guidelines.

- Merit pay plans should be pilot tested before full-scale implementation.

- While policy guidelines are needed to ensure fairness in merit pay decisions, too many guidelines may prevent a clear link between pay and performance.

Many of these recommendations for the federal government are relevant to private-sector employees as well. Further developments in this area should be closely monitored to see to what extent they contribute to desirable merit pay outcomes. Merit pay has been a large-scale social experiment by the federal government and should be a continuing source of valuable ideas for many organizations.

In summary, merit pay decisions, like most personnel decisions, are subject to a number of laws and regulations. To ensure compliance with these laws and regulations, the auditing of merit pay decisions should be a routine practice in organizations. The audit should consist of an investigation as to the degree to which actual merit pay decisions correspond with the provisions of the law. The auditing of merit pay decisions should be fully integrated into other legal compliance-review procedures in the organization. This integration step is necessary to convey to employees that managers are just as accountable for merit pay decisions under the law as they are for other business decisions.

Summary of Major Points

1. *Procedural Justice.* The effectiveness of a merit pay plan depends on the perceived fairness of the procedures used to establish merit increases, as well as the amounts allocated to merit increases. Rules that foster perceptions of procedural justice include consistent allocations, bias suppression, accurate decisions, correctable decisions, representation by the recipient, and ethical treatment.

2. *Appeals Procedure.* One concrete method for establishing procedural justice is to provide an appeals procedure for those employees concerned with their merit increase.

3. *Communications.* For merit pay communications to be effective, they need to be made consistent with the principles of interactional justice and come from a credible source. One promising medium for communicating merit pay information is a newsletter.

4. *Pay Secrecy.* An open merit pay plan is not necessarily superior to a closed merit pay plan. Under an open plan, satisfaction may be greater, but reward differentiation that is true to performance may be less likely to occur.

5. *Split Roles.* The research to date does not favor split roles over combined reviews. Discussions of salary should not be prohibited during developmental reviews.

6. *Role of the Allocator.* The allocator of merit pay has the central role in merit decisions. Steps must be taken by the organization to ensure that allocators have the knowledge, skills, and motivation to make solid merit pay decisions. Training and accountability should help to achieve this objective.

7. *Laws and Regulations.* Merit pay decisions must be made in accordance with laws and regulations as well as company policy. Major laws and regulations that have a bearing on merit pay are set forth in the following acts: Title VII of the 1964 Civil Rights Act, Equal Pay Act, Age Discrimination in Employment Act, National Labor Relations Act, and Merit Pay Reform Act.

Conclusions

It has been emphasized throughout the book that the relationship between pay and performance must be *perceived* as well as documented if merit pay is to be successful. The key element in ensuring that employees perceive the relationship between pay and performance is the administration of the merit pay plan. More than any other part of the merit pay process, the administration of the merit pay plan has a bearing on the perceived relationship between pay and performance. For there to be a perceived relationship between pay and performance, three events must take place.

First, the merit pay plan must be made highly visible to employees. For example, policies regarding merit pay could be communicated in a newsletter. Merit pay should be discussed during the appraisal of employee performance. Information that should be communicated is the possible range of merit increases, the actual range and average merit increase, and the individual's particular merit increase. The individual increases granted to all other employees should not be communicated.

This recommendation of limited openness in merit pay decisions may seem to contradict a major theme of the book, which is that the perceived link between pay and performance is as important as the actual link. You could argue that merit decisions must be totally open or public for the perceived link to be clear to employees. Most certainly, as shown in Chapter 2, there is a large body of motivational theory to substantiate the argument that merit pay decisions should be open. However, while an open system is a worthy goal to pursue, it is still premature to put a totally open merit system into operation in most organizations.

Both research and practice suggest that the current state of affairs in most organizations is not yet conducive to open merit pay decisions. In many organizations, rating errors such as those described in Chapter 4 continue to go unchecked. As a result, employees often get very similar merit increases regardless of actual performance levels. Under these circumstances, making public the merit increases of all employees may well diminish rather than enhance the perception that pay is based on performance. In short, performance must be adequately measured before open merit systems can be effectively used.

Second, the merit pay system needs to be seen as a fair one. Steps that can be taken to ensure fairness are creating an appeals procedure, training raters, using valid performance measures, following laws and regulations, and encouraging participation by employees in the development of the merit pay plan.

Third, supervisors must be equipped to make the actual link between performance and pay. At a minimum, supervisors need to be trained in the merit pay process and be held accountable for clearly establishing a link between pay and performance for their subordinates. Unfortunately, training and accountability being implemented by a small number of organizations. These procedures appear, however, to hold great promise and should be used more frequently. Merit pay plans will not be as effective as they could be until organizations become willing to commit the time and financial resources needed to train supervisors and hold them accountable for merit pay decisions.

To improve current administrative practices, the following priority ordering of activities seems reasonable. The most immediate concern should be the development of performance standards with sound validity properties and a corresponding merit pay system that is perceived to be fair. The next concern should be the proper use of these standards and systems by supervisors. Finally, and only after the preceding steps have been taken, organizations should take steps toward a more open system of merit pay decisions. If the previous two steps have been taken, open merit systems have the potential to strengthen the perceived link between pay and performance. If the previous two steps have not been taken, an open pay system may actually weaken the perceived relationship between pay and performance.

7

Evaluating Merit Pay Outcomes

This final chapter of the book focuses on the second stage of the merit pay process as shown in Figure 1.1. This stage consists of the relationship between merit increases and subsequent outcomes such as performance and satisfaction. You would expect to find that if a merit pay plan had been carefully developed and administered, merit increases allocated under the plan would lead to desirable outcomes. That is, if pay increases are linked to previous performance, then pay increases will lead to improved subsequent performance as well as other desirable outcomes.

The reason that the evaluation stage is so important is that it provides feedback to the organization on the extent to which merit pay is indeed producing desirable outcomes. If it is not, the evaluation process should reveal why and what needs to be done to correct the problem. Wallace (1990) found that one distinguishing characteristic of organizations with successful, as opposed to unsuccessful, incentive pay plans is evaluation of the outcomes associated with the plan. Organizations with successful plans devote resources toward evaluating actual outcomes rather than taking the results of the plan on "blind faith." Simply put, evaluation is a key step in managing the merit pay process. Without taking this step, it is doubtful that an organization can successfully manage the merit pay process.

In evaluating the results, or outcomes, of a merit pay plan, two issues are of primary importance and are covered first in this chapter. The first issue is defining and measuring favorable outcomes. The second is developing procedures that will be used to collect data on merit pay outcomes. Following a discussion of these two issues, a summary of the existing evaluation research is presented, organized by procedures and outcomes. This final section provides a more detailed answer to the question posed in the first chapter: "Are merit pay plans successful?"

Outcomes

A criterion model for evaluating merit pay plans is shown in Figure 7.1. As shown in this figure, there are a variety of outcomes for merit pay systems, and these outcomes can be grouped along two dimensions. One dimension is the level at which the desired outcome takes place—individual or business unit. You would expect that a well-developed and administered plan would

Figure 7.1
Criterion Model for Evaluating Merit Pay Plans

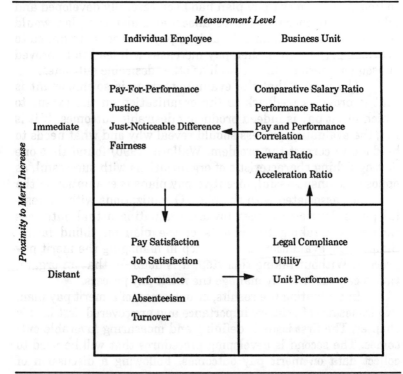

Source: R. Heneman (1991). Reprinted with permission.

have a positive impact on individuals in the organization as well as on business units or collections of individuals in the organization. Another dimension is the proximity of the outcome to the merit pay increase. While some outcomes would occur close in time to the merit pay increase, others may be more distant, taking place at a later point in time. These dimensions can be used to sort the various outcomes associated with merit pay into four categories.

Immediate Business Unit Outcomes

Merit pay plans are likely to have an immediate impact on two areas of compensation in organizational business units—position and movement of employees within the pay range. Outcomes in each of these areas can be assessed with a variety of indicators as shown in Figure 7.1.

Comparative Salary Ratio. The position of employees within the pay range is captured in what is called the comparative salary ratio, or "compa-ratio." It is simply the average salary for employees in the business unit divided by the midpoint. The midpoint is usually established around the market average. Merit increases, if rolled into base salaries, will increase average salaries and therefore increase the compa-ratio. In turn, if maximum salary levels are not adjusted upward, the higher the compa-ratio, the less merit pay will be available for performance in the next round of merit increases, as discussed in Chapter 5. As a result, if compa-ratios are very high in an organization, it may be difficult to motivate future performance using merit pay alone because employees are "maxed out," or close to the top of the pay range. In a sense, the compa-ratio may serve as an upper boundary to performance as an outcome, because it limits the size of increases. (See Chapter 5 for a complete discussion of compa-ratios.)

Performance Ratio. Another ratio that goes along with the compa-ratio in evaluating merit pay plans is the performance ratio (Goodale & Mouser, 1978). It is the average performance rating divided by the midpoint performance rating. The performance ratio can be used to see whether the value of the compa-ratio reflects actual employee performance. If pay increases in an organization are indeed based on performance, there should be a strong positive relationship between performance ratios and compa-ratios in business units. If you find instead a business unit where the performance ratio is high but the compa-ratio is low, employees may not be receiving all the pay they deserve based on their performance. This discrepancy may be due to a variety of reasons, including low maximums for the pay range or artificially deflated increases given by the allocator. Performance ratios like compa-ratios send a signal as to the actual tie between pay and performance.

Pay and Performance Correlations. Perhaps the most straightforward way to assess whether merit pay practice follows merit pay policy is to calculate the actual correlation between pay and performance for each business unit. The stronger the correlation between merit increases and performance ratings, the stronger the actual link between pay and performance. Whether this corresponds to employees' perceptions of the link between pay and performance is another matter, as discussed in Chapter 2.

Reward Ratio. The concept of a reward ratio comes from Hunter and Silverman (1980). It refers to a ratio found in merit pay guidecharts which can be compared across business units. The ratio is the largest merit increase granted for excellent performance divided by the lowest merit increase for average or satisfactory performance. Stronger links between pay and performance can be inferred in those business units with larger reward ratios. Some organizations define acceptable reward ratios. For example, at one time the federal Office of Personnel Management (OPM) defined acceptable reward ratios as falling in the range from 2 to 1 through 4 to 1 for the highest performance level over the average or satisfactory level (Hunter & Silverman, 1980). Hence, the OPM could audit federal agencies for compliance with this desired ratio in setting up guidecharts and allocating increases.

Acceleration Ratio. An acceleration ratio (Hunter & Silverman, 1980) is the merit increase that can be granted for employees in the highest portion of the pay range (e.g., fourth quartile), divided by the merit increase for employees in the lowest portion of the pay range (e.g., first quartile). The larger the ratio is, the longer it will take employees to progress or accelerate through the pay grade. A large or small ratio may or may not be desirable depending on the tradeoff between reward and cost orientation for organizations, as discussed in Chapter 5.

Immediate Individual Employee Outcomes

Another set of criteria is also fairly immediate, but is measured at the level of the individual employee rather than at the level of the business unit. These criteria primarily relate to employees' perceptions of the merit pay plan.

Pay-for-Performance Perceptions.   As stated throughout the book, the perceived relationship between pay and performance is as important as the actual relationship between these two variables. To measure these perceptions, a multiple-item measure was developed by R. Heneman et al. (1988), based on the work of Perry and Pearce (1983). This measure of pay-for-performance perceptions is shown in Table 7.1. In a study of hospital employees, this measure had modest reliability (R. Heneman et al., 1988).

Justice Perceptions.   Included here are measures of distributive and procedural justice (discussed in Chapter 6). The former focuses on the fairness of the reward allocation while the latter focuses on the fairness of procedures used to determine reward allocation (Greenberg, 1986 & 1987a). Folger and Konovsky (1989) developed measures of distributive and procedural justice with good internal consistency reliability for a study of manufacturing employees. The procedural justice measure is multidimensional, consisting of questionnaire items for feedback, planning, recourse, and observation.

Just-Noticeable Differences (JND).   A JND refers to the size of a pay increase that is needed to "make a difference" in influencing employee attitudes and behaviors (H. Heneman & Ellis, 1982). This concept is described in greater detail in Chapter 5. Over the years, a variety of one-item measures have been created to tap this concept. Unfortunately, when one-item measures are used, internal consistency reliability cannot be assessed. A multiple-item measure, which may allow for assessment of internal consistency reliability, was developed by

Table 7.1
Measure of Pay-for-Performance Perceptions

	Strongly Disagree	Disagree	Neutral	Agree	Strongly Agree
1. If I perform especially well on my job, it is likely that I would get a pay raise	1	2	3	4	5
2. The best workers in the hospital get the highest pay raises	1	2	3	4	5
3. The pay raises that I receive on my job make me work harder	1	2	3	4	5
4. High performers and low performers seem to get the same pay raises	1	2	3	4	5

Source: R. Heneman, Greenberger, & Strasser (1988). Reprinted with permission.

Note: Item 4 is reverse scored to 1 = 5, 2 = 4, 3 = 3, 4 = 2, 5 = 1.

Hinrichs (1969) and is reported in detail in an appendix to Rambo and Pinte (1989).

Pay Fairness. Many years ago, Belcher (1979) made the distinction between pay fairness and pay satisfaction. Fairness refers to an individual's reaction to his or her pay increase relative to the amount received by others. Satisfaction refers to an individual's reaction to the amount received relative to what he or she believes the amount should have been. Scarpello (1988) has developed a measure of pay fairness and reports that, for a sample of manufacturing employees, perceptions of fairness and satisfaction are strongly related under some, but not all, circumstances. Hence, organizations may choose to measure both pay satisfaction and pay fairness.

Distant Individual Employee Outcomes
Other outcomes are also at the individual level of measurement, but are more distant than the individual's immediate perceptions

of the merit pay system. These more distant criteria include affective and behavioral reactions to the merit pay plan.

Job Performance. One obvious distant individual employee outcome is job performance. Job performance is a behavioral reaction to merit pay. As discussed throughout the book, an increase in performance is a major goal of merit pay plans. The measurement of job performance is covered in Chapter 4.

Along with an increase in the *level* of performance, another desirable merit pay outcome is an increase in the *consistency* of performance over time. Depending on the person (Henry & Hulin, 1987) and the job (Rambo, Chomiak, & Price, 1983), you would expect an incentive pay plan, such as merit pay, to lead to more stable performance over time (Rothe, 1978). In a six-year study of chippers and grinders in a foundry, Vinchur, Schippman, Smalley, and Rothe (1991) found evidence that performance was fairly stable over time under a piece-rate incentive plan. This line of argument suggests that for a merit pay plan to be considered successful, it should produce not only a one-time increase in performance but should sustain performance at an increased level over time. To assess the degree to which this takes place, performance needs to be assessed on a repeated, regular basis.

Job Satisfaction. One affective reaction to work is known as job satisfaction. This reaction comes from the employee's assessment of what *is* versus what *should be* vis-a-vis the conditions surrounding work and the work itself (Locke, 1976). Although there are many measures of job satisfaction, two have stood the test of time and have sound reliability properties. Because they have been used extensively by organizations, these measures have produced normative data, available for comparison purposes. One of the conditions of work assessed by each of the two measures is pay. The two measures are the Minnesota Satisfaction Questionnaire (MSQ) (Weiss, Davis, England, & Lofquist, 1967) and the Job Descriptive Index (JDI) (Smith, Kendall, & Hulin, 1969). If a measure of overall satisfaction is desired, the JDI and MSQ, which target specific components of work, need to be supplemented with an overall measure of job satisfaction. An overall measure of job satisfaction and its relationship to the MSQ is described in Scarpello and Campbell (1983).

Pay Satisfaction. One specific condition implicit in work is pay, and a questionnaire has been developed to measure satisfaction with pay. This questionnaire is known as the Pay Satisfaction Questionnaire (PSQ) and was developed by H. Heneman and Schwab (1985). It is a measure of employees affective reactions to pay. The PSQ is shown in Figure 7.2. As shown in the questionnaire, pay satisfaction can be viewed as having four dimensions. Satisfaction with pay level is the perceived satisfaction with direct wages and salaries. Satisfaction with pay raises refers to the perceived satisfaction with changes in pay level. Satisfaction with structure/administration is defined as perceived satisfaction with the internal pay hierarchy and the methods used to distribute pay. Satisfaction with benefits concerns perceived satisfaction with indirect payments to employees. Although normative data are sparse for this measure, it has excellent reliability properties and is targeted directly at pay rather than other facets of work (Scarpello, Huber, & Vandeberg, 1988).

Absenteeism. Absenteeism may decrease with merit pay because it is typically one aspect of performance that is monitored by organizations. The less absent an employee is from work, the better his or her performance. The better his or her performance, the larger the merit increase. In turn, this larger merit increase should continue to motivate reduced absenteeism in the future.

A wide variety of measures has been used to assess the incidence of absence from work, including measures of magnitude, frequency, and duration. These measures and others are summarized in Rhodes and Steers (1990). Perhaps the best known and most widely used measure of absence comes from the continuing survey by the Bureau of National Affairs (BNA, 1983; Mincer, 1977). The formula as follows:

$$\frac{\text{Number of employee days lost through job absence during the month}}{(\text{Average number of employees}) \times (\text{Number of workdays})} \times 100$$

Comparative data on absence, using this formula, are reported in the *BNA's Bulletin to Management*. As noted in H. Heneman,

Figure 7.2
The Modified Pay Satisfaction Questionnaire (PSQ)

The statements below describe various aspects of your pay. For each statement decide how satisfied or dissatisfied you feel about your pay, and put the number in the corresponding blank that best indicates your feeling. To do this, use the following scale:

1	2	3	4	5
Very Dissatisfied	Dissatisfied	Neither Satisfied Nor Dissatisfied	Satisfied	Very Satisfied

1. My take-home pay.	L
2. My benefit package.	B
3. My most recent raise.	R
4. Influence my supervisor has on my pay.	R
5. My current salary.	L
6. Amount the company pays toward my benefits.	B
7. The raises I have typically received in the past.	R
8. The company's pay structure.	S/A
9. Information the company gives about pay issues of concern to me.	S/A
10. My overall level of pay.	L
11. The value of my benefits.	B
12. Pay of other jobs in the company.	S/A
13. Consistency of the company's pay policies.	S/A
14. Size of my current salary.	L
15. The number of benefits I receive.	B
16. How my raises are determined.	R
17. Differences in pay among jobs in the company.	S/A
18. How the company administers pay.	S/A

Source: H. Heneman (1985). Copyright © Herbert G. Heneman, III and Donald P. Schwab, 1983. Reprinted with permission.

Note: L = level, B = benefits, R = raise, S/A = structure/administration.

Schwab, Fossum, and Dyer (1989), this formula underestimates absenteeism because absences of less than a day are not included, and long-term absences are counted only through the first four days. Also, it does not distinguish between voluntary and involuntary absenteeism. You would expect merit pay to have a greater impact on voluntary absenteeism, that is, absence under the control of the individual employee. Hence, organizations may wish to supplement the BNA formula with a measure of voluntary absence frequency.

Turnover.   Another behavioral reaction to merit pay, along with performance and absenteeism, is turnover, or people leaving the organization. Turnover may be reduced with merit pay because people may be more satisfied with their pay. Turnover, like absenteeism, can be measured in a number of ways. These measures are summarized in Mobley (1982). The most well-known measure of turnover is shown in the following formula (Mincer, 1977):

$$\frac{\text{Number of separations during month}}{\text{Average number of employees on payroll during month}} \times 100$$

As with the measure of absenteeism, the BNA also reports comparative data on turnover, using this formula, in its *Bulletin*. Primarily, it is a measure of voluntary turnover, but some involuntary turnover (dismissals) are also included (H. Heneman et al., 1989). You would expect merit pay to more greatly influence voluntary than involuntary turnover. Hence, one might supplement this measure with a measure of voluntary turnover when evaluating merit pay plans.

Distant Business Unit Outcomes

A final category of outcomes is that of distant outcomes related to the business unit level rather than the individual employee level. These outcomes are assessed using more financial-oriented measures of business unit success as well as measures of compliance with the law.

Legal Compliance.   One important standard that must be met in a merit pay plan is compliance with the laws and regulations covered in Chapter 6. To monitor compliance, merit pay plans can be periodically audited at the business unit level. Such an audit would consist of correlating performance ratings and merit increases with the protected-class categories of age, race, sex, color, religion, and national origin to ensure that differences in merit increases are not due to protected-class status.

Utility. Another standard that can be used at the business unit level is known as utility, or the financial return on performance increases linked to merit pay. Landy, Farr, and Jacobs (1982) presented a utility formula that can be applied to merit pay decisions (R. Heneman, 1990). In essence, financial returns on merit pay dollars are calculated by comparing the dollar value of the subsequent performance of those who receive versus those who do not receive merit increases, after the costs of merit pay have been subtracted out. Utility represents the dollar value of a merit pay plan to an organization based on the performance of employees after merit pay has been implemented. Caution should be taken, however, in using the utility standard, as it is still in the exploratory stages for merit pay.

Bearing this cautionary note in mind, Sterling (1990) conducted an informative utility analysis on the monetary returns associated with a merit pay plan for a set of data used by Schwab and Olson (1990). This data set consisted of data for 157 employees in a simulated organization. To estimate the dollar value of a merit pay program, he used the following formula based on the work of Schmidt, Hunter, and Pearlman (1982):

$$\Delta U = TNd\,t\,SD_y - NC$$

ΔU = the dollar value of the merit pay program

  T = the number of years duration of the effect of merit pay on subsequent performance

  N = the number of individuals who received merit pay

  d_t = the true difference in job performance between the average employee who received merit pay and the average employee who did not receive merit pay in standard deviation units

SD_y = the standard deviation of job performance in dollars of the group not receiving merit pay

  C = the cost of the merit pay program per employee

Based on some fairly reasonable estimates of these parameters from the Schwab and Olson (1990) and Schmidt et al. (1982) studies, Sterling (1990) found that the dollar value of a merit pay program is slightly over $3 million, or approximately $1.0 million a year assuming that the value of T is three years.

This figure may be somewhat of an overestimate, as he estimated C (or cost) to be zero. He assumed that there were no costs to the program because merit pay represents a more efficient use of the costs associated with existing pay programs. Even if this is the case, there may be some administrative costs in shifting from a traditional pay plan with across-the-board increases to a merit pay plan. As shown throughout the book, there are costs associated with the design, implementation, and evaluation of a merit pay plan, above and beyond the costs of merit pay increases. Hence, the $3 million figure may need to be adjusted downward for a more accurate estimate.

It should also be noted that the data used to derive this estimate of the expected utility of a merit pay plan were simulated in a Monte Carlo study (Schwab & Olson, 1990). It remains to be seen what the estimated utility of merit pay will be in actual organizational settings. Nevertheless, the Sterling (1990) study is a good beginning.

Unit Performance. Another set of standards has to do with the effectiveness of the business unit. Several cost-accounting measures could be used to assess the impact of merit increases on the financial performance of business units. Rock (1983) reviews three financial measures of performance that could be used. The first measure comes from a standard profit-and-loss statement and is earnings per share (EPS). A second measure is return on equity (ROE), which can be obtained from profit-and-loss statements as well as balance sheets. Both these measures can be tracked over time, or in relation to other companies. Hence, they could be compared before and after the introduction of a merit pay plan, or compared to similar companies without a merit pay plan. According to Rock (1983), advantages to using EPS and ROE as standards is that they are fairly easy to measure and communicate.

A major disadvantage of EPS and ROE is that they do not adequately capture performance during periods of high interest charges, high replacement costs, and high inflation. In effect, measures of earnings such as EPS and ROE may be illusory during these periods because they fail to show how "real" the earnings are (Rock, 1983). Another disadvantage with using EPS and ROE as standards is that they are difficult to assess at the operating-unit level (as opposed to the corporate level).

Given these disadvantages, some organizations are using cash-flow indicators of business unit performance instead. Although more difficult to measure and communicate, they can account for economic influences outside the control of the organization, such as inflation, and also can be measured at both the corporate and operating-unit level (Rock, 1983). Good examples of this approach come from Ubelhart (1990).

One cash-flow indicator is cash-flow return on investment (CFROI), which is the ratio of cash flow over time to cash investment. Another cash flow indicator is business value, which is CFROI-adjusted for the growth or contraction of assets. It should be noted that these cash flow indicators and others are fairly new. Hence, they need to be carefully reviewed with financial specialists before use, because there are no established formats and procedures (Ubelhart, 1990).

Relations Among Outcomes and the Need for Multiple Outcomes

The arrows drawn in Figure 7.1 suggest that the categories of outcomes are related to one another in a logical manner. Immediate business unit outcomes should lead to immediate individual employee outcomes. For example, an individual's perceptions of pay, such as pay for performance, are likely to be influenced by his or her position in the pay grade and potential for merit increases, as indicated by reward and acceleration ratios. Immediate individual employee outcomes should, in turn, lead to distant individual employee outcomes. That is, individuals' perceptions of the merit pay plan will influence their affective reactions to the plan (e.g., pay satisfaction) as well as their behaviors at work (e.g., performance). Distant individual employee outcomes should then contribute to distant business unit outcomes. Performance, for example, would be expected to have an impact on the financial success of the business unit. Distant business unit outcomes should in turn influence immediate business unit performance. Reward ratios, for example, may be larger when the business unit has greater financial success. These relationships among the categories suggest the importance of using multiple outcomes in assessing merit pay plans.

More specifically, there are two reasons to evaluate merit pay plans with multiple criteria. First, the outcomes of a merit pay plan are unlikely to be all positive or negative. A more likely scenario is that a merit pay plan may be successful along some lines and not others. Multiple criteria will differentiate between areas of success and weakness. For example, Gomez-Mejia and Balkin (1989) reported on a merit pay plan that had a positive effect on performance measured at the business unit level, but did not have an effect on performance measured at the individual level.

Second, multiple criteria can be used to show or diagnose *why* merit pay leads to desirable or undesirable results. For example, a correlation between merit increases and perceptions of pay fairness is interesting, but not very useful. It would be very useful, however, to see that perceptions of pay fairness are the result of the acceleration ratio and, in turn, pay fairness perceptions have led to lower levels of absenteeism, contributing to the bottom line performance of the business unit.

Form of the Relationship Between Merit Pay and Outcomes

It is sometimes implicitly assumed that there is a linear or one-for-one return on merit pay increases. Most statistical tests of the relationship between satisfaction (pay or job) and merit increases are based on a linear model. As pointed out by Porter, Greenberger, and R. Heneman (1990), however, there are several reasons to expect that the relationship between merit increases and satisfaction measures is nonlinear. These reasons are summarized in Figure 7.3.

As shown in Graph B, there may be diminishing marginal returns (Bernoulli, 1964). This is, each additional dollar spent on merit pay may mean less of an increase in satisfaction because each additional dollar contributes less and less to the total available for consumption. Alternatively, based on the work in psychophysics by Stevens (1959), each additional dollar of a merit increase may contribute to greater amounts of satisfaction as shown in Graph C. The reason for increasing amounts of satisfaction in Graph C is that each additional dollar results in a feeling of increased recognition and status from the organization.

As shown in Graphs D and E, satisfaction may be greater for some merit increases than others. In Graph D, the "Matthew Effect" is represented (Gabris & Mitchell, 1988) and suggests that satisfaction is lowest when an average merit increase is granted, because the employee is likely to feel that pay is being

Figure 7.3
Theorized Relationships: Pay Satisfaction to Actual Pay

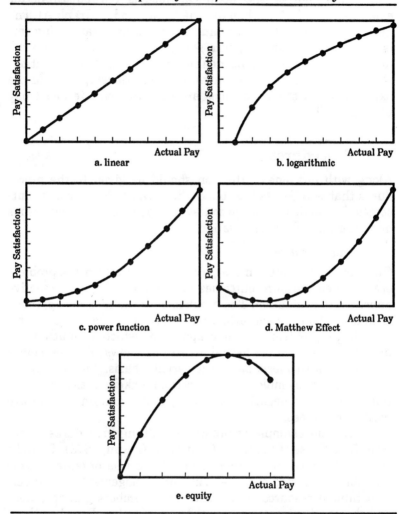

Source: Porter, Greenberger, & R. Heneman (1990). Reprinted with permission.

taken from him or her to go to better performers. (See Chapter 2 for additional information on the Matthew Effect.) In Graph E, an equity effect is depicted (Adams, 1965) in which perceptions of overreward may produce decreased satisfaction with increasing levels of merit pay.

In a very limited test of these models, Porter et al. (1990) found that one of the nonlinear models (Graph E) better explained satisfaction than did the linear model (Graph A). The authors concluded that in evaluating merit pay plans using satisfaction as the outcome, care should be taken to examine the form of the relationship for nonlinear as well as linear relationships. The possibility of nonlinear relationship should be explored when other outcomes are used to evaluate merit pay plans as well.

Procedures

Along with outcomes, attention should be given to the procedures that will be used to collect the data needed to assess outcomes. In particular, attention should be given to audit issues and internal and external validity.

Audit Issues

One way to evaluate a merit pay plan is to wait until a problem occurs, then measure outcomes of the plan. This is a reactive approach to evaluation. The problem with the reactive approach is that by the time you evaluate, it may be too late to correct a very large problem. Another approach, which is much more proactive, is to conduct formal audits or reviews of the outcomes associated with merit pay on a periodic basis. Audit data are then fed back to employees and decision makers in the organization to improve negative outcomes, and maintain or improve positive outcomes.

A good example of proactive auditing procedures comes from Blue Cross of Southern California (Cowan, 1978). To audit the effectiveness of its plan, a task force was organized. This task force consisted of 50 percent line management and 50 percent human resource staff. Task force members gathered data on behavioral outcomes associated with the plan. Based on these data, they developed a list of possible problems, both long and short term, and possible solutions. This information was then fed back to line managers and used to develop action plans to resolve the potential problems revealed. Part of the action plan included steps to be taken by individual managers to audit the effectiveness of the merit pay plan in their business unit.

Having employee representation as well as management and human resource representation on the audit task force is desirable. It is especially important when employees' affective reactions to the plan are measured as a part of the audit. Surveying employees' attitudes may heighten their expectations concerning the merit pay plan. Having employee representation on the audit task force creates a channel to give employees feedback on their concerns and to communicate what can be done in response to these concerns, what additional information needs to be gathered, or why nothing can be done about a particular issue.

Study Design Considerations

It is one thing for an employer to show a *relationship* between merit increases and outcomes, but it another for an employer to show that measured outcomes are the *result* of merit increases and that we are likely to find the same results in other settings. Attention must be given to the concepts of internal and external validity when collecting outcome data to have confidence in the results. The greater the internal and external validity of a study, the greater the confidence we can place in the results.

Internal Validity. In evaluating a merit pay plan, the objective is to see to what extent merit pay caused a change in the outcome variables of interest. In the context of merit pay, internal validity refers to the extent to which merit pay rather than other factors caused a change in outcomes. Probably the most frequently used method to assess this is a *one-shot case study* in which outcomes are measured only after merit pay is implemented. Although this method is better than no evaluation at all, it is not much better. A one-shot case study fails to answer the question, "Did a *change* in outcomes take place?" High or low outcome scores after merit increases may be due to the fact that outcomes were already high or low before merit increases were granted.

To see if a change in outcomes took place, a better method of data collection is a *pretest-posttest design.* Here, outcomes of interest are measured before (pretest) and after (posttest) merit increases. By using a pretest and posttest, it is possible to assess whether a change in outcomes actually took place or whether outcomes remained the same as before, regardless of merit increases. Although a pretest-posttest design is better than a one-shot case study, it is not without problems. In particular, while this design answers the question of whether a change took place, it does not answer the question of whether the change was due to merit pay or to something else.

A variety of factors other than merit pay could be responsible for the change in outcomes from the pretest to posttest. These rival explanations for the change (or lack thereof) are detailed in Campbell and Stanley (1966). These other factors are known as "threats" to internal validity, where internal validity refers to the question, "To what extent does merit pay cause certain outcomes?" Threats to internal validity include, but are not limited to, history, maturation, and instrumentation (Campbell & Stanley, 1966). These factors or others may be responsible for changes in outcomes rather than merit pay. *History* refers to events in addition to merit pay that took place between the pretest and posttest. Examples might include changes in technology, human resource practices, or supervision. *Maturation* refers to changes in studied employees. For example, with the passage of time, employees may become more mature or better at managing impressions. *Instrumentation* refers to changes in the measuring instruments or persons using them. Examples might include using different raters or different standards of performance for the pretest and posttest.

One way to minimize these threats is to use a *control group*. What this means is that in evaluating merit pay, two groups are used. An experimental group receives merit pay while a control group does not receive merit pay. A comparison can be made between the experimental and control group to see to what extent a change in outcomes is due to merit pay. This method is known as a *pretest-posttest control group design*. The only difference between the experimental and control group is that merit pay is given to the experimental group. Hence, any differences in outcomes should be attributable to merit pay.

To make the comparison between experimental and control groups meaningful, employees need to be randomly assigned to each group. Random assignment is another way to minimize threats to internal validity. Each employee has the same chance of being in the experimental and control group, which minimizes differences in employees as the explanation for differences in outcomes.

There are two obvious problems, from an administrative standpoint, with the pretest-posttest control group design. First, it is difficult, if not impossible, to allow some employees to be eligible for a merit increase while others are not eligible. Second, random assignment may not be possible. To illustrate these two problems, imagine how you would feel if your boss came up to you and a coworker and told you that you would not be eligible for a merit increase but your coworker would be. It is doubtful that you would feel much better if your boss then told you that it was simply a random decision for purposes of research and that you shouldn't take the decision personally!

There are two other designs that can be used to minimize these administrative problems. However, they do not minimize the threats to internal validity as well as a pretest-posttest control group design with random assignment to the experimental and control groups.

One alternative design is a *nonequivalent control group design*. With this design, a pretest and posttest is administered to an experimental and control group. Employees are not, however, assigned on a random basis. Instead, intact work groups are assigned as experimental and control groups. For example, division A of an organization would receive a new merit pay plan, while division B would not receive the new plan until later when the evaluation is completed. The problem with this design, is that the groups are not equivalent and, hence, differences in outcomes may be due to differences in groups. To minimize this possibility, the groups in the evaluation study could be "matched" as well as possible to increase the possibility of equivalence. Employees in the studied sample would be matched along characteristics believed to influence merit pay outcomes. For example, there may be reason to expect that seniority is related to performance. To control for the effects of seniority, an equivalent number of employees with various seniority levels could be included in the studied experimental and control groups. It should be noted that although matching help to minimize differences between groups, it is impossible to perfectly match groups along all variables likely to have an impact on outcomes.

A second design that can be used to minimize administrative problems is a *time-series design*. With a time-series design, a control group is not used. Instead, multiple pretests and multiple posttests are used. In effect, the experimental group also serves as the control through the use of multiple measures. You could more strongly infer that merit pay led to specific outcomes when the only change in outcomes took place after the introduction of merit pay rather than before, during, and after merit pay. While it may be advantageous from an administrative standpoint to use a time-series design, it is not possible to totally rule out history as an explanation for the change.

External Validity. In addition to being concerned about internal validity, attention also needs to be directed toward external validity in conducting an evaluation of merit pay. External validity raises the question, "To what extent can we generalize the results of the evaluation to other employee groups, settings, and merit pay plans?" In other words, just because a merit pay plan has a specific set of outcomes under one set of circumstances does not automatically mean it will have the same outcomes under another set of circumstances.

There are also threats to external validity which, when minimized, allow us to generalize the results of the evaluation to other circumstances. This generalizability is an important aspect of evaluation, as it allows organizations to predict outcomes across business units. Also, it is important as it allows organizations to assess the extent to which the results of merit pay studies at other organizations are relevant to their own organizations.

Campbell and Stanley (1966) again provide a detailed description of threats to external validity. First, the selection of employees to be evaluated is a concern. A merit pay plan that works well for managers, for example, may not work well for lower level employees. If merit pay is to be used for multiple employee groups, then representatives from each group may need to be included in the evaluation study.

Second, merit pay plans may coincide with other new programs. That is, merit pay may be introduced to the organization at the same time as another human resource intervention, such as training. As a result, it may be difficult to know if outcomes are attributable to merit pay or to training. Whenever possible, merit pay should be evaluated independently of other interventions. Also, it should not be automatically assumed that the results of one type of merit plan (e.g., lump-sum, as described in Chapter 5) will generalize to settings with another type of plan (e.g., a traditional merit pay plan).

Third, studied employees' outcomes may have more to do with the fact that they are being studied than the fact that they are receiving merit pay. That is, employees may be reacting to the novel setting rather than to the merit increases received. To guard against this possibility, multiple posttests can be conducted. You would expect that if the outcomes were due to the novelty of the situation, the novelty would diminish over time. When multiple tests are used, however, another problem may arise. Employees in the evaluation study may become sensitized to what is expected by the organization and respond accordingly.

In summary, when designing a study to evaluate the effectiveness of merit pay, data collection procedures need to account for both internal and external threats to validity. Consideration must be given to using a pretest, control group, random or matched assignment, representative sample, and multiple posttests. Although there are risks to using these methods in evaluating merit pay, the study results are more usable than when these methods are not used, as in a one-shot case study.

A Practical Illustration. When reading about study design considerations for the first time, you may walk away feeling somewhat overwhelmed by the technical jargon. There is indeed a fair amount of it. The technical language has been included in this book, however, because the reader may encounter this jargon when reading merit pay studies or interacting with people who conduct evaluation studies on merit pay. Although the labels and phrases are somewhat cumbersome, they are very relevant in terms of applicability. Perhaps the best way to demonstrate the applicability of study design considerations is to put yourself in the role of an executive who is charged with deciding whether to use a merit pay plan for the first time.

As a first step, you may read previous merit pay studies, as suggested in Chapter 1. Also, you may be approached by consultants who would like you to try their particular approach to merit pay. The first question you should ask about the studies you are reviewing and of the consultants is "What evidence is there that the merit pay plan leads to improved performance?" At this point you may read or be told: "Productivity was 120 percent after the introduction of the merit pay plan." At first blush, this seems encouraging. Upon careful consideration of study design issues, however, you conclude that this statement is meaningless. Why? Because if there is no indication that a pretest of productivity was conducted before the plan was implemented, the study results cannot support the claim. For all you know, based on this statement, productivity may have declined from the 150 percent productivity level that existed prior to the merit pay plan.

Next, you may turn to yet another study which shows a substantial increase in productivity from the pretest to the posttest. The use of a pretest gives you a greater sense of confidence in this merit pay plan than in the previous one. A careful reading shows, however, that along with the implementation of a merit pay plan, during the period of time from the pretest to the posttest, a new training program was also implemented. You now correctly conclude that while a productivity increase did occur, you cannot be confident that the change in productivity was actually due to merit pay rather than training. Why? There was no control group for comparing the group of similarly trained employees that did not receive merit pay to the experimental group.

In yet another study, you find a similar increase in productivity from pretest to posttest. This time, however, a control group was used. One group received merit pay, and the other did not. Hence, you can feel much more confident in the results found for this merit pay plan. You are still rightfully troubled, however, by the fact that more senior-level people were in the merit pay experimental group than in the control group. That is, there was no random assignment of employees. How might seniority be a problem? Senior people in organizations tend to receive higher salaries, and the higher salaries may have caused a productivity increase rather than merit pay. On the plus side, you are pleased to see that employees in the studied organization are similar to the ones in your own organization, and that productivity was tracked for an extended period of time after an initial merit increase was granted to employees. Hence, a representative sample was studied, and the results were not from a one-time-only evaluation.

Overall, this final study probably would give you the greatest level of confidence of the three described. You may decide to use this plan as the basis for setting up a merit pay plan for your organization. The next steps to take would be to make sure the plan is feasible, adapt it to your circumstances, and implement it. But *before* you implement it, you may again want to consider study design issues. In particular, you can replicate the pretest/posttest design with a control group evaluation design in your organization. Moreover, you can carefully match employees by seniority in the experimental and control groups by levels of seniority to eliminate your major concern with the previous study. As can be seen from this example, study design considerations are critical to sound business decisions concerning evaluation.

Review of Empirical Studies Evaluating Merit Pay Plans

In Chapter 1, an initial attempt was made to answer the question, "Are merit pay plans successful?" The answer was a tentative and qualified "yes," based on a survey of compensation professionals by Peck (1984). As shown in Table 2.1, it is possible to tie pay to previous performance. This has been demonstrated in diverse organizations. The extent to which this link then leads to favorable outcomes is less certain. As will be shown in this final section of the book, there is a great deal of variance in the success of merit pay plans when gauged by outcomes subsequent to merit pay. This should not come as a surprise, however, given the care that must be taken in the assessment of the desirability and feasibility of merit pay, the development and administration of a merit pay plan, and the evaluation of a merit pay plan.

A summary of the empirical studies evaluating outcomes associated with merit pay is shown in Table 7.2. This table is also supplemented by a summary of empirical studies that have evaluated merit pay in the federal government as shown in Tables 7.3 and 7.4. In reviewing these summary tables, several aspects of the procedures used and outcomes reported stand out.

Procedures

One notable procedural feature is the heavy reliance placed on managerial employees in the public sector. Managers have been studied in school districts, transit agencies, states, cities, counties, municipalities, and especially in federal government agencies. The plus side of relying so heavily on this one type of participant is that it allows an in-depth look at how merit pay plans operate and affect individuals. The downside, however, is external validity. The results may not generalize to other employee groups or to other sectors of the economy. In reviewing these summaries, also keep in mind that the less than optimal results obtained with merit pay in the federal government may not necessarily generalize to private-sector organizations.

A second notable procedural feature is how little attention has been given to evaluating merit pay against business unit outcomes. Most of the evaluation studies have instead concentrated on individual outcomes. While these outcomes are indeed important, they provide an incomplete look at the overall effectiveness of merit pay plans. More research is needed on the effects of merit pay on business unit outcomes.

A third notable feature is the relative lack of controls in the research designs that have been used. In only 10 of the studies shown in Table 7.2 was any attempt made to control for extraneous factors. In five studies, a nonequivalent control group was used (Daley, 1987; Fox, 1989; Greene & Podsakoff, 1978; Schay, 1988; Schneider & Olson, 1970). In another four studies, a time-series design was used (Alan & Rosenberg, 1986; Pearce et al., 1985; Kopelman & Reinharth, 1985; Scott et al., 1987). An attempt was made to statistically control for extraneous factors in one study (Jenkins & Lawler, 1981). Given the lack of control over extraneous factors, it is not possible to assign strict causality to merit pay for the outcomes reported. Threats to internal validity need to be kept in mind in reviewing many of these evaluation studies.

Outcomes

The outcomes reported for merit pay in these evaluation studies do little to alter the conclusion reached in Chapter 1 that merit pay plans are, overall, moderately effective. Merit pay seems to be consistently related to positive attitudes, but has not been consistently

Table 7.2
Summary of Studies Evaluating Outcomes of Merit Pay Plans

Authors	Participants	Organizations	Criteria	Procedure	Results[a]
Alan and Rosenberg (1986)	2230 managers	New York City government	Performance ratings	Performance measured for 3 consecutive years after implementation of plan	Performance ratings increased over the 3 year period at an unspecified level of significance
Bullock (1983)	380 employees	Engineering division of a southeastern public utility	Pay satisfaction and job satisfaction	Pay and job satisfaction measured before and after implementation of merit pay plan	Merit award status did not significantly predict changes in pay satisfaction, but did significantly predict increases in job satisfaction.
Cherrington, Reitz, and Scott (1971)	90 undergraduate business-student volunteers	Academic institution	Relationship between satisfaction and performance perceptions	Comparison of three pay plans: random rewards, positively contingent rewards, and negatively contingent rewards	Positive relationship between satisfaction and performance for positively contingent rewards, and negative relationship for negatively contingent rewards
Daley (1987)	315 mid-level managers and senior executives	Federal government	Motivation as defined by items measuring equity, intrinsic satisfaction, and perceived performance-reward relationship	Comparison of employees that received and did not receive merit pay	Intrinsic satisfaction and equity the same for both groups; perceived performance-reward relationship significantly greater for recipients of merit pay
Deadrick and Scott (1987)	222 transit directors	Urban Mass Transportation Administration	Employee motivation	Employee motivation measured at varying years after implementation of merit pay plans	Increased employee motivation was the most frequently mentioned benefit of merit pay programs.

(continued)

Table 7.2 (continued)

Authors	Participants	Organizations	Criteria	Procedure	Results[a]
Fox (1989)	378 employees in professional or managerial positions	States, counties, and municipalities	Organizational commitment	Comparison of experimental group who received merit pay increases versus matched control group who received other forms of increases	Stronger positive correlation between merit pay and commitment for the experimental than control group
Gaertner, Gaertner, and Akinnusi (1984)	213 management employees	Five sites of the Environmental Protection Agency and the Mine Safety and Health Administration	Anticipated reactions to implementation of a merit pay plan	Comparison of organizations with organic and mechanistic structures	Reactions from managers in the organic organization were significantly less positive than managers in the mechanistic organization.
Giles and Barrett (1971)	157 professional level personnel	Medium-sized eastern electronics company	Satisfaction with merit increase	Perceived merit increase and satisfaction measured at same time	Satisfaction increased as a power function of perceived merit increase.
Gomez-Mejia and Balkin (1989)	175 scientists and engineers	Research and development laboratories in the Boston area	Pay satisfaction, withdrawal cognition, project performance, individual performance	Participants responded to questionnaire about characteristics and effectiveness of pay system	Merit pay had a significant positive impact on group but not individual performance.
Greene (1973)	62 first-line managers	Marketing and financial divisions of a large manufacturing company	Job satisfaction and performance	Organization had a merit pay plan. All criteria measured at two different time periods	Performance causes merit pay. Job satisfaction does not cause performance. Merit pay and performance cause job satisfaction

Authors	Participants	Organizations	Criteria	Procedure	Results[a]
Greene and Podsakoff (1978)	Plant 1: 456 operative-level employees and 37 first-line managers. Plant 2: 592 operative-level employees and 45 first-level supervisors	Two paper mill plants of a large manufacturer	Performance and satisfaction	Comparison of plant 1 (pay based on seniority) and plant 2 (pay based on merit) before and after merit pay was removed at plant 1. Participants matched by personal and job characteristics	Performance decreased and satisfaction increased in plant 1 compared to plant 2.
H. Heneman and Young (1988)	96 school administrators	Public school district in medium-sized midwestern city	Reactions to performance appraisal process, reactions to merit plan, and motivation	Criteria measured before and after implementation of merit plan	Above-average reactions to performance appraisal process before and after plan implementation. Reactions to plan and motivation below average before and after plan implementation
R. Heneman, Greenberger, and Strasser (1988)	104 nursing, technical, professional, and managerial employees	Midwest hospital	Pay-for-performance perceptions, and pay satisfaction	Criteria measured in hospital with an informal merit plan	Positive relationship between pay-for-performance perceptions and pay satisfaction
Hills, Scott, and Markham (1988)	About 673 nonunion office employees in managerial, professional, technical, & clerical positions	Mass transit organization	Pay increase satisfaction and pay-performance correlations.	Criteria were measured before and after implementation of a new guide chart emphasizing pay-for-performance philosophy.	Correlations between pay and performance increased as a result of new guidechart. Pay increase satisfaction was significantly lower for those employees who receive the lowest performance ratings and are highest in the pay grade.

(continued)

Table 7.2 (continued)

Authors	Participants	Organizations	Criteria	Procedure	Results[a]
Jenkins and Lawler (1981)	58 skilled machinists	Small manufacturer of tool and die equipment	Job satisfaction, pay satisfaction, performance, and pay-for-performance perceptions	Criteria measured before and after implementation of merit plan	Job satisfaction and pay satisfaction increased.
Kahn and Sherer (1990)	92 middle to upper level managers	Corporate offices and main production facility in a moderate size production firm	Performance ratings	Performance measured before and after merit increase	No significant increase in performance
Kopelman (1976)	210 design and development engineers	Three large technology-based companies	Motivation, performance, satisfaction, and relationship between pay and performance	All three plants had a merit-pay system. All criteria were measured at two different time periods.	Motivation, performance, and satisfaction were positively related to the pay-performance relationship.
Kopelman and Reinharth (1982)	1,165 white-collar employees with nonsupervisory responsibilities	Ten branches of a large financial institution	Performance of organizational subunit, range of salary increases, and the tie between performance and rewards	Ten subunits evaluated. Same unspecified type of merit plan was used in each branch. Performance was measured at two different time periods.	Positive relationship between the range of salary increases and subunit performance. Performance reward relationship was more strongly related to subsequent levels of subunit performance than to concurrent levels of performance.

Authors	Participants	Organizations	Criteria	Procedure	Results[a]
Miceli and Near (1988)	About 2000 middle managers and executives	22 departments and agencies of the federal government	Correlations between reception of merit award and motivation and satisfaction with employer, pay level, and pay system	Criteria measured approximately 2 years after implementation of merit pay plan	Positive correlations for merit with motivation, satisfaction with employer, and satisfaction with pay system. Negative correlation between merit and pay level
Pearce and Perry (1983)	About 160 managers and supervisors	Five diverse federal agencies	Value of pay, relationship between effort and performance, and relationship between performance and rewards	Perceptions measured before and after the implementation of a new performance-appraisal and merit-pay system	Pay was seen as an important reward, but the absolute level of importance declined. The expectation that effort will lead to performance decreased, and the expectation that performance will lead to rewards decreased.
Pearce, Stevenson, and Perry (1985)	Ranged from 12 to 73 employees and managers	20 local and branch social security administration offices	Four objective measures of office level productivity	Monthly time series data collected for about 48 months. Three interventions: (1) merit pay orientation and training (2) merit pay plan implemented (3) merit pay awarded	No significant increase in performance for any of the performance measures after any of the interventions
Schay (1988)	About 2072 employees in scientific, technical, administrative, and clerical positions	Research and development laboratories in the U.S. Navy	Pay-for-performance perceptions and pay satisfaction	Criteria administered before and after implementation of a merit plan. Criteria for experimental groups compared with criteria for matched control groups	Pay-for-performance perceptions increased for the experimental groups and did not change for the control groups. Pay satisfaction did not change for the experimental groups and decreased for the control groups.

(continued)

Table 7.2 *(continued)*

Authors	Participants	Organizations	Criteria	Procedure	Results[a]
Schneider and Olson (1970)	146 registered nurses	Two midwestern hospitals	Effort, pay satisfaction, relationship between effort and intrinsic rewards	Comparison of hospital 1 (pay based on effort and performance) and hospital 2 (pay based on service)	Effort was greater in hospital 1 than in hospital 2. Effort was positively related to intrinsic rewards in hospital 1, but not in hospital 2. The positive relationship between pay satisfaction and effort was greater in hospital 1 than in hospital 2.
Scott, Hills, Markham and Vest (1987)	Approximately 800 employees eligible for a merit pay plan	Large transit authority on the west coast	Performance ratings and satisfaction	Performance measured for 3 consecutive years; satisfaction measured once; merit pay plan in place for an unspecified period of time	Performance ratings increased over 3 year time period; majority of participants dissatisfied with their last pay raise
Wisdom and Patzig (1987)	26 public sector managers 1130 private sector managers	Respondents to National Survey of Supervisory Management Practices	Employee performance	Comparison of private and public sector manager's perceptions	Perceptions of employee performance were higher for private than public sector managers.

Source: R. Heneman (1990). Adapted with permission.

[a] Only statistically significant results ($p < .05$) are reported unless otherwise specified.

Table 7.3
Summary of Empirical Studies on the Federal Merit Pay System (FMPS)

Source	INTENDED OUTCOMES			
	To Relate Pay to Performance	To Provide Flexibility in Recognizing Good Performance with Cash Awards	To Motivate Merit Pay Employees	To Improve Productivity, Timeliness and Quality of Work
Daley, 1987. "Merit Pay Enters with a Whimper: The Initial Federal Civil Service Reform Experience"	Merit pay is not perceived as equitable; raises are too small.		Merit pay did not heighten survey measures of motivation.	Merit pay recipients perceived their agency to be no more responsive or effective than non-recipients.
Gaertner and Gaertner, 1984. "Performance Evaluation and Merit Pay: Results in the Environmental Protection Agency and the Mine Safety and Health Administration"			Improvement in accuracy of performance standards and overall appraisal	No positive impact on perceived agency effectiveness or employee work behavior
Gaertner and Gaertner, 1984. "Performance Contingent Pay for Federal Managers"	Not perceived to be rewarding people fairly with significant raises		Performance standards and appraisal improve work planning and accomplishment.	No positive impact on perceived agency effectiveness or employee work behavior
O'Toole and Churchill, 1982. "Implementing Pay-for-Performance: Initial Experiences"	Subjectivity and lack of resources undermine pay-for-performance relationship.		Enhances communication on goals and job expectations	Inconclusive

(continued)

Table 7.3 (*continued*)

Source	To Relate Pay to Performance	To Provide Flexibility in Recognizing Good Performance with Cash Awards	To Motivate Merit Pay Employees	To Improve Productivity, Timeliness and Quality of Work
Pagano, 1985. "An Exploratory Evaluation of the Civil Service Reform Act's Merit Pay System for the GS 13-15s"	Small sample of pool managers complained the monetary reward was not worth the amount of paperwork and energy expended.			
Pearce and Perry, 1983. "Federal Merit Pay: A Longitudinal Analysis"	No improvement in the pay-for-performance contingency after merit pay		Performance criteria were clearer, but may not reflect agency effectiveness.	
Pearce and Porter, 1986. "Employee Responses to Formal Performance Appraisal Feedback"			Relatively low (satisfactory) ratings caused a significant drop in organizational commitment.	
Pearce, Stevenson and Perry, 1985. "Managerial Compensation Based on Organizational Performance: A Time-Series Analysis of the Impact of Merit Pay"				No significant effect on organizational performance

Source	To Relate Pay to Performance	To Provide Flexibility in Recognizing Good Performance with Cash Awards	To Motivate Merit Pay Employees	To Improve Productivity, Timeliness and Quality of Work
Perry, Hanzlik and Pearce, 1982. "Effectiveness of Merit-Pay-Pool Management"	Modification of appraisal ratings to achieve agency merit pay goals reduced credibility of the system.			
U.S. General Accounting Office, 1984. A 2-Year Appraisal of Merit Pay in Three Agencies	Non-performance factors influenced size of merit increases more than necessary.	Provision of cash awards highly variable across agencies	Standards perceived to be fair, job related, and consistent with organizational goals	
U.S. General Accounting Office, 1981. Serious Problems Need to Be Corrected Before Federal Merit Pay Goes Into Effect			Performance appraisals have limitations, including overly quantitative standards and lack of pre-testing.	OPM method for computing merit pay would exceed former costs by $58 to $74 million.
U.S. Merit Systems Protection Board, 1981. Status Report on Performance Appraisal and Merit Pay Among Mid-Level Employees	Half of all employees perceived a moderate to strong effect on performance.		Employees perceived ratings as fair and accurate, but not very helpful.	

Source: Perry (1988). Reprinted with permission.

Table 7.4.
Assessment of the Performance Management and Recognition System (PMRS)

INTENDED OUTCOMES

Source	To Relate Pay to Performance	To Provide Flexibility in Recognizing Good Performance with Cash Awards	To Motivate Merit Pay Employees	To Improve Productivity, Timeliness and Quality of Work
Perry and Petrakis, 1987. "Can Merit Pay Improve Performance in Government?"	Employees who achieved high monetary rewards in 1985 were more likely to perform at high levels in the next rating period.	About 2/3 of the sample received performance awards.		Rewards were poor discriminators between "stayers" and "leavers."
Perry, Petrakis and Miller, 1989. "Federal Merit Pay, Round II: An Analysis of the Performance Management and Recognition System"	Lagged monetary rewards were positively and significantly related to performance ratings in 1986 but not 1987.	About 2/3 of the sample received performance awards.		
U.S. General Accounting Office, 1987. Pay for Performance: Implementation of the Performance Management and Recognition System	Non-performance factors that caused inequities under merit pay continue to exist in PMRS.	Fifty percent of respondents found the amounts of performance awards inadequate.	Performance standards for many employees were issued more than 30 days into the appraisal period.	

Source	To Relate Pay to Performance	To Provide Flexibility in Recognizing Good Performance with Cash Awards	To Motivate Merit Pay Employees	To Improve Productivity, Timeliness and Quality of Work
U.S. Merit Systems Protection Board, 1987. *Performance Management and Recognition System: Linking Pay to Performance*	Slightly less than half of employees perceived better performance leading to more pay.		Performance standards were perceived to be fair and accurate.	
U.S. Merit Systems Protection Board, 1988. *Toward Effective Performance Management in the Federal Government*	Same as MSPB (1987)		Same as MSPB (1987)	Higher turnover rates for employees rated "unacceptable" and "minimally successful"
U.S. Office of Personnel Management, 1987. *Performance Management and Recognition System*	Agencies reported reinforcement of linkage between pay and performance.	Size and amount of funding for performance awards increased.	Quality of performance standards a problem; not stated in measurable terms and did not differentiate between performance levels	
U.S. Office of Personnel Management, 1988. *Performance Management and Recognition System: FY 1986 Performance Cycle*	Performance ratings were inflated and average rating levels increased with grade level.	Performance awards were granted to most GM employees.		

Source: Perry (1988). Reprinted with permission.

shown to be related to improved subsequent performance. Given the potential problems with internal and external validity in many of these studies, the conclusion that merit pay plans are moderately effective should remain a tentative conclusion.

As just noted, merit pay outcomes have been fairly favorable for employee attitudes, with the notable exception of the federal government. Merit pay plans have been shown to be related to actual and perceived correlations between pay and performance (Daley, 1987; Hills et al., 1988; Kopelman, 1976; Kopelman & Reinharth, 1982; Schay, 1988). Positive relationships for pay-for-performance perceptions with pay satisfaction (R. Heneman et al., 1988) and job satisfaction (Kopelman, 1986) have been reported. That is, the stronger the perception that pay is related to performance, the higher the level of pay and job satisfaction. Merit pay plans have also been shown to be related to measures of job and pay satisfaction (Bullock, 1983; Giles & Barrett, 1971; Greene & Podsakoff, 1978; Jenkins & Lawler, 1981; Miceli & Near, 1988; Schay, 1988) and commitment (Fox, 1989).

The results to date on the relationship between merit pay and subsequent motivation and performance are not encouraging. This is seen in the results reported in Tables 7.3 and 7.4 for the federal government. Disappointing results have been reported in other organizational settings as well (e.g., H. Heneman & Young, 1988; Kahn & Sherer, 1990). It should be noted, however, that not *all* of the results have been disappointing. Improved performance at the *group* level has been associated with merit pay (Kopelman & Reinharth, 1982; Gomez-Mejia & Balkin, 1989), as have perceptions of improved motivation (Miceli & Near, 1988; Deadrick & Scott, 1987). While the goal is to be able to pinpoint which characteristics of merit pay plans are associated with which desirable behavioral or attitudinal outcomes, it is not possible to do so at this stage. As discussed by R. Heneman (1990), a shortfall in the current merit pay research is the limited information about the actual characteristics of the merit pay plan in the reporting of merit pay studies.

One glaring omission in the research on outcomes associated with merit pay is the relationship between merit pay and absenteeism and turnover. Almost no research has been conducted on the impact of merit pay on absenteeism and turnover, yet there is ample reason to believe that merit pay would lead to reduced levels of absence and turnover. The reason for this belief is shown in Figure 7.4.

In most cases, merit pay is not a one-time bonus, but is instead an addition to base pay. As a result, merit pay increases show a positive relationship with pay levels (H. Heneman, 1973). In other words, a merit increase in one year contributes to a larger base salary in the next year. The impact of merit pay on pay level has been overlooked in much of the merit pay research since 1973. But, it has been consistently reported in the pay satisfaction literature that, as would be expected, pay satisfaction is greater when pay level is larger (H. Heneman, 1985). When pay satisfaction is high, it has also been shown in the pay satisfaction literature that absenteeism and turnover are both decreased. What these results suggest is that if absenteeism and turnover had been included more often as outcomes in merit pay evaluation studies, the results of these merit pay studies may have been more favorable than the results presented in Table 7.2, where absenteeism and turnover were not studied.

The major conclusion from this review of empirical studies evaluating merit pay outcomes is that organizations should evaluate the results of their merit pay plans rather than relying solely on the results of these reviewed studies. The studies reviewed here are suggestive of probable results, but are limited

Figure 7.4
Impact of Merit Pay on Absenteeism and Turnover

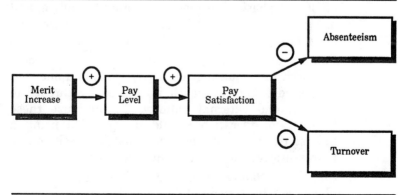

in number, show inconsistent findings, and include potential threats to internal and external validity. Given the constraints of this current research, organizations are well advised to conduct their own evaluation studies.

Summary of Major Points

1. *Merit Pay Outcomes.* A variety of merit pay outcomes can be used to evaluate the results of a merit pay plan. These outcomes can be categorized as immediate versus distant to the merit increase, and measured at the individual versus the business unit level.

2. *Relations Among Outcomes and Need for Multiple Outcomes.* Merit pay outcomes are not independent of one another. Instead, they exert an influence on one another. Multiple outcomes should be used in evaluating merit pay to show *how* and *why* merit pay plans are successful or not successful.

3. *Nonlinear Relationships Between Merit Pay and Outcomes.* A one-for-one return on merit pay outcomes for each dollar of merit increases should not be automatically assumed. Instead, tests are recommended to explore the possibility of nonlinear forms of the relationship between merit increases and outcomes.

4. *Proactive Versus Reactive Audits.* Audits of the results of merit pay plans should be conducted proactively, on an ongoing basis. If a reactive approach is taken, and merit pay plans are only audited when a problem arises, it may be too late to correct the problem.

5. *Validity of Evaluation Research.* The most common approach to evaluating merit pay plans is a one-shot case study. This approach is limited by threats to internal and external validity. To minimize these threats, consideration should be given to using a pretest, control group, random or matched assignment, representative sample, and multiple posttests.

6. *Empirical Studies on Outcomes.* Overall, merit pay plans seem to be moderately successful, as merit pay is consistently related to favorable employee attitudes

and less consistently related to improved performance. This overall assessment is tentative, however, given the threats to internal and external validity in this body of research.

Conclusions

The most disappointing aspect of merit pay is that very few evaluation studies have been conducted to tell us how effective these plans are to organizations. Virtually all organizations have merit plans, and virtually all operate on blind faith that their plans are working. It is strongly recommended that organizations conduct regular evaluation studies on the effectiveness of their merit pay plans.

Another disappointing aspect of merit pay is the limitations inherent in the current existing evaluation research, which make interpretation of the results difficult. There is a need for *more* research and a need for *better* research as well. Better evaluation research would broaden the evaluated outcomes to include outcomes at the business-unit level as well as at the individual level. Better evaluation research would also have better research design to minimize the threats to internal and external validity, which are too often present in most existing evaluation efforts.

On a more positive note, the evaluation research that has been conducted does show that merit pay shows promise as a method of incentive pay. Merit pay almost always appears to be related to pay and job satisfaction, and sometimes is associated with improved performance. This record can probably be improved with a better understanding of how merit pay works. As pointed out throughout the book, to better understand merit pay you need to recognize that: (1) the merit pay process must be managed, (2) a balance must be struck between performance and cost considerations, (3) the link between past performance and pay is a necessary but insufficient condition to establish a link between pay and improved future performance, and (4) the relationship between pay and performance must be perceived as well as documented.

Today, there is considerable use of merit pay plans. However, much more can and should be done with these plans from both research and practice perspectives. From a research perspective, much greater attention needs to be given to the institutional arrangements that govern merit pay decisions. Many have now researched the relationship between pay and performance. Some are now examining the informal arrangements in the work environment that influence the relationship between pay and performance. Certainly, this new direction in research, focusing on more informal arrangements, is important and should continue. A good example is the recent attention given to organizational, or office, politics as they relate to merit increases. We undoubtedly need more and better research on this fact of organizational life. What is still missing, however, in merit pay research is a more thorough investigation of formal institutional arrangements that also influence the pay and performance relationship. Using again the example of politics formal political actions taken by institutions also have a bearing on merit pay and deserve greater attention.

As discussed elsewhere in this book, the formal procedures specified for merit pay by the federal government have had a large impact on merit pay decisions and the reactions of federal government employees. Institutional arrangements such as these can be found in many other organizations as well. For example, everyone seems to have merit pay guidecharts, but we know little about what factors are considered by policy makers in setting up these guidecharts and to what extent they are actually followed by managers.

In terms of practice, more remains to be done with merit pay plans as well. First and foremost, as emphasized in this chapter, we must stop operating on the basis of "blind-faith" and, instead, begin conducting evaluation studies. Along with the need for more evaluations, there is also a need for more creativity and experimentation with merit pay plans. For example, merit pay could be used as a short-term, as well as a long-term, reward strategy. For example, to reinforce the application of materials learned in a training program, merit pay could be allocated in increments as employees get closer and closer to the desired behavior back on the job. This type of arrangement would presumably have advantages over a one-shot cash bonus granted for a single instance of effective behavior after training. Short-term merit pay could, in effect, be made contingent on a performance management plan for one part of a job. This is just one example of the more innovative use of merit pay. Organizations may become more willing to experiment with variations on traditional merit pay plans as they come to view the evaluation of merit pay as an integral part of the merit pay process, and an effective tool in managing the process.

References

Adams, J.S. (1965). Inequity in social exchange. In L.R. Berkowitz (Ed.), *Advances in experimental social psychology, volume 2* (pp. 267-299). New York: Academic Press.

Aiken, L.R. (1980). Content validity and reliability of single items on questionnaires. *Educational and Psychological Measurement, 40,* 950-959.

Alexander, R.A. & Barrett, G.A. (1982). Equitable salary increase judgments based upon merit and nonmerit considerations: A cross-national comparison. *International Review of Applied Psychology, 31,* 443-454.

Allan, P. & Rosenberg, S. (1986). An assessment of merit pay administration under New York City's managerial performance evaluation system: Three years of experience. *Public Personnel Management, 15,* 297-309.

Alloy, J.L. (1988, August 1). A move to pay workers the old-fashioned way. *Business First Magazine, Columbus, 4* (45), 4-5.

Balkin, D.B. (1989). Union influences on pay policy: A survey. *Journal of Labor Research, 10,* 299-307.

Balkin, D.B. & Gomez-Mejia, L.R. (1984). Determinants of R and D compensation in the high tech industry. *Personnel Psychology, 37,* 635-650.

Balkin, D.B. & Gomez-Mejia, L.R. (1987). The strategic use of short-term and long-term pay incentives in the high technology industry. In D.B. Balkin & L.R. Gomez-Mejia (Eds.), *New perspectives on compensation* (pp. 237-246). Englewood Cliffs, NJ: Prentice Hall.

Balkin, D.B. & Gomez-Mejia, L.R. (1990). Matching compensation and organizational strategies. *Strategic Management Journal, 4,* 153-169.

Ball, S.A. & Heneman, R.L. (1988). *Accurate performance ratings: There is hope.* Paper presented at the Annual Conference of the Human Resource Management and Organizational Behavior Conference, Long Beach, CA.

Balzer, W.K., Doherty, M.E. & O'Connor, R.J. (1989). Effects of cognitive feedback on performance. *Psychological Bulletin, 106,* 410-433.

Banks, C.G. & Roberson, L. (1985). Performance appraisers as test developers. *Academy of Management Review, 10,* 128-142.

Bannister, B.D. & Balkin, D.B. (1990). Performance evaluation and compensation feedback messages: An integrated model. *Journal of Occupational Psychology, 63,* 97-111.

Barkin, S. (1948). Labor's attitude toward wage incentive plans. *Industrial and Labor Relations Review, 1,* 553-572.

Barkin, S. (1970). Wage incentive problems in arbitration. *Labor Law Journal, 21* (1), 22-27.

Baron, J.N., Dobbin, F.R. & Jennings, P.D. (1986). War and peace: The evolution of modern personnel administration in U.S. industry. *American Journal of Sociology, 92,* 350-383.

Bartlett, C.J. (1983). What's the difference between valid and invalid halo? Forced choice measurement without forcing a choice. *Journal of Applied Psychology, 68,* 218-226.

Bartol, K.M. & Martin, D.C. (1989). Effects of dependence, dependency threats, and pay secrecy on managerial pay allocations. *Journal of Applied Psychology, 74,* 105-113.

Bartol, K.M. & Martin, D.C. (1990). When politics pays: Factors influencing managerial compensation decisions. *Personnel Psychology, 43,* 599-610.

Basnight, T.A. (1980). Designing master or "ideal" pay-performance matrices. *Compensation Review, 12* (4), 44-50.

Bass, B.M. (1968). Ability, values, and concepts of equitable salary increases in exercise compensation. *Journal of Applied Psychology, 52,* 299-303.

Beer, M. & Gery, G.J. (1972). Individual and organizational correlates of pay system preferences. In H.L. Tosi, R.J. House, & M.D. Dunnette (Eds.), *Managerial motivation and compensation* (pp. 325-349). East Lansing, MI: MSU Business Studies.

Belcher, D.W. (1979). Pay equity or pay fairness? *Compensation Review, 11* (2), 31-37.

Belcher, D.W. (1980). Pay and performance. *Compensation Review, 12* (3), 14-20.

Berger, C.J. & Schwab, D.P. (1980). Pay incentives and pay satisfaction. *Industrial Relations, 19,* 206-210.

Bernardin, H.J. & Klatt, L.A. (1985). Managerial appraisal systems: Has practice caught up to the state of the art? *The Personnel Administrator, 30* (11), 71-86.

Bernoulli, D. (1984). Exposition of a new theory on the measurement of risk. In G.A. Miller (Ed.), *Mathematics and psychology.* New York: Wiley.

Bernstein, A. (July 15, 1991). Joe Sixpack's grip on corporate America. *Business Week,* pp. 108-109.

Binning, J.F. & Barrett, G.V. (1989). Validity of personnel decisions: A conceptual analysis of the inferential and evidential bases. *Journal of Applied Psychology, 74,* 478-494.

Birnbaum, M.H. (1983). Perceived equity of salary policies. *Journal of Applied Psychology, 68,* 48-59.

Bishop, J. (1987). The recognition and reward of employee performance. *Journal of Labor Economics, 5,* 36-56.

Borman, W.C. (1978). Exploring upper limits of reliability and validity in job performance ratings. *Journal of Applied Psychology, 63,* 135-144.

Borman, W.C. & Dunnette, M.D. (1975). Behavior-based versus trait-oriented performance ratings: An empirical study. *Journal of Applied Psychology, 60,* 561-565.

Brennan, E.J. (1985). The myth and the reality of pay for performance. *Personnel Journal, 64* (3), 73-75.

Brenner, O.C. & Bertsch, T. M. (1983). Do assertive people prefer merit pay? *Psychological Reports, 52,* 595-598.

Bretz, R.D., Jr. & Milkovich, G.T. (1989). *Performance appraisal in large organizations: Practice and research implications (working paper 89-17).* Center for Advanced Human Resource Studies, School of Industrial and Labor Relations, Cornell University, Ithaca, NY.

Brockner, J. (1988). *Self-esteem at work.* Lexington, MA: Lexington.

Brogden, H.E. & Taylor, E.K. (1950). A theory and classification of criterion bias. *Educational and Psychological Measurement, 10,* 159-186.

Brown, C. (1990). Firms choice of method of pay. *Industrial and Labor Relations Review, 43* (No. 3, Special Issue), 165S-182S.

Brunker, G.P. (1982). The potential for performance-based benefit plans. *Compensation Review, 14* (3), 23-32.

Bullock, R.J. (1983). Participation and pay. *Group and Organization Studies, 8,* 127-136.

Bureau of National Affairs (ongoing). *Bulletin to management.* Washington, DC: Author.

Bureau of National Affairs (1983). *Performance appraisal programs* (Personnel Policies Forum Survey No. 135). Washington, DC: Author.

Bureau of National Affairs (1988). Changing pay practices: New developments in employee compensation. *Labor Relations Week, 2* (24), 1-200.

Campbell, D.T. & Fiske, D.W. (1959). Convergent and discriminant validation by the multitrait-multimethod matrix. *Psychological Bulletin, 56,* 81-105.

Campbell, D.T. & Stanley, J.C. (1966). *Experimental and quasi-experimental designs for research.* Chicago: Rand-McNally.

Campbell, J.P. (1990). Modeling the performance prediction problem in industrial and organizational psychology. In M.D. Dunnette and L.M. Hough (Eds.), *Handbook of industrial and organizational psychology, second edition, volume I* (pp. 687-732). Palo Alto, CA: Consulting Psychologists.

Carell, M.R. & Dittrich, J.E. (1978). Equity theory: The recent literature, methodological considerations, and new directions. *Academy of Management Review, 3,* 202-210.

Carnevale, A.P. (1991). *America and the new economy.* Washington, DC: American Society for Training and Development and U.S. Department of Labor.

Carroll, S.J. (1987). Business strategies and compensation systems. In D.B. Balkin & L.R. Gomez-Mejia (Eds.), *New perspectives on compensation* (pp. 343-355). Engelwood Cliffs, NJ: Prentice Hall.

Cimini, M.H. (1990). Developments in industrial relations. *Monthly Labor Review, 113* (3), 63-66.

Cimini, M.H. (1991). Developments in industrial relations. *Monthly Labor Review, 114* (5), 43-47.

Cherrington, D.J., Reitz, H.J. & Scott, W.E., Jr. (1971). Effects of contingent and noncontingent rewards on the relationship between satisfaction and task performance. *Journal of Applied Psychology, 55,* 531-536.

Clark, J.B. (1889). The possibility of a scientific law of wages. *Publications of the American Economic Association, 4,* 39-69.

Clark, T.B. & Wachtel, M. (1988, June). The quiet crisis goes public. *Government Executive,* 14-21.

Cleveland, J.N., Murphy, K.R. & Williams, R.E. (1989). Multiple uses of performance appraisal: Prevalence and correlates. *Journal of Applied Psychology, 74,* 130-135.

Cohen, D.K. & Murname, R.J. (1980). The merits of merit pay. *Public Interest, 80,* 3-30.

Cook, F.W. (1987). Rethinking compensation practices in light of economic conditions. *Personnel, 27* (1), 46-51.

Cooper, W.H. (1981). Conceptual similarity as a source of illusory halo in job performance ratings. *Journal of Applied Psychology, 66,* 302-307.

Cotton, J.L. & Cook, M.S. (1982). Meta-analyses and the effects of various reward systems: Some different conclusions from Johnson et al. *Psychological Bulletin, 92,* 176-183.

Cowan, P. (1978). How Blue Cross put pay-for-performance to work. *Personnel Journal, 57* (5), 250-269.

Daley, D. (1987). Merit pay enters with whimper: The initial federal civil service reform experience. *Review of Public Personnel Administration, 7* (2), 72-79.

Dansereau, F., Graen, G. & Haga, W.J. (1975). A vertical dyad-linkage approach to leadership within formal organizations. *Organizational Behavior and Human Performance, 13,* 46-78.

Deadrick, D.L. & Scott, K.D. (1987). Employee incentives in the public sector: A national survey of urban mass transit authorities. *Public Personnel Management, 16,* 135-143.

Deci, E.L. (1972). The effects of contingent and noncontingent rewards and controls on intrinsic motivation. *Organizational Behavior and Human Performance, 8,* 217-229.

DeNisi, A.S., Cafferty, T.P. & Meglino, B.M. (1984). A cognitive view of the performance appraisal process: A model and research propositions. *Organizational Behavior and Human Performance, 33,* 360-396.

DeNisi, A.S., Robbins, T. & Cafferty, T.P. (1989). Organization of information used for performance appraisals: Role of diary keeping. *Journal of Applied Psychology, 74,* 124-129.

Dienesch, R.M. & Liden, R.C. (1986). Leader-member exchange model of leadership: A critique and further development. *Academy of Management Review, 11,* 618-634.

Distefano, M.K., Pryer, M.O.W. & Erffmeyer, R.C. (1983). Application of content validity methods to the development of a job-related performance rating criterion. *Personnel Psychology, 36,* 621-631.

Dorfman, P.W., Stephen, W.G. & Loveland, J. (1986). Performance appraisal behaviors: Supervisor perceptions and subordinate reactions. *Personnel Psychology, 39,* 579-598.

Dossett, D.L. (1989). Dimensional characteristics of behaviorally based performance ratings. *Journal of Management Systems, 1,* 51-66.

Downs, C.W. & Moscinski, P. (1979). *A survey of appraisal processes and training in large corporations.* Paper presented at the Annual Academy of Management Meetings, Atlanta, GA.

Dreher, G.F. (1981). Predicting the salary satisfaction of exempt employees. *Personnel Psychology, 34,* 579-589.

Dyer, L.D. & Parker, D.F. (1975). Classifying outcomes in work motivation research: An examination of the intrinsic-extrinsic dichotomy. *Journal of Applied Psychology, 60,* 455-458.

Dyer, L.D. & Theriault, R. (1976). The determinants of pay satisfaction. *Journal of Applied Psychology, 61,* 596-604.

Elkouri, F. & Elkouri, E.A. (1973). *How arbitration works.* Washington, DC: The Bureau of National Affairs.

Evans, W.A. (1970). Pay for performance: Fact or fable? *Personnel Journal, 49* (9), 726-731.

Farh, J.L. & Dobbins, G.H. (1989). Effects of comparative performance information on the accuracy of self-ratings and agreement between self- and supervisory ratings. *Journal of Applied Psychology, 74,* 606-610.

Farmer, C.R. (1978). Merit pay: Viable? *Personnel, 16* (5), 57-63.

Fay, C.H. (in press). Salary budgeting and planning: Enhancing the process through the use of the computer. In M. Rock (Ed.), *Handbook of wage and salary administration.* New York: McGraw-Hill.

Feldman, J.M. (1981). Beyond attribution theory: Cognitive processes in performance appraisal. *Journal of Applied Psychology, 66,* 127-148.

Ferris, G.R., Russ, G.S. & Fandt, P.M. (1989). Politics in organizations. In R.A. Giacalone & P. Rosenfeld (Eds.), *Impression management in the organization* (pp. 143-170). Hillsdale, NJ: Erlbaum.

Flanagan, J.L. (1954). The critical incident technique. *Psychological Bulletin, 51,* 327-358.

Florida Power Corporation: Focus on performance. (1985). *Training, 22* (11), 57-60.

Folger, R. & Konovsky, M.A. (1989). Effects of procedural and distributive justice on reactions to pay raise decisions. *Academy of Management Journal, 32,* 115-130.

Fossum, J.A. (1976). Publicity or secrecy: Pay and performance effects on satisfaction. *Proceedings of the Academy of Management,* 270-272.

Fossum, J.A. & Fitch, M.K. (1985). The effects of individual and contextual attributes on the size of recommended salary increases. *Personnel Psychology, 38,* 587-603.

Foster, K. & Lynn, K.V. (1978). Dividing up the "merit" increase pie for management. *Personnel Administrator, 23* (5), 42-48.

Fox, S.F. (1989). Intergenerational differences, merit pay, and loyalty in a state and local government. *Review of Public Personnel Administration, 9* (2), 15-27.

Frank, R.H. (1984). Are workers paid their marginal products? *The American Economic Review, 74,* 549-571.

Freedman, S.M. (1978). Some determinants of compensation decisions. *Academy of Management Journal, 21,* 397-409.

Freedman, S.M. & Montanari, J.R. (1980). An integrative model of managerial reward allocation. *Academy of Management Review, 5,* 381-390.

Freeman, R.B. (1982). Union wage practices and wage dispersion within establishments. *Industrial and Labor Relations Review, 36,* 3-21.

Friedman, B.A. & Cornelius, E.T. III. (1976). Effect of rater participation in scale construction on the psychometric characteristics of two rating scale formats. *Journal of Applied Psychology, 61,* 210-216.

Gabor, A. (June 5, 1989). Catch a falling star system. *U.S. News & World Report,* pp. 43-44.

Gabris, G.T. & Mitchell, K. (1988). The impact of merit raise scores on employee attitudes: The Matthew Effect of performance appraisal. *Public Personnel Management, 17,* 369-382.

Gabris, G.T., Mitchell, K. & McLemore, R. (1985). Rewarding individual and team productivity: The Biloxi merit bonus plan. *Public Personnel Management, 14,* 231-244.

Gaertner, K.H. & Gaertner, G.H. (1984). Performance evaluation and merit pay: Results in the Environmental Protection Agency and Health Administration. In P.I. Ingraham & C. Ban (Eds.), *Legislating bureaucratic change: The Civil Service Reform Act of 1978* (pp. 87-111). Albany, NY: State University of New York.

Gaertner, G.H., Gaertner, K.H. & Akinnusi, D.M. (1984). Environment, strategy, and the implementation of administrative change: The case of civil service reform. *Academy of Management Journal, 27,* 525-543.

Gardner, J.W. (1961). *Excellence.* New York: Harper.

Garland, H. (1973). The effects of piece-rate underpayment and over-payment on job performance: A test of equity theory with a new induction procedure. *Journal of Applied Social Psychology, 3,* 325-334.

Georgopoulos, B.S., Mahoney, G.M. & Jones, N.W. (1957). A path-goal approach to productivity. *Journal of Applied Psychology, 41,* 345-353.

Gerhart, B.A. & Milkovich, G.J. (in press). Salaries, salary growth, and promotions of men and women in a large, private firm. In R. Michael & H. Hartman (Eds.), *Pay equity: Empirical inquiries.* Washington, DC: National Academy Press.

Ghiselli, E.E., Campbell, J.P. & Zedeck, S. (1981). *Measurement theory for the behavioral sciences.* San Francisco: W.H. Freeman.

Giles, B.A. & Barrett, G.V. (1971). Utility of merit increases. *Journal of Applied Psychology, 55,* 103-109.

Giles, W.F. & Mossholder, K.W. (1990). Employee reactions to contextual and session components of performance appraisal. *Journal of Applied Psychology, 75,* 371-377.

Gomez-Mejia, L.R. & Balkin, D.B. (1989). Effectiveness of individual and aggregate compensation strategies. *Industrial Relations, 28,* 431-445.

Goodale, J.G. & Mouser, M.W. (1981). Developing and auditing a merit pay system. *Personnel Journal, 60* (5), 391-397.

Goodman, P.S. (1975). Effect of perceived inequity on salary allocation decisions. *Journal of Applied Psychology, 60,* 372-375.

Gordon, D.F. (1974). A neo-classical theory of Keynsian unemployment. *Economic Inquiry, 12* (4), 431-459.

Gordon, M.E. & Johnson, W.A. (1982). Seniority: A review of its legal and scientific standing. *Personnel Psychology, 35,* 255-280.

Gould, S. & Penley, L.E. (1984). Career strategies and salary progression: A study of their relationships in a municipal bureaucracy. *Organizational Behavior and Human Performance, 34,* 244-265.

Green, S.G. & Liden, R.C. (1980). Contextual and attributional influences on control decisions. *Journal of Applied Psychology, 65,* 453-458.

Greenberg, J. (1986). Determinants of perceived fairness of performance evaluations. *Journal of Applied Psychology, 71,* 340-342.

Greenberg, J. (1987a). A taxonony of organizational justice theories. *Academy of Management Review, 12,* 9-22.

Greenberg, J. (1987b). Reactions to procedural justice in payment distributions: Do the means justify the ends? *Journal of Applied Psychology, 72,* 55-61.

Greenberg, J. & McCarty, C.L. (1990). *The interpersonal aspects of procedural justice: A new perspective on pay fairness.* Paper presented at the Spring Meeting of the Industrial Relations Research Association, Buffalo, NY.

Greene, C.N. (1973). Causal connections among managers' merit pay, job satisfaction, and performance. *Journal of Applied Psychology, 58,* 95-100.

Greene, C.N. & Podsakoff, P.M. (1978). Effects of removal of a pay incentive: A field experiment. *Academy of Management Proceedings, 38,* 206-210.

Greiner, J.W., Bell, L. & Hatry, H.P. (1975). *Employee incentives to improve state and local government in productivity.* Washington, DC: National Commission on Productivity and Work Quality.

Guzzo, R.A. & Bondy, J.S. (1983). *A guide to worker productivity experiments in the United States: 1976-1981.* Scarsdale, NY: Work in America Institute.

Haire, M., Ghiselli, E.E. & Gordon, M.E. (1967). A psychological study of pay. *Journal of Applied Psychology Monograph, 51,* (Whole No. 636).

Hall, J.L., Posner, B.Z. & Harder, J.W. (1989). Performance appraisal systems: Matching practice with theory. *Group and Organization Studies, 14,* 51-69.

Hamner, W.C. (1975). How to ruin motivation with pay. *Compensation Review, 7* (4), 17-27.

Handshear, N.A. (1988). News preferred over mystery—members favor Merit Review News. *American Compensation Association News, 31* (5), 10.

Handshear, N.A. (1989). Personal communication.

Hansen, W.L. (1988). Merit pay in structured and unstructured salary systems. *Academe, 74* (6), 10-13.

Henderson, R. (1980). *Performance appraisal: Theory to practice.* Englewood Clifs, NJ: Prentice Hall.

Heneman, H.G. III (1973). Impact of performance on managerial pay levels and pay changes. *Journal of Applied Psychology, 58,* 128-130.

Heneman, H.G. III (1985). Pay satisfaction. In K.N. Rowland & G.R. Ferris (Eds.), *Research in personnel and human resources management, volume 3,* (pp. 115-139). Greenwich, CT: JAI Press.

Heneman, H.G. III & Ellis, R.A. (1982). Correlates of just-noticeable differences in pay increases. *Labor Law Journal, 34,* 533-538.

Heneman, H.G. III & Schwab, D.P. (1979). Work and rewards theory. In D. Yoder & H.G. Heneman, Jr. (Eds.) *ASPA handbook of personnel and industrial relations* (pp. 6-1–6-22). Washington, DC: Bureau of National Affairs.

Heneman, H.G. III & Schwab, D.P. (1985). Pay satisfaction: Its multidimensional nature and measurement. *International Journal of Psychology, 20,* 129-141.

Heneman, H.G. III, Schwab, D.P., Fossum, J.A. & Dyer, L.D. (1989). *Personnel/human resource management.* Homewood, IL: Irwin.

Heneman, H.G. III, Schwab, D.S., Standal, J.T., & Peterson, R.B. (1978). Pay comparisons: Dimensionality and predictability. *Academy of Management Proceedings, 38,* 211-215.

Heneman, H.G. III & Young, I.P. (1988). *Evaluation of school district administrator's reactions to a merit pay program.* Paper presented at the National Academy of Management Meetings, Anaheim, CA.

Heneman, R.L. (1984a). *The effects of rating format and rater training on performance rating accuracy and the motivation to rate accurately.* Unpublished doctoral dissertation, Michigan State University, East Lansing, MI.

Heneman, R.L. (1984b). *Pay for performance: Exploring the merit system* (Work in America Institute/Studies in Productivity #38). New York: Pergamon.

Heneman, R.L. (1986). The relationship between supervisory ratings and results-oriented measures of performance: A meta-analysis. *Personnel Psychology, 39,* 811-826.

Heneman, R.L. (1988). Traits, behaviors, and rater training: Some unexpected results. *Human Performance, 1,* 85-98.

Heneman, R.L. (1990). Merit pay research. In G.R. Ferris & K.M. Rowland (Eds.), *Research in personnel and human resources management, Vol. 8,* (pp. 203-262). Greenwich, CT: JAI Press.

Heneman, R.L. (1991). Evaluating the effectiveness of merit pay: A criterion model. *Proceedings of the 34th Annual Meeting of the Midwest Academy of Management, 34,* 121-126.

Heneman, R.L. & Cohen, D.J. (1988). Supervisory and employee characteristics as correlates of employee salary increases. *Personnel Psychology, 41,* 345-360.

Heneman, R.L., Greenberger, D.B., & Anonyuo, C. (1989). Attributions and exchanges: The effects of interpersonal factors on the diagnosis of employee performance. *Academy of Management Journal, 32,* 466-476.

Heneman, R.L., Greenberger, D.B., & Strasser, S. (1988). The relationship between pay-for-performance perceptions and pay satisfaction. *Personnel Psychology, 41,* 745-759.

Heneman, R.L. & Wexley, K.N. (1983). The effects of time delay in rating and amount of information observed on performance rating accuracy. *Academy of Management Journal, 26,* 677-686.

Heneman, R.L., Wexley, K.N. & Moore, M.L. (1987). Performance-rating accuracy: A critical review. *Journal of Business Research, 15,* 431-448.

Henry, R.A. & Hulin, C.L. (1987). Stability of skilled performance across time: Some generalizations and limitations on utilities. *Journal of Applied Psychology, 72,* 457-462.

Herman, J.B. (1973). Are situational contingencies limiting job attitude-job performance relationships? *Organizational Behavior and Human Performance, 10,* 208-224.

Herrnstein, R.J. (1990). Behaviors, reinforcement, and utility. *Psychological Science, 1,* 217-224.

Hills, F.S., Scott, D.K. & Markham, S.E. (1988). *Pay system structure as a moderator of the pay-performance relationship and employee pay increases satisfaction.* Paper presented at the National Academy of Management Meetings, Anaheim, CA.

Hinkin, T.R., Podsakoff, P.M. & Schriesheim, C.A. (1987). The mediation of performance-contingent "compensation" by supervisors in work organizations: A reinforcement perspective. In D.B. Balkin & L.R. Gomez-Mejia (Eds.), *New perspectives on compensation* (pp. 196-210). Englewood Cliffs, NJ: Prentice Hall.

Hinrichs, J.R. (1969). Correlates of employee evaluations of pay increases. *Journal of Applied Psychology, 53,* 481-489.

Hobson, C.J., Mendel, R.M. & Gibson, F.W. (1981). Clarifying performance appraisal criteria. *Organizational Behavior and Human Performance, 28,* 164-188.

Holliman, S.D. (1983). *Merit pay: The federal government's pay-for-performance experience.* Unpublished master's thesis, Naval Postgraduate School, Monterey, CA.

How one company has taken pay for performance to the max: Performance based benefits (1989). *Compensation and Benefits Managers Report* (Prentice Hall Professional Newsletter) *3* (20), 149-151.

Huber, V.L., Neale, M.A. & Northcraft, G.B. (1987). Judgment by heuristics: Effects of ratee and rater characteristics and performance standards on performance-related standards. *Organizational Behavior and Human Decision Processes, 40,* 149-169.

Hulin, C.L. (1982). Some reflections on general performance dimensions and halo rating error. *Journal of Applied Psychology, 67,* 165-170.

Hunter, R.W. & Silverman, B.R.S. (1980). Merit pay in the federal government. *Personnel Journal, 59,* 1003-1007.

Hurwich, A.C. (1986). Strategic compensation designs that link pay to performance. *Journal of Business Strategy, 7* (3), 79-83.

Hyde, A.C. (1988). The new environment for compensation and performance in the public sector. *Public Personnel Management, 17,* 351-357.

Ilgen, D.R., Fisher, C.D. & Taylor, M.S. (1979). Consequences of individual feedback on behavior in organizations. *Journal of Applied Psychology, 64,* 349-371.

Ivancevich, J.M. (1983). Contrast effects in performance evaluations and reward practices. *Academy of Management Journal, 26,* 465-476.

Jackson, S.E., Schuler, R.S. & Rivero, J.C. (1989). Organizational characteristics as predictors of personnel practices. *Personnel Psychology, 42,* 727-786.

James, L.R. (1973). Criterion models and construct validity for criteria. *Psychological Bulletin, 80,* 75-83.

Jenkins, D.G., Jr., (1986). Financial incentives. In E.A. Locke (Ed.), *Generalizing from laboratory to field settings* (pp. 167-180). Lexington, MA: D.C. Heath.

Jenkins, D.G., Jr. & Lawler, E.E. III (1981). Impact of employee participation in pay plan development. *Organizational Behavior and Human Performance, 28,* 111-128.

Jick, T.D. (1979). Mixing qualitative and quantitative methods: Triangulation in action. *Administrative Science Quarterly, 24,* 602-611.

Johnson, D.W., Maruyama, G., Johnson, R., Nelson, D. & Skon, L. (1981). Effects of cooperative, competitive, and individualistic goal structures on achievement: A Meta-analysis. *Psychological Bulletin, 89,* 47-62.

Johnson, M. & Kasten, K. (1983). Meritorious work and faculty rewards: An empirical test of the relationship. *Research in Higher Education, 19,* 49-71.

Kahn, L.M. & Sherer, P.D. (1990). Contingent pay and managerial performance. *Industrial and Labor Relations Review, 43* (No. 3 Special Issue), 107S-120S.

Kanter, R.M. (1987). From status to contribution: Some organizational implications of the changing basis for pay. *Personnel, 17* (1), 12-37.

Katz, L.F. (1986). Efficiency wage theories: A partial evaluation. In S. Fischer (Ed.), *National Bureau of Economics Research macroeconomics annual* (pp. 235-276). Cambridge, MA: The MIT Press.

Katzell, R.A., Beinstock, P. & Faerstein, P. (1977). *A guide to worker productivity experiments in the United States: 1971-1975.* Scarsdale, NY: Work in America Institute.

Kaufman, B.E. (1989). Models of man in industrial relations research. *Industrial and Labor Relations Review, 43,* 72-88.

Kaun, D.E. (1984). Faculty advancement in a nontraditional university environment. *Industrial and Labor Relations Review, 37,* 592-606.

Kavanaugh, M.J., Mackinney, A.L. & Wolins, L. (1971). Issues in a managerial performance: Multitrait-multimethod analyses of ratings. *Psychological Bulletin, 75,* 34-39.

Keely, M. (1978). A contingency framework for performance evaluation. *Academy of Management Review, 3,* 428-438.

Kennedy, C.W., Fossum, J.A. & White, B.J. (1983). Empirical comparison of within-subjects expectancy theory models. *Organizational Behavior and Human Performance, 20,* 124-143.

Kidder, L., Bellettirie, G. & Cohn, E.S. (1977). The effects of anonymity on reward allocations made by women and men. *Journal of Experimental Social Psychology, 13,* 70-80.

King, L.M., Hunter, J.E. & Schmidt, F.L. (1980). Halo in a multidimensional, forced-choice performance evaluation scale. *Journal of Applied Psychology, 65,* 507-516.

Kleiner, M.M. & Bouillon, M.L. (1988). Providing business information to production workers: Correlates of compensation and profitability. *Industrial and Labor Relations Review, 41,* 605-617.

Klimoski, R. & Inks, L. (1990). Accountability forces in performance appraisal. *Organizational Behavior and Human Decision Processes, 45,* 194-208.

Koch, J.V. & Chizmar, J.F. (1973). The influence of teaching and other factors upon absolute salaries and salary increases at Illinois State University. *The Journal of Economic Education, 5,* 27-34.

Komaki, J. (1986). Applied behavior analysis and organizational behavior: Reciprocal influence of the two fields. In B. Staw & L.L. Cummings (Eds.), *Research in organizational behavior, volume 8,* (pp. 297-334). Greenwich, CT: JAI Press.

Konrad, A.M. & Pfeffer, J. (1990). Do you get what you deserve? Factors affecting the relationship between productivity and pay. *Administrative Science Quarterly, 35,* 258-285.

Kopelman, R.E. (1976). Organizational control system responsiveness, expectancy theory constructs, and work motivation: Some interrelations and causal connections. *Personnel Psychology, 29,* 205-220.

Kopelman, R.E. & Reinharth, L. (1982). Research results: The effect of merit-pay practices on white collar performance. *Compensation Review, 14* (4), 30-40.

Koys, D.J., Keaveny, T.J. & Allen, R.E. (1989). Demographic and attitudinal predictors of preferences for alternative pay increase policies. *Proceedings of the Thirty-Second Annual Meeting of the Midwest Academy of Management, 32,* 159-163.

Krefting, L.A., Newman, J.M. & Krzystofiak, F. (1987). What is a meaningful pay increase? In D.B. Balkin & L.R. Gomez-Mejia (Eds.), *New perspectives on compensation* (pp. 135-140). Englewood Cliffs, NJ: Prentice Hall.

Krefting, L.A. & Mahoney, T.A. (1977). Determining the size of a meaningful pay increase. *Industrial Relations, 16,* 83-93.

Kroeck, K.G., Avolio, B.J., Small, R.L. & Einstein, W.O. (1987). Shifts in resource allocation preference following panel discussion. *Journal of Management, 13,* 713-724.

Krueger, A.B. & Summers, L.H. (1988). Efficiency wages and interindustry wage structure. *Econometrica, 56,* 259-293.

Kruglanski, A.W. (1989). The psychology of being "right": The problem of accuracy in social perception and cognition. *Psychological Bulletin, 106,* 395-409.

Landau, S.B. & Leventhal, G.S. (1976). A simulation study of administrator's behavior toward employees who receive job offers. *Journal of Applied Social Psychology, 6,* 291-306.

Landy, F.J. (1986). Stamp collecting versus science: Validation as hypothesis testing. *American Psychologist, 41,* 1183-1192.

Landy, F.J., Barnes, J.L. & Murphy, K.R. (1978). Correlates of perceived fairness and accuracy of performance evaluations. *Journal of Applied Psychology, 63,* 751-754.

Landy, F.J. & Farr, J.L. (1980). Performance rating. *Psychological Bulletin, 87,* 72-107.

Landy, F.J., Farr, J.L. & Jacobs, R.R. (1982). Utility concepts in performance measurement. *Organizational Behavior and Human Performance, 30,* 15-40.

Landy, F.J., Vance, R.J., Barnes-Farrel, J.L. & Steele, J.W. (1980). Statistical control of halo error in performance ratings. *Journal of Applied Psychology, 65,* 501-506.

Latham, G.P. & Wexley, K.N. (1981). *Increasing productivity through performance appraisal.* Reading, MA: Addison-Wesley.

Lawler, E.E. III (1965). Manager's perceptions of their subordinates' pay and of their superiors' pay. *Personnel Psychology, 18,* 413-422.

Lawler, E.E. III (1971). *Pay and organizational effectiveness: A psychological view.* New York: McGraw-Hill.

Lawler, E.E. III (1972). Secrecy and the need to know. In H.L. Tosi, R.J. House & M.D. Dunnette (Eds.), *Managerial motivation and compensation* (pp. 455-476). East Lansing, MI: MSU Business Studies.

Lawler, E.E. III (1976). Comments on Herbert H. Meyer's "The pay for performance dilemma." *Organizational Dynamics, 4* (1), 73-75.

Lawler, E.E. III (1981). *Pay and organization development.* Reading, MA: Addison-Wesley.

Lawler, E.E. III, & Hackman, J.R. (1969). Impact of employee participation in the development of pay incentives plans: A field experiment. *Journal of Applied Psychology, 53,* 467-471.

Lawler, E.E. III, Mohrman, A.M., Jr. & Resnick, S.M. (1984). Performance appraisal revisited. *Organizational Dynamics, 12,* 20-35.

Lawshe, C.H. (1975). A quantitative approach to content validity. *Personnel Psychology, 28,* 563-575.

Lawther, W.C., Bernardin, H.J., Traynham, E. & Jennings, K. (1989). Implications of salary structure and merit pay in the fifty American states. *Review of Public Personnel Administration, 9* (2), 1-14.

Lazear, E. & Rosen, S. (1981). Rank order tournaments as an optimum labor contract. *Journal of Political Economy, 89,* 841-864.

Lerner, M.J. (1982). The justice motive in human relations and the economic model of man: A radical analysis of facts and fictions. In V. Derlega & J. Grezlak (Eds.), *Cooperation and helping behavior: Theories and research* (pp. 121-145). New York: Academic Press.

Leventhal, G.S. (1976). The distribution of rewards and resources in groups and organizations. In L. Berkowitz & E. Walster (Eds.), *Equity theory: toward a general theory of social interaction. Advances in experimental social psychology, volume 9* (pp. 92-131). New York: Academic Press.

Leventhal, G.S., Michaels, J.W. & Sanford, C. (1972). Inequity and interpersonal conflict: Reward allocation and secrecy about reward as methods of preventing conflict. *Journal of Personality and Social Psychology, 23,* 88-102.

Leventhal, G.S., Karuza, J. & Fry, W.R. (1980). Beyond fairness: A theory of allocation preferences. In J. Mikula, (Ed.), *Justice and Social interaction,* (pp. 167-218). New York: Springer-Verlag.

Levine, D. (1989). Efficiency wages in Weitzmans share economy. *Industrial Relations, 28,* 321-333.

Levine, E.L., Ash, R.A., Hall, H. & Sistrunk, F. (1983). Evaluation of job analysis methods by experienced job analysts. *Academy of Management Journal, 26,* 339-347.

Lincoln, J.F. (1951). *Incentive management.* Cleveland: The Lincoln Electric Company.

Locke, E.A. (1968). Towards a theory of task motivation and incentives. *Organizational Behavior and Human Performance, 3,* 157-189.

Locke, E.A. (1976). The nature and causes of job satisfaction. In M.D. Dunnette (Ed.), *Handbook of industrial and organizational psychology* (pp. 297-349). Chicago: Rand-McNally.

Locke, E.A., Bryan, J.F. & Kendall, L.M. (1968). Goals and intentions as mediators of the effects of monetary incentives on behavior. *Journal of Applied Psychology, 52,* 104-121.

Locke, E.A., Feren, D.B., McCaleb, V.M., Shaw, K.N. & Denny, A.J. (1980). The relative effectiveness of motivating employee performance. In K.D. Duncan, M.M. Gruneberg & D. Wallis (Eds.), *Changes in working life,* (pp. 363-388). New York: John Wiley & Sons.

Longenecker, C.O., Sims, H.P., Jr. & Gioia, D.A. (1987). Behind the mask: The politics of employee appraisal. *Academy of Management Executive, 1,* 183-193.

Lump-sum salary increases. (1983). *Small Business Report, 8,* (6), 9-10.

Luthans, F. & Kreitner, R. (1975). *Organizational behavior modification.* Glenview, IL: Scott, Foresman.

Magnusen (1987). Faculty evaluation, performance, and pay. *Journal of Higher Education, 58,* 516-529.

Mahoney, T.A. (1964). Compensation preferences of managers. *Industrial Relations, 3,* 135-144.

Majors, B. (1988). Gender, justice, and the psychology of entitlement. *Review of Personality and Social Psychology, 7,* 124-148.

March, J.G. & Olson, J.P. (1983). Organizing political life: What administrative organization tells us about government. *American Political Science Review, 77* (6), 281-296.

Markham, S.E. (1988). Pay-for-performance dilemma revisited: Empirical example of the importance of group effects. *Journal of Applied Psychology, 73,* 172-180.

Marriott, R. (1962). An exploratory study of merit rating payment systems in three factories. *Occupational Psychology, 36,* 179-214.

Martin, D.C. (1987). Factors influencing pay decisions: Balancing managerial vulnerabilities. *Human Relations, 40,* 417-430.

Martin, D.C., Bartol, K.M. & Levine, M.J. (1987). The legal ramifications of performance appraisal. *Employment Relations Law Journal, 26,* 12-16.

McBriarty, M.A. (1988). Performance appraisal: Some unintended consequences. *Public Personnel Management, 17,* 421-433.

McDonnell Douglas Corporation. (1987). *Merit review notes.* St. Louis: Author.

Medoff, J.L. & Abraham, K.G. (1980). Experience, performance, and earnings. *Quarterly Journal of Economics, 95,* 703-736.

Medoff, J.L. & Abraham, K.G. (1981). Are those paid more really more productive? The case of experience. *Journal of Human Resources, 16,* 186-216.

Meindl, J.R. (1989). Managing to be fair: An exploration of values, motives, and leadership. *Administrative Science Quarterly, 34,* 252-276.

Mento, A.J., Steel, R.P. & Karren, R.J. (1987). A meta-analytic study of goal setting on task performance: 1966-1984. *Organizational Behavior and Human Decision Processes, 39,* 52-83.

Merit pay systems in the public sector: A tale of two cities (1984). *Management Review, 73* (10), 46-47.

Meyer, H.H. (1975). The pay-for-performance dilemma. *Organizational Dynamics, 3* (1), 55-61.

Meyer, H.H. (1987). How can we implement a pay-for-performance policy successfully? In D.B. Balkin & L.R. Gomez-Meija (Eds.), *New perspectives on compensation* (pp. 179-186). Englewood Cliffs, NJ: Prentice Hall.

Meyer, H.H. & Walker, W.B. (1961). Need for achievement and risk preference as they relate to attitudes toward reward systems and performance appraisal in an industrial setting. *Journal of Applied Psychology, 51,* 251-256.

Meyer, H.H., Kay, E. & French, J.R.P. (1965). Split roles in performance appraisal. *Harvard Business Review, 43,* 123-129.

Miceli, M.P. & Lane, M.C. (1991). Antecedents of pay satisfaction: A review and extension. In K.M. Rowland & G.R. Ferris (Eds.), *Research in personnel and human resources management, vol. 9* (235-309). Greenwich, CT: JAI Press.

Miceli, M.P. & Near, J.P. (1988). *Correlates of satisfaction with pay level and pay system in pay-for-performance plans.* Paper presented at the National Academy of Management Meetings, Anaheim, CA.

Miles, R.E. & Snow, C.C. (1978). *Organizational strategy, structure, and process.* New York: McGraw-Hill.

Milkovich, G.T. (1987). Compensation systems in high-technology companies. In D.B. Balkin & L.R. Gomez-Meija (Eds.), *New perspectives on compensation* (pp. 269-277). Englewood Cliffs, NJ: Prentice Hall.

Milkovich, G.T. & Newman, J.M. (1987). *Compensation, 2 ed.* Plano, TX: Business Publications.

Miller, E.C. (1979). Pay for performance. *Personnel, 15* (7), 4-11.

Mincer, M.G. (1977). Job absence and turnover: A new source of data. *Monthly Labor Review, 100* (10), 24-31.

Miner, J.B. (1980). *Theories of organizational behavior.* Hinsdale, IL: Dryden.

Minken, S.L. (1988). Does lump-sum pay merit attention? *Personnel Journal, 67* (6), 77-83.

Minority employees call for GM boycott (June 26, 1989). *The Ohio State Lantern,* p. 2.

Mitchell, D.J.B. (1989). *Human resource management: An economic approach.* Boston: PWS-KENT.

Mitchell, D.J.B., Lewin, D. & Lawler, E.E. III (1990). Alternative pay systems, firm performance, and productivity. In A.S. Blinder (Ed.), *Paying for productivity: A look at the evidence* (pp. 15-94). Washington, DC: The Brookings Institution.

Mitchell, T.R. (1974). Expectancy models of job satisfaction, occupational preference, and effort: A theoretical, methodological, and empirical appraisal. *Psychological Bulletin, 81,* 1053-1077.

Mobley, W.H. (1982). *Employee turnover: Causes, consequences, and control.* Reading, MA: Addison-Wesley.

Mohrman, A.J. Jr., Resnick-West, S.M. & Lawler, E.E. III (1989). *Designing performance appraisal systems.* San Francisco: Jossey-Bass.

Molloy, P.J. (1989). *Press release.* Detroit: General Motors Corporation.

Moore, M.L. & Heneman, R.L. (1983). *Performance assessment and critical skills model for the rehabilitation management system.* East Lansing, MI: Office of Management Practices, Department of Management and Budget, State of Michigan.

Moran (1986). Equitable salary administration in high-tech companies. *Compensation and Benefits Review, 18* (5), 31-40.

Mount, M.K. (1987). Coordinating salary action and performance appraisal. In D.B. Balkin & L.R. Gomez-Mejia (Eds.), *New perspectives on compensation* (pp. 187-195). Englewood Cliffs, NJ: Prentice Hall.

Mowday, R.T. (1979). Equity theory predictions of behavior in organizations. In R.M. Steers and L.W. Porter (Eds.), *Motivation and work behavior, 2 ed* (pp. 124-146). New York: McGraw-Hill.

Mulvey, P.W. (1991). *Pay system satisfaction: An exploration of the construct and predictors.* Unpublished doctoral dissertation, The Ohio State University, Columbus, Ohio.

Murphy, K.R. & Balzer, W.K. (1989). Rater errors and rating accuracy. *Journal of Applied Psychology, 74,* 619-624.

Murphy, K.R. & Cleveland, J.N. (1991). *Performance appraisal: An organization's perspective.* Boston: Allyn & Bacon.

Murphy, K.R., Garcia, M., Kerkar, S., Martin, C. & Balzer, W.K. (1982). Relationship between observational accuracy and accuracy in evaluating performance. *Journal of Applied Psychology, 67,* 320-325.

Nalbantian, H.R. (1987). Incentive compensation in perspective. In H.R. Nalbantian (Ed.), *Incentives, cooperation, and risk sharing* (pp. 3-43). Totowa, NJ: Rowman & Littlefield.

Napier, N.K. & Latham, G.P. (1986). Outcome expectancies of people who conduct performance appraisals. *Personnel Psychology, 39,* 827-837.

Nathan, B.R. & Cascio, W.F. (1986). Technical and legal standards. In R.A. Berk (Ed.), *Performance assessment* (pp. 1-50). Baltimore: Johns Hopkins Press.

Nathan, B.R. & Tippins, N. (1990). The consequences of halo "error" in performance ratings: A field study of the moderating effect of halo on test validation results. *Journal of Applied Psychology, 75,* 290-296.

National Research Council (1991). *Pay-for-performance: Evaluating performance appraisal and merit pay.* Washington, DC: National Academy Press.

Naughton, K. (August 31, 1990). Chrysler's merit raises rile UAW. *The Detroit News,* p. 1.

Nigro, L.G. (1981). Attitudes of federal employees toward performance appraisal and merit pay: Implications for CSRA implementation. *Public Administration Review. 41,* 84-86.

O'Dell, C.O. (1987). *Major findings from people, performance, and pay.* Scottsdale, AZ: American Productivity Center and American Compensation Association.

O'Hara, K., Johnson, C.M. & Beehr, T.A. (1985). Organizational behavior management in the private sector: A review of empirical research and recommendations for further investigation. *Academy of Management Review, 10,* 848-864.

Ordine, B. (October 29, 1990). QB ratings confounding, controversial. *The Columbus Dispatch,* p. 4C.

Organ, D. (1988). *Organizational citizenship behavior: The good soldier syndrome.* Lexington, MA: DC Heath.

Osburn, H.G., Timmreck, C. & Bigby, D. (1981). Effect of dimensional relevance on accuracy of hiring decisions by employment interviewers. *Journal of Applied Psychology, 67,* 320-325.

O'Toole, D.E. & Churchill, J.R. (1982). Implementing pay-for-performance: Initial experiences. *Review of Public Personnel Administration, 2* (3), 13-28.

Ott, J.S. (1989). *The organizational culture perspective.* Chicago: The Dorsey Press.

Overstreet, J.S. (1985). The case for merit bonuses. *Business Horizons, 15* (3), 53-58.

Pacific Gas and Electric Co. (1989). *The 1989 management incentive program and information on the 1989 merit plan and the performance recognition program.* San Francisco, CA: Author.

Padgett, M.Y. & Ilgen, D.R. (1989). The impact of ratee performance characteristics on rater cognitive processes and alternative measures of rater accuracy. *Organizational Behavior and Human Decision Processes, 44,* 232-260.

Pagano (1985). An exploratory evaluation of the Civil Service Reform Act's merit pay system for GS 13-15S: A case study of the U.S. Department of Health and Human Services. In D.H. Rosenbloom (Ed.), *Public personnel policy: The politics of civil service* (pp. 161-182). Port Washington, NY: Associated Academic Press.

Patten, T.H. Jr. (1976). Linking financial rewards to employee performance: The roles of OD and MBO. *Human Resource Management, 15* (1), 2-17.

Patten, T.H. Jr. (1977). Pay for performance or placation? *The Personnel Administrator, 22* (9), 26-29.

Pearce, J.L. (1987). Why merit pay doesn't work: Implications from organization theory. In D.B. Balkin & L.R. Gomez-Mejia (Eds.), *New perspectives on compensation* (pp. 169-178). Englewood Cliffs, NJ: Prentice Hall.

Pearce, J.L. & Perry, J.L. (1983). Federal merit pay: A longitudinal analysis. *Public Administration Review, 43,* 315-325.

Pearce, J.L. & Porter, L.W. (1986). Employee repsonses to formal performance appraisal feedback. *Journal of Applied Psychology, 71,* 211-218.

Pearce, J.L., Stevenson, W.B. & Perry, J.L. (1985). Managerial compensation based on organizational performance: A time series analysis of the effects of merit pay. *Academy of Management Journal, 28,* 261-278.

Peck, C. (1984). *Pay and performance: The interaction of compensation and performance appraisal* (Research Bulletin No. 155). New York: The Conference Board.

Perry, J.L. (1986). Merit pay in the public sector: The case for a failure of theory. *Review of Public Personnel Administration, 7* (1), 57-69.

Perry, J.L. (1988). Making policy by trial and error: Merit pay in the federal service. *Policy Studies Journal, 17* (2), 389-405.

Perry, J.L., Hanzlik, M.C. & Pearce, J.L. (1982). Effectiveness of merit-pay-pool management. *Review of Public Personnel Administration, 2* (3), 5-12.

Perry, J.L. & Pearce, J.L. (1983). Initial reactions to federal merit pay. *Personnel Journal, 62* (3), 230-237.

Perry, J.L. & Pearce, J.L. (1985). Civil Service reform and the politics of performance appraisal. In D.H. Rosenbloom (Ed.), *Public personnel policy: The politics of civil service* (pp. 146-160). Port Washington, NY: Associated Academic Press.

Perry, J.L. & Petrakis, B.A. (1987). *Can merit pay improve performance in government?* Paper presented at the Annual Research Conference of the Association for Public Policy Analysis and Management.

Perry, J.L. & Petrakis, B.A. (1988). Can pay for performance succeed in government? *Public Personnel Management, 17,* 359-366.

Perry, J.L., Petrakis, B.A. & Miller, T.K. (1989). Federal merit pay, Round II: An analysis of the performance management and review system. *Public Administration Review, 49,* 29-37.

Perry, T.A. (1990). Staying within the basics. *HR Magazine, 35* (11), 73-76.

Personiak, M.E. (1984). White-collar pay determination under range-of-rate systems. *Monthly Labor Review, 107* (12), 25-30.

Personnel Policies Forum (1981). *Wage and salary administration* (PPF Survey No. 131). Washington: The Bureau of National Affairs.

Peters, R. & Atkin, R. (1980). The effects of open pay systems on allocation of salary increases. *Academy of Management Proceedings, 40,* 293-297.

Porter, L.W. & Lawler, E.E. III (1968). *Managerial attitudes and behavior.* Homewood, IL: Irwin.

Porter, G., Greenberger, D.B. & Heneman, R.L. (1990). Pay and pay satisfaction: A comparison of economic, political, psychological, and psychophysical predictions. *Academy of Management Best Paper Proceedings, 50,* 289-293.

Prince, J.B. & Lawler, E.E. III (1986). Does salary discussion hurt the developmental performance appraisal? *Organizational Behavior and Human Decision Processes, 37,* 357-375.

Pulakos, E.D., Schmitt, N. & Ostroff, C. (1986). A warning about the use of a standard deviation across dimensions within ratees to measure halo. *Journal of Applied Psychology, 71,* 29-32.

Quinn, J.B. (June 3, 1991). The hard new facts of pay. *Newsweek,* p. 44.

Raff, D.M.G. & Summers, L.H. (1987). Did Henry Ford pay efficiency wages? *Journal of Labor Economics, 5,* 557-586.

Rainey, H.G. (1979). Perceptions of incentives in business and government: Implications for civil service reform. *Public Administration Review, 39,* 440-448.

Rambo, W.W., Chomiak, A.M. & Price, J.M. (1983). Consistency of performance under stable conditions at work. *Journal of Applied Psychology, 68,* 78-87.

Rambo, W.W. & Pinto, J.N. (1989). Employees' perceptions of pay increases. *Journal of Occupational Psychology, 62,* 135-145.

Rhodes, S.R. & Steers, R.M. (1990). *Managing employee absenteeism.* Reading, MA: Addison-Wesley.

Rock, R.H. (1983). Pay for performance: A concept in search of standards. *Directors and Boards, 7* (3), 15-17.

Rock, R.H. (1988). Performance management: Chasing the right bottom line. In R.L. Rock (Ed.), *Handbook of wage and salary administration* (pp. 31-1–32-2). New York: McGraw-Hill.

Rosen, S. (1985). Implicit contracts: A survey. *Journal of Economic Literature, 23,* 1144-1175.

Rothe, H.F. (1946). Output rates among butter wrappers: I. Work curves and their stability. *Journal of Applied Psychology, 30,* 199-211.

Rothe, H.F. (1978). Output rates among industrial workers. *Journal of Applied Psychology, 63,* 40-46.

Rothstein, H.R. (1990). Interrater reliability of job performance ratings: Growth to asymptote level with increasing opportunity to observe. *Journal of Applied Psychology, 75,* 322-327.

Rozelle, R.M. & Baxter, J.C. (1981). Influence of role pressures on the perceiver: Judgments of videotaped interviews varying judge accountability and responsibility. *Journal of Applied Psychology, 66,* 437-441.

Saal, F.E., Downey, R.G. & Lahey, M.A. (1980). Rating the ratings: Assessing the psychometric quality of rating data. *Psychological Bulletin, 88,* 413-428.

Sackett, P.R., Zedeck, S. & Fogli, L. (1988). Relations between measures of typical and maximum job performance. *Journal of Applied Psychology, 73,* 482-486.

Salop, S.C. (1979). A model of the natural rate of unemployment. *American Economic Review, 69,* 117-125.

Scarpello, V. (1988). *Pay satisfaction and pay fairness: Are they the same?* Paper presented at the Third Annual Conference of the Society for Industrial and Organizational Psychology, Inc. (Division 14 of the American Psychological Association), Dallas, TX.

Scarpello, V. & Campbell, J.P. (1983). Job satisfaction: Are all the parts there? *Personnel Psychology, 36,* 577-600.

Scarpello, V., Huber, V. & Vanderberg, R.J. (1988). Compensation satisfaction: Its measurement and dimensionality. *Journal of Applied Psychology, 73,* 163-171.

Schay, B.W. (1988). Effects of performance contingency pay on employee attitudes. *Public Personnel Management, 17* (2), 237-250.

Scheele, A. (January 1991). How to get the raise you want (No matter what the boss says at first). *Working Woman,* 71.

Schefflen, K.C., Lawler, E.E. III & Hackman, J.R. (1971). Long-term impact of employee participation in the development of pay incentive plans: A field experiment revisited. *Journal of Applied Psychology, 55,* 182-186.

Schlesinger, J.M. (January 26, 1988). GM's new compensation plan reflects general trend tying pay to performance. *Wall Street Journal,* pp. 1.

Schmidt, F.L., Hunter, J.E., Outerbridge, A.N. & Goff, S. (1988). Joint relation of experience and ability with job performance: Test of three hypotheses. *Journal of Applied Psychology, 73,* 46-57.

Schmidt, F.L., Hunter, J.E. & Pearlman, K. (1982). Assessing the economic impact of personnel programs on workforce productivity. *Personnel Psychology, 35,* 333-346.

Schmitt, N.W. & Klimoski, R.J. (1991). *Research methods in human resource management.* Cincinnati: South-Western.

Schmitt, N.W. & Stults, D.M. (1986). Methodology review: Analysis of multitrait-multimethod matrices. *Applied Psychological Measurement, 10,* 1-22.

Schneider, B. & Olson, L.K. (1970). Effort as a correlate of organizational reward system and individual values. *Personnel Psychology, 23,* 313-326.

Schneier, C.E. (1974). Behavior modification: A review and critique. *Academy of Management Journal, 17,* 528-548.

Schneier, C.E. (1989a). Implementing performance management and recognition and rewards (PMRR) systems at the strategic level: A line management-driven effort. *Human Resource Planning, 12* (3), 205-220.

Schneier, C.E. (1989b). Capitalizing on performance management, recognition, and reward systems. *Compensation and Benefits Review, 22* (2), 20-30.

Scholl, R.W., Cooper, E.A. & McKenna, J.F. (1987). Referent selection in determining equity perceptions: Differential effects on behavioral and attitudinal outcomes. *Personnel Psychology, 40,* 113-124.

Schuster, J.R., Colletti, J.A. & Knowles, L., Jr. (1973). The relationship between perceptions concerning magnitudes of pay and the perceived utility of pay: Public and private organizations compared. *Organizational Behavior and Human Performance, 9,* 110-119.

Schwab, D.P. (1980). Construct validity in organizational behavior. In L.L. Cummings & B.M. Staw (Eds.), *Research in organizational behavior, volume 2* (pp. 1-37). Greenwich, CT: JAI Press.

Schwab, D.P. (1988). Predicting salary levels and salary increments: An examination of merit system inequities. In D.P. Schwab (Chair), *Determinants and consequences of merit pay programs: Interorganizational illustrations.* Symposium conducted at the Annual Academy of Management Meetings, Anaheim, CA.

Schwab, D.P., Olian-Gottlieb, J. & Heneman, H.G. III (1979). Between-subjects expectancy theory research. *Psychological Bulletin, 86,* 139-147.

Schwab, D.P. & Olson, C.A. (1990). Merit pay practices: Implications for pay-performance relationships. *Industrial and Labor Relations Review, 43* (No. 3 Special Issue), 237S-256S.

Schwadel, F. (July 5, 1990). Chain finds incentives a hard sell. *The Wall Street Journal,* pp. B1, B4.

Scott, D.W., Hills, F.S., Markham, S.E. & Vest, M.J. (1987). *Evaluating a pay-for-performance program at a transit authority.* Paper presented at the National Academy of Management Meetings, New Orleans, LA.

Scott, W.E. Jr., Farh, J.L. & Podsakoff, P.M. (1988). The effects of "intrinsic" and "extrinsic" reinforcement contingencies on task behavior. *Organizational Behavior and Human Decision Processes, 41,* 405-425.

Seals, D. (1984). Making employee pay a strategic issue. *Financial Executive, 52* (10), 40-41.

Seithal, W.W. & Emens, J.S. (1983). Calculating merit increases: A structured approach. *Personnel, 36* (5), 56-68.

Sherer, P.D., Schwab, D.P. & Heneman, H.G. III (1987). Managerial salary-raise decisions: A policy capturing approach. *Personnel Psychology, 40,* 27-38.

Sibson and Company, Inc. (1989). *Compensation planning survey, 1989.* Princeton, NJ: Author.

Silverman, B.R.S. (1981). Developmental pay: Forerunner to merit pay in the federal government. *Compensation Review, 13* (2), 25-36.

Silverman, B.R.S. (1983). Why the merit pay system failed in the federal government. *Personnel Journal, 62* (4), 294-302.

Silverman, S.B. & Wexley, K.N. (1984). Reaction of employees to performance appraisal interviews as a function of their participation in scale development. *Personnel Psychology, 37,* 703-710.

Skinner, B.F. (1953). *Science and human behavior.* New York: McMillan.

Smith, D.E. (1986). Training programs for performance appraisal: A review. *Academy of Management Review, 11,* 22-40.

Smith, M.L., O'Dowd, E.J. & Christ, G.M. (1987). Pay for performance: One company's experience. *Compensation and Benefits Review, 18,* 19-27.

Smith, P.C. & Kendall, L.M. (1963). Retranslation of expectations: An approach to the construction of unambiguous anchors for rating scales. *Journal of Applied Psychology, 47,* 149-155.

Smith, P.C., Kendall, L.M. & Hulin, C.L. (1969). *The measurement of satisfaction in work and retirement.* Chicago: Rand McNally.

Sovereign K.L. (1989). *Personnel law, 2 ed.* Englewood Cliffs, NJ: Prentice Hall.

Stayer, R. (1990). How I learned to let my workers lead. *Harvard Business Review, 68* (6), 65-72.

Sterling, C.L. (1990). *A utility analysis framework for merit pay systems.* Unpublished manuscript. Columbus, College of Business, Ohio State University.

Stevens, S.S. (1959). Measurement, psychophysics, and utility. In C.W. Churchman & P. Ratoosh (Eds.), *Measurement: Definitions and theories.* New York: Wiley.

Stiglitz, J.E. (1987). The design of labor contracts: The economics of incentives and risk sharing. In H.R. Nalbantian (Ed.), *Incentives, cooperation, and risk sharing* (pp. 47-68). Totowa, NJ: Rowman & Littlefield.

Stokes, D.M. (1981). A new mathematical approach to merit-based compensation systems. *Compensation Review, 13* (4), 43-55.

Stonich, P.J. (1984). The performance measurement and reward system: Critical to strategic management. *Organizational Dynamics, 16,* 45-57.

Sullivan, J.F. (1988). The future of merit pay programs. *Compensation and Benefits Review, 20* (3), 22-30.

Sulsky, L.M. & Balzer, W.K. (1988). Meaning and measurement of performance rating accuracy: Some methodological and theoretical concerns. *Journal of Applied Psychology, 73,* 497-506.

Teel, K.S. (1986). Are merit raises really based on merit? *Personnel Journal, 64* (3), 88-95.

Thaler, R.H. (1989). Interindustry wage differentials. *Journal of Economic Perspectives, 3* (2), 181-193.

Thorndike, R.L. (1949). *Personnel selection.* New York: Wiley.

Tobin, J. (1985). Neoclassical theory in America: J.B. Clark and Fisher. *The American Economic Review, 75* (6), 28-38.

Todd, J.T., Thompson, P.H. & Dalton, G.W. (1974). Management control of personnel. *Journal of Accountancy, 137,* 34-40.

Tubbs, M.E. (1986). Goal setting: A meta-analysis examination of the empirical evidence. *Journal of Applied Psychology, 71,* 474-483.

Turban, D.B. & Jones, A.P. (1988). Supervisor-subordinate similarity: Types, effects and mechanisms. *Journal of Applied Psychology, 73,* 228-234.

Two automakers resume merit pay increases (1981). *Monthly Labor Review, 104* (7), 47.

Ubelhart, M.C. (1990). What goes 'round comes 'round: The emergence of shareholder value measures in executive compensation. *Compensation and Benefits Management, 6,* 313-318.

Ungson, G.R. & Steers, R.M. (1984). Motivation and politics in executive compensation. *Academy of Management Review, 9,* 313-323.

U.S. Congress (1981). *Serious problems need to be corrected before federal merit pay goes into effect.* Report of the Comptroller General of the United States. FPCD-81-73 (September 11).

U.S. General Accounting Office (1981). *Serious problems need to be corrected before federal merit pay goes into effect.* (FPCD-81-73). Washington, DC: Author.

U.S. General Accounting Office (1984). *A two-year appraisal of merit pay in three agencies* (GGD-84-1). Washington, DC: U.S. Government Printing Office.

U.S. General Accounting Office (1987). *Pay for performance: Implementation of the performance management and recognition system* (GGD-87-28). Washington, DC: U.S. Government Printing Office.

U.S. Merit Systems Protection Board (1981, June). *Status report on performance appraisal and merit pay among mid-level employees.* Washington, DC: Author.

U.S. Merit Systems Protection Board (1987). *Performance management and recognition system: Linking pay to performance.* Washington, DC: Author.

U.S. Merit Systems Protection Board (1988). *Toward effective performance management in the federal government.* Washington, DC: Author.

U.S. Office of Personnel Management (1987). *Performance management and recognition system.* Washington, DC: Author.

U.S. Office of Personnel Management (1988). *Performance management and recognition system: FY1986 performance cycle.* Washington, DC: Author.

Van Adelsberg, H. (1978). Relating performance evaluation to compensation of public-sector employees. *Public Personnel Management, 7* (2), 72-79.

Varadarajan, P. & Futrell, C. (1984). Factors affecting perceptions of smallest meaningful pay increases. *Industrial Relations, 23,* 278-286.

Vecchio, R.P. & Terborg, J.R. (1987). Salary increment allocation and individual differences. *Journal of Occupational Behavior, 8,* 37-43.

Vest, M.J., Hills, F.S. & Scott, K.D. (1989). *Determinants of instrumentality beliefs in a merit pay system.* Paper presented at the National Academy of Management Meetings, Washington, DC.

Vinchur, A.J., Schippmann, J.S., Smalley, M.D. & Rothe, H.F. (1991). Productivity consistency of foundry chippers and grinders: A six-year field study. *Journal of Applied Psychology, 76,* 134-136.

Vines, L.S. (1989). GM offers $3 million to settle suit. *Human Resource Executive, 3* (3), 8.

Vroom, V.H. (1964). *Work and motivation.* New York: Wiley.

Waldman, S. & Roberts, B. (November 14, 1988). Grading merit pay. *Newsweek,* pp. 45-46.

Wallace, M.J. (1990). *Rewards and renewal: America's search for competitive advantage through alternative pay strategies.* Scottsdale, AZ: American Compensation Association.

Wanous, J.P., Keon, T.L. & Latack, J.C. (1983). Expectancy theory and occupational/organizational choices: A review and test. *Organizational Behavior and Human Performance, 32,* 66-86.

Weekly, J.A. & Gier, J.A. (1989). Ceilings in the reliability and validity of performance ratings: The case of expert raters. *Academy of Management Journal, 32,* 213-222.

Weeks, D.A. (1976). *Compensating employees: Lessons from the 1970s* (Report No. 707). New York: The Conference Board.

Weiner, N. (1980). Determinants and behavioral consequences of pay satisfaction: A comparison of two models. *Personnel Psychology, 33,* 741-757.

Weiss, D.J., Dawis, R.V., England, G.W. & Lofquist, L.H. (1967). *Manual for the Minnesota satisfaction questionnaire.* Minneapolis: Minnesota Studies in Vocational Rehabilitation, Bulletin 45.

Wexley, K.N. & Youtz, M.A. (1985). Raters' beliefs about others: Their effects on rating errors and rating accuracy. *Journal of Occupational Psychology, 58,* 265-275.

Whyte, W.F. (1955). *Money and motivation.* New York: Harper, 1955.

Wildstrom, S.H. (May 19, 1986). Reagan's bombshell for civil servants: Merit pay. *Business Week,* p. 61.

Winstanley, N.B. (1978). Comment on Patten's "Pay for performance or placation." *The Personnel Administrator, 23* (5), 49-52.

Wisdom, B. & Patzig, D. (1987). Does your organization have the right climate for merit? *Public Personnel Management, 16* (2), 127-133.

Wright, P.M. (1989). Testing the mediating role of goals in the incentive-performance relationship. *Journal of Applied Psychology, 74,* 699-705.

Wyatt Company (1987). *Salary management practices in the private sector.* U.S. Advisory Committee on Federal Pay in cooperation with the American Compensation Association, Philadelphia, PA.

Wyatt Company (1989). Results of the 1989 Wyatt performance management survey. *The Wyatt Communicator,* Fourth Quarter, 4-18.

Zedeck, S. & Smith, P.C. (1968). A psychophysical determination of equitable payment. *Journal of Applied Psychology, 52,* 343-347.

Index